*The*

# SAPR-PBIS™ MANUAL

# *The*

# SAPR-PBIS™ MANUAL

## A Team-Based Approach to Implementing Effective Schoolwide Positive Behavior Interventions and Supports

by

**Bridget Walker, Ph.D.**
Seattle University
Seattle, Washington

and

**Douglas Cheney, Ph.D.**
University of Washington
Seattle, Washington

·P A U L·H·
BROOKES
PUBLISHING CO.®
www.brookespublishing.com

Baltimore • London • Sydney

·PAUL·H·
BROOKES
PUBLISHING CO.®
www.brookespublishing.com

**Paul H. Brookes Publishing Co.**
Post Office Box 10624
Baltimore, Maryland 21285-0624

www.brookespublishing.com



Manufactured in the United States of America by
Versa Press, Inc., East Peoria, Illinois.

*The Self-Assessment and Program Review for Positive Behavior Interventions and Supports (SAPR-PBIS™)* is intended for one-time use and can be purchased in packages of 10 (ISBN-13: 978-1-59857-251-3). To order, contact Brookes Publishing Co., 1-800-638-3775; http://www.brookespublishing.com.

**Library of Congress Cataloging-in-Publication Data**

Walker, Bridget Anne.
The SAPR-PBIS™ manual : a team-based approach to implementing effective schoolwide positive behavior interventions and supports / by Bridget Walker and Douglas Cheney.
p. cm.
Includes bibliographical references and index.
ISBN-13: 978-1-59857-170-7 (pbk.) — ISBN-10: 1-59857-170-2 (pbk.)
1. School discipline—Handbooks, manuals, etc. 2. Problem children—Behavior modification—Handbooks, manuals, etc. 3. Conduct disorders in children—Treatment—Handbooks, manuals, etc. 4. School improvement programs—Handbooks, manuals, etc. 5. Group work in education—Handbooks, manuals, etc. I. Cheney, Douglas, 1949– II. Title.
LB3012.W334 2012
371.39'3–dc23 2012012292

British Library Cataloguing in Publication data are available from the British Library.

2016 2015 2014 2013 2012

10 9 8 7 6 5 4 3 2 1

# Contents

# About the Authors

**Bridget Walker, Ph.D.** (walkerb@seattleu.edu), is Assistant Professor in the Master in Teaching Program at Seattle University. She has been involved in the field of education for more than 20 years as a special education teacher and behavior specialist as well as a consultant and trainer. Dr. Walker completed her doctorate at the University of Washington (UW) in 2006. While at the UW, she coordinated the BEACONS (Behavior, Emotional, and Academic Curriculum On the Needs of Students) project and the Check, Connect, and Expect project as part of the UW Behavior Research Center. Dr. Walker has helped more than 30 schools throughout the state of Washington develop schoolwide positive behavior intervention and support programs. In addition, she has consulted with numerous schools and districts, helping them assess and improve their programs and supports at the intensive level for students with, or at risk of developing, emotional and behavioral disabilities.

Dr. Walker is the author of several articles on positive behavior interventions and supports and on supporting students with challenging behaviors in schools and treatment settings; she is also the author of two book chapters on effective programs for students with emotional and behavioral disabilities in the context of the philosophical framework of therapeutic Re-EDucation. She is Past President of the Washington Re-EDucation Association (WAREA), a nonprofit agency that she helped found in 1998, as well as Past President of the American Re-EDucation Association. She is also a Regional Coordinator and Master Trainer for the Life Space Crisis Intervention Institute in Maryland.

In 2011, she was awarded the PBIS Champion award by the Northwest Positive Behavior Interventions and Supports Network (NWPBIS) for her ongoing work in helping schools effectively implement PBIS to support the success of all students.

**Douglas Cheney, Ph.D.** (dcheney@uw.edu), is Professor of Special Education at the University of Washington (UW), Seattle, where he directs the master's program to prepare teachers for educating students with emotional or behavioral disabilities. Dr. Cheney also codirected UW's doctoral training program in positive behavior interventions and supports (PBIS); Washington's Behavior Research Center on effective behavioral interventions; the Check, Connect, and Expect project; and Washington's PBIS Network between 2001 and 2010. Dr. Cheney has been a consultant to numerous school districts and five state departments; he co-chaired Washington's Statewide Task Force on Behavioral Disorders from 1997 to 1999, which provided a blueprint for the state's PBIS model. He has extensive research experience, having been awarded more than $10 million of funds from the U.S. Department of Education and from state departments of education and mental health in Oregon, New Hampshire, and Washington for more than 20 years.

Dr. Cheney has served as co-editor of *The Journal of Emotional and Behavioral Disorders* and associate editor for *Intervention in School and Clinic.* He was on the editorial boards of *Behavior Disorders* and *Beyond Behavior.* He was President of the Council for Children with Behavior Disorders, a division of the Council for Exceptional Children (CEC), from 1998 to 1999 and Convention Chair for CEC's international conventions in Denver in 2012 and San Antonio in 2013. Dr. Cheney directed the Institute on Emotional Disabilities at Keene State College, New Hampshire, from 1992 to 1997 and was a special education teacher and administrator from 1974 to 1989. In 2010, he was awarded a PBIS Lifetime Achievement Award by the Northwest Positive Behavior Interventions and Supports Network for his PBIS work in schools both nationally and regionally.

# Foreword

Bridget Walker and Douglas Cheney offer in this handbook a systematic process for improving implementation of schoolwide positive behavior interventions and supports (SWPBIS). The handbook represents an important approach for establishing a positive social culture in schools. We have long followed a process in which school personnel received training on effective academic, behavioral, and organizational strategies only to be left alone after training with the hard job of finding the time and resources to implement those practices in their school. Walker and Cheney provide in this text the ability to use repeated assessment of the key evaluation question: "Are we doing what we said we would do?" They offer a simple format for asking this question and the more important guidance on how to use the information to actually improve schools.

Walker and Cheney build on the recommendation from Clancy (2010) to incorporate "participatory evaluation" to achieve more complete and more effective use of SWPBIS. The handbook begins by focusing the reader on the need to improve the social culture of schools and the direct link between investing in social behavior and improving academic outcomes. SWPBIS is one approach for achieving the goal of improving a schoolwide social culture. The evidence that SWPBIS is needed, possible, and effective has grown dramatically since 2005 (Bradshaw, Koth, Thornton, & Leaf, 2009; Bradshaw, Mitchell, & Leaf, 2010; Horner et al., 2009; Horner, Sugai, & Anderson, 2009). It is now clear that schools are more effective (both socially and academically) if they do the following:

1. Define a small set of clearly articulated behavioral expectations for the whole school.
2. Teach and acknowledge these behavioral expectations much as they would academic behavior.
3. Establish clear and predictable consequences for problem behavior that both 1) reduce the likelihood that problem behavior will be inadvertently rewarded and 2) reduce the likelihood that problem behavior will interrupt the educational opportunities of all other students.
4. Invest in academic and behavior supports at multiple tiers of intensity, with 1) basic support for all students; 2) more focused support for those who need a small amount of additional assistance; and 3) intensive, individualized support for those students who require exceptional academic and/or behavioral assistance.
5. Collect and use data for decision making.
6. Build the organizational systems (teams, feedback loops, policies) needed to support effective behavioral and academic practices.

The Self-Assessment and Program Review for Positive Behavior Interventions and Supports (SAPR-PBIS™) is a self-assessment measure used by a school team with the help of its district PBIS coach. The SAPR-PBIS is needed because SWPBIS has many components and takes 2–4 years to put into place. SWPBIS is not something that can be reviewed during a brief workshop and implemented the next week. The need to build consensus across families, faculty, and students takes time. The need to adapt SWPBIS practices to "fit" the local school community, culture, and context takes time. The need to carefully retain what the school already does well and add only helpful features takes time. Unfortunately, time has a way of sapping the essence from many a good idea. In this text, Walker and Cheney offer a simple, clear message, and a practical way to achieve it.

The message is, "To achieve functional change, measure regularly if you are implementing what you say you want to do, and use that information to build an action plan that will bring you closer to your goal." This familiar message is supplemented with the SAPR-PBIS, which is the practical tool for assessing SWPBIS and repeatedly building the action steps that will help a school achieve the core features of SWPBIS.

The first four chapters of the book provide a rationale and framework for using repeated self-assessment as a tool for implementing the core features of SWPBIS and response to intervention (RTI). The need for a leadership team is reviewed. The importance of linking academic and behavior supports is clarified, and strategies for overcoming common roadblocks are reviewed. Chapter 5 provides a summary of the 10 evidence-based practices that are at the heart of the SAPR-PBIS protocol.

1. Policies and procedures
2. Prevention and screening
3. Staff development
4. Behavioral expectations
5. Response to discipline referrals
6. Academic and social supports provided
7. Functional behavioral assessment as needed
8. Data collected and analyzed
9. Families as partners
10. Comprehensive plans for intensive needs

These 10 practices will not be new to many readers and will be especially familiar to those readers with a history of implementing SWPBIS and/or RTI. The goal of this text is not to introduce new educational practices but to introduce the SAPR-PBIS as a tool for improving implementation of well-established practices.

Walker and Cheney help the reader with specific examples of SAPR-PBIS scoring and use. They also offer description of how the SAPR-PBIS has been used with success across 23 schools in Washington State. The messages from this text are both a challenge and a guide. We are challenged to move from "wanting" to do better to actually doing those things that will benefit students. We are guided toward this goal through the vision of an active, participatory process in which common goals are established, evidence-based practices are identified and taught, and the hard work of implementation is supported through regular and transparent cycles in which the school team assesses current status, builds a practical action plan, implements the plan, and then repeats the process with another assessment. In companion with this ongoing cycle of improvement, the team continually monitors if students are benefiting (both academically and socially).

The promise of SAPR-PBIS is a path toward substantive and durable improvement in the effectiveness of schools. Given research since the 1980s, we know a great deal about the core features of effective education. In many ways our real struggle today is with finding efficient and effective ways to do what we know works. Walker and Cheney use the 10 practices that are at the heart of SWPBIS as a framework for defining 1) what is needed, 2) what is possible, and 3) a clear path for achieving the vision they define for effective and efficient school settings. Their approach is reflective of other, useful self-assessment options (Team Implementation Checklist [Sugai, Horner, Lewis-Palmer, Rossetto Dickey, 2011] and Benchmarks of Quality [Kincaid, Childs, & George, 2010]) for assisting the implementation of SWPBIS. Together, these new participatory evaluation efforts are setting a new standard for using data to make our schools more effective learning environments.

*Robert H. Horner, Ph.D.*
*Professor of Special Education*
*University of Oregon*
*Eugene, Oregon*

## REFERENCES

Bradshaw, C., Koth, C., Thornton, L., & Leaf, P. (2009). Altering school climate through school-wide positive behavioral interventions and supports: Findings from a group-randomized effectiveness trial. *Prevention Science, 10*, 100–115.

Bradshaw, C.P., Mitchell, M.M., & Leaf, P.J. (2010). Examining the effects of school-wide positive behavioral interventions and supports on student outcomes: Results from a randomized controlled effectiveness trial in elementary schools. *Journal of Positive Behavior Interventions, 12*, 133–148.

Clancy, M. (2010). *Participatory evaluation in programs for students with emotional and behavioral disabilities.* Unpublished doctoral dissertation, Seattle University.

Horner, R.H., Sugai, G., & Anderson, C.M. (2010). Examining the evidence base for school-wide positive behavior support. *Focus on Exceptionality, 42*(8), 1–14.

Horner, R., Sugai, G., Smolkowski, K., Eber, L., Nakasato, J., Todd, A., & Esperanza, J., (2009). A randomized, wait-list controlled effectiveness trial assessing school-wide positive behavior support in elementary schools. *Journal of Positive Behavior Interventions, 11*, 133–145.

Kincaid, D., Childs, K., & George, H. (2010). *School-wide Benchmarks of Quality* (Rev. ed.). Unpublished instrument, University of Southern Florida, Tampa.

Sugai, G., Horner, R.H., Lewis-Palmer, T., & Rossetto Dickey, C. (2011, May). *Team Implementation Checklist, Version 3.1.* Eugene, OR: University of Oregon, Educational & Community Supports.

# Preface

The past 2 decades of educational research and practice have produced many positive and productive approaches to changing the use of discipline from a punitive exclusionary approach to an integrated instructional approach. We have been fortunate to have worked with scores of educators during these decades who have worked tirelessly in their efforts to improve their own instructional approaches for students' social behavior. This work has primarily been done in Washington state as a part of the BEACONS (Behavior, Emotional, and Academic Curriculum On the Needs of Students) project. BEACONS began as a demonstration project at four schools in Washington state as a result of a statewide task force on behavior that encouraged the use and evaluation of the three-tiered model of behavioral support that was described by Walker et al. (1996). The same model was adopted by Drs. Horner and Sugai at the Office of Special Education Programs Center on Positive Behavior Interventions and Supports (PBIS) at the University of Oregon in 1997, and BEACONS's schools became some of the early exemplars for the positive behavior interventions and supports (PBIS) national network.

Our learning regarding the systems-level integration of the PBIS initiative grew exponentially as we worked with Washington state schools and interacted with other state leaders at national meetings about PBIS. In particular, we were taken by the notion that discipline had to change from externally imposed actions on a student for wrongdoing to the more contemporary idea that discipline is a systematic set of learning experiences that guide students to improving their self-discipline and character. Discipline involves learning an effective set of social skills that is needed to achieve important social and academic outcomes. Within schools, it means that social expectations must be systematically taught, monitored, and reinforced to benefit students socially and academically.

One other enduring lesson from the PBIS initiative has been the emphasis on data-based decision making. Researchers have long based their academic efforts on data-based outcomes, but the switch to school staff taking the lead on generating their own data to demonstrate important change, particularly in the area of behavior, became a rally cry for schools practicing PBIS. We therefore relied on those who were responsible for implementing school change (i.e., the school staff) in their own evaluation process. The literature refers to this process as participatory evaluation (PE). PE involves key stakeholders establishing important benchmarks to shape meaningful results for their school. We found PE to be an effective tool for organizational change within the PBIS process to evaluate the level of implementation of evidence-based practices. In addition, PE provided a framework for implementing and reviewing the status of key instructional practices over time. As discussed in much of the PBIS literature, an assessment framework based on key stakeholders' data can develop a climate of organizational reflection and decision making that contributes to sustained school improvement.

We have been impressed by the PBIS Technical Assistance Center's ability to develop practical and efficient assessment tools that readily fit the PBIS process. In our earliest work in BEACONS, we introduced our school leadership teams to tools such as the School-wide Evaluation Tool (SET; Sugai, Lewis-Palmer, Todd, & Horner, 2001) and the School-Wide Information System (SWIS; May et al., 2000) to inform their decision making. In a profound manner, school staff are now becoming more informed decision makers by looking at and acting on discipline data that they have gathered and analyzed with efficient tools. Thus, one of our goals in BEACONS was to develop and provide schools with another practical measure for assessing implementation of practices at all three tiers of the PBIS model. An outcome of this goal was this work, The Self-Assessment and Program Review for Positive Behavior Interventions and Supports (SAPR-PBIS™).

The purpose of this manual is to provide PBIS leadership teams and staff both an assessment tool and a corresponding manual that provides a set of action-oriented items to enhance their PBIS efforts. We have found that an additional component of effective PBIS implementation is the ability of the leadership team to enter into difficult discussions and end with productive ideas. To this end, we emphasize the notion of learning conversations in this manual. Learning conversations occur for teams that address difficult issues by carefully exploring conflicting perspectives by asking for evidence to support one's opinion. This loops the conversation of perspective back to the data at hand for decision making. Leadership teams that employ this conversational approach are found to be more effective at exploring options and achieving outcomes. In addition, they develop more trust between team members, become a more effective leadership body, and cultivate a more adept ability to influence the entire school staff to implement the suggested PBIS practices with fidelity.

This manual provides educators with the process for having effective team conversations while monitoring their PBIS implementation. The leadership team is charged with evaluating 10 key practices across each school year. The evaluation can occur once or twice yearly depending on the team's interest and ability to conduct the SAPR-PBIS evaluation. In Chapter 4, we provide the leadership team with a description of how to effectively use this tool to assess, graph, and monitor ongoing implementation of PBIS practices. This system is therefore based on a cyclical approach to assess, implement, evaluate, refine, improve, and reassess school PBIS practices. Schools using the SAPR-PBIS in our demonstration projects have found high levels of staff satisfaction and improved student outcomes in their overall social behavior. Administrators have commented that the use of the SAPR-PBIS and its recommended action items has lead to decreases in office discipline referrals and allowed them more time to focus on their role in instructional leadership and supervision of staff.

The purpose of Chapter 5 is to link the assessment of the 10 essential PBIS practices to action items and resources for the school staff. These recommendations are offered so that school leadership teams can work more independently once they have participated in their initial PBIS training. We have found that it is not always feasible for school teams to enlist the aid of consultants or trainers to work with them at their school. Budgets are tight, time is limited, and in many states, PBIS consultants are few and far between. Having a manual that links assessment to practice can be an effective alternative to ongoing training or engaging consultants. There are many online resources that a team can access, and often a staff member with behavioral expertise can take the lead of translating these practices and developing a plan for school implementation.

We hope the SAPR-PBIS is received as an effective and efficient tool for improving school practices in the social domain. Coupling the social-behavioral recommendations in this manual with those in the response to intervention work in the academic domain should assist school staff and students in enhancing their outcomes. In an era that focuses on academic excellence and corresponding social proficiency, the need for this manual is evident. We wish the user of this manual the best of skill and good fortune as you work on improving school practice to the benefit of all students.

## REFERENCES

May, S., Ard, W., Todd, A., Horner, R., Glasgow, A., Sugai, G., & Sprague, J. (2000). *School-Wide Information System (SWIS)*. Eugene: University of Oregon, Educational and Community Supports.

Sugai, G., Lewis-Palmer, T., Todd, A., & Horner, R. (2001). *School-wide Evaluation Tool (SET)*. Eugene, OR: Author.

Walker, H.M., Horner, R.H., Sugai, G., Bullis, M., Sprague, J.R., Bricker, D., & Kaufman, M.J. (1996). Integrated approaches to preventing antisocial behavior patterns among school-age children and youth. *Journal of Emotional and Behavioral Disorders*, *4*, 194–209.

# SAPR-PBIS™ at a Glance

| | |
|---|---|
| Type of tool | A self-assessment process for school leadership teams to evaluate their implementation of schoolwide positive behavior interventions and supports (SWPBIS) |
| Intervals | Two times per year |
| Areas screened | 10 practices that represent the building blocks of effective SWPBIS |
| Number of items | *Individual Form:* 62 items on 10 scales<br>*Team Meeting Form:* 10 scales and 1 planning sheet (Action Plan) |
| Sample item | *Individual Form:* Rate on a scale of 1–5 the extent to which the following indicator is in place: "The behavioral expectations and schoolwide program are regularly communicated to families."<br>*Team Meeting Form:* "Place a tally mark to reflect each of the scores of individual team members, and circle the box that reflects the scores from most team members." |
| Who completes it | Professionals (administrators, school psychologists, behavior specialists, classroom teachers) |
| Who scores it | Professionals (administrators, school psychologists, behavior specialists, classroom teachers) |
| Time to complete | 30 minutes for Individual Form (completed independently)<br>60–90 minutes for Team Meeting Form (completed over the course of a meeting) |
| Time to score | ~5 minutes, completed within the team meeting |
| Scores provided | Overall ratings in 10 key practice areas to help identify 3 or more priorities for improvement. |
| What the scores tell you | Discrepancies in individual scores can indicate areas where better communication or training is needed; overall practice scores and indicator scores should be used to provide goals and priorities for improving implementation of SWPBIS. |
| Photocopiable | No |
| Languages | English |
| Training required | Minimal |
| Norm referenced | No |
| Criterion referenced | Yes |
| Standardization sample | 23 schools, with 150 individual staff members |
| Reliability | Total internal reliability = .96; each scale > .76 (range .76–.95) |
| Validity | Content validity was completed though literature review and expert panel review. Construct validity was established by correlating scores with the School-wide Evaluation Tool (SET). |
| Years in development | 9 years |

# Acknowledgments

The Self-Assessment and Program Review for Positive Behavior Interventions and Supports (SAPR-PBIS™) is the result of the efforts of numerous individuals who worked diligently on the BEACONS (Behavioral, Emotional, and Academic Curriculum On the Needs of Students) project from 1998 to 2007. During this time, funding was provided by the U.S. Office of Special Education Programs (OSEP), Washington's Office of the Superintendent of Public Instruction (OSPI), and the Washington Education Association. We would like to thank representatives of those agencies for their assistance and support for this work. In particular, we would like to thank Lou Danielson and our project officers at OSEP, Selete Avoke and Tom Hanley; Lou Colwell and Doug Gill at OSPI; and Christie Perkins and Pat Steinberg at the Washington Education Association. Our collaborator, now at North Carolina State University, Scott Stage, and our research assistants, Erika Blood, Craig Blum, Andrea Flower, Wendy Iwaszuk, Hal Jackson, Wyeth Jesse, Tran Templeton, and Gita Upreti, provided their time and effort in conceptualizing and implementing the research for the SAPR-PBIS. Finally, we would like to thank the teachers, administrators, paraprofessionals, parents, and guardians in the 23 schools throughout Washington State who helped implement the project. In particular, we would like to thank our regional and school district coordinators, Susan Dahlquist, Vicki Fisher, Heidi Hyta, Melinda Jennings, Amy Jesse, Kent McIntosh, Pat Mullen, Irene Olson, Dale Petersen, and Tricia Robles. Finally, we wish to express our gratitude to Rebecca Lazo, Senior Acquisitions Editor at Brookes Publishing Co., who recognized the importance of the SAPR-PBIS and persisted in bringing the SAPR-PBIS into publication. This work could not have been completed without the many hardworking professionals who helped, and we greatly appreciate their involvement and support.

*To Dr. Walker's husband, Scott Condon,*
*and Dr. Cheney's wife, Elayne Puzan.*
*We dedicate this work with our tremendous thanks*
*for their steadfast patience and enduring support.*
*None of our efforts could be possible without them.*

SAPRpbis™ 1

# School Improvement and the Three-Level Support Model

Schools are faced with tremendous challenges as they attempt to meet the social and academic needs of an increasingly diverse student body. For example, issues with poverty, cultural and linguistic diversity, mobility, disability, and economic recession all press schools to use their resources in a creative and productive manner to meet student needs. When facing these challenges, it has become well established that student learning and behavior are inextricably linked (U.S. Department of Education, 2005). A priority has therefore been placed on putting together practices in schools that can address both areas of a student's development. When a school can find approaches that decrease the disruptive behavior of students and that strengthen instructional practices, struggling students are much more likely to improve their academic and social outcomes (Sutherland, Lewis-Palmer, Stichter, & Morgan, 2008).

Two initiatives, positive behavior interventions and supports (PBIS) and response to intervention (RTI), have provided a framework and legislative underpinning for developing a positive approach to addressing the academic and behavioral domains. The RTI initiative began due to concerns that the discrepancy formula for identifying students with learning disabilities was not a productive educational approach. In the discrepancy approach, results from intelligence and achievement tests were compared to determine whether there was a significant difference between a student's ability and performance. Students who were struggling with reading, written expression, or mathematics and who had a significant discrepancy between ability and performance could be identified with a learning disability. Many teachers and researchers were frustrated with the discrepancy approach because it lacked reliability and validity and forced educators to wait until third grade or thereafter to attain a measure of achievement and performance (Bender & Shores, 2007). A more proactive approach such as RTI, based on early intervention and assessment practices, was considered to be more responsive and helpful in determining how students were responding to instruction.

The move toward RTI has numerous proponents that can be traced back to Heller, Holtzman, and Messick's (1982) call for special education to consider whether students were receiving quality instruction and valid assessments. Early research that set a foundation for RTI included Bergan's (1977) research on problem solving and peer comparisons and Deno and Mirkin's (1977) curriculum-based measurement (CBM). These approaches set target goals for a student's behavioral or academic improvement and monitored whether instructional or behavioral intervention assisted the student in meaningful change. Much research has been implemented to support both the problem solving and CBM approaches, but RTI reached a critical moment in 2004 when the Individuals with Disabilities Education Act was reauthorized (Individuals with Disabilities Education Improvement Act [IDEA] of 2004, PL 108-446).

Due to concerns over the issue that the discrepancy model did not address the early identification of students with learning disabilities, the National Joint Committee on Learning Disabilities wrote a letter to the U.S. Department of Education's Office of Special Education Programs (OSEP) in 1997 to recommend alternative approaches to testing and teaching students with learning difficulties (Bradley, Danielson, & Doolittle, 2007). A Learning Disabilities Initiative was established to attain a consensus on how students with learning disabilities would be identified and instructed. The work on the Learning Disabilities Initiative culminated in the 2004 reauthorization of IDEA (PL 108-446) when the longstanding requirement to use the discrepancy approach was modified to allow the use of the RTI approach. Local educational agencies were permitted to use a process for identifying learning disabilities that was based on how a child responded to evidence-based practices as part of the evaluation process. This change in language allowed states to investigate RTI models.

IDEA 2004 also continued an emphasis on improving educational practice in the area of behavior. In IDEA 1997, the use of "positive behavior interventions and supports" was defined as a more proactive approach for any student whose "behavior impedes his or her learning, or the learning of others" (IDEA 1997, PL 105-17, § 614 [d][3][B][I]). IDEA 2004 requires school teams to conduct a functional behavioral assessment (FBA) and develop or modify a behavior intervention plan for students whose behavior has been found to be a manifestation of his or her disability (IDEA 2004, PL 108-446, § 616 [k][1][C] or [G]). Language was written into IDEA 1997 to fund a national technical assistance center. The center was founded at the University of Oregon and is known as the OSEP Center on Positive Behavior Interventions and Supports (OSEP Center on PBIS; see http://www.pbis.org).

RTI's focus on progress monitoring and quality instruction for students with learning difficulties, and the PBIS approach of effective behavioral intervention, have complemented each other, and states have sought models to implement these initiatives. Most state education agencies have statements on how a three-tiered model of prevention and/or intervention can be used in schools. PBIS is viewed as a comprehensive approach to providing schoolwide supports and interventions for all students, as well as an early intervention approach for individual students' problem behavior (Learning First Alliance, 2001; McNamara & Hollinger, 2003; Sugai & Horner, 1999). Based on the work of public health and prevention science, PBIS focuses on addressing systemic issues in schools to positively address the areas of discipline, academic performance, and social-emotional development for all students. A major construct of the PBIS model is that there are three levels of prevention or intervention that should correspond with a continuum of supports and interventions for the school's students (Sprague, Sugai, Horner, & Walker, 1999; U.S. Department of Education, 2000; Walker et al., 1996). An example of a universal intervention is the teaching and reinforcing of schoolwide expectations. Sprague et al. (1999) theorized that approximately 80% of the students in a school will need no further interventions or supports when systems at this level are positive, consistent, and well established.

Those working on implementing both RTI and PBIS have found that these approaches are not "off the shelf" assessment or intervention programs for students. No one model of RTI has risen to the top for universal adoption, nor has any specific PBIS curriculum been recommended by the federal government. OSEP has, however, recommended a basic framework for conducting the RTI/PBIS process that involves developing and using a three-tiered model in schools. The tiers include one for all students (universal), one for students who are unresponsive to the school's universal instructional approaches and are showing learning and/or behavioral difficulties (secondary, targeted), and one that is individualized and intensive for students with significant academic and/or behavioral problems (tertiary). Students are expected to receive high-quality services at Tiers 1 and 2 for at least 8–12 weeks before being referred for services at Tier 3 (Bradley et al., 2007).

With this process being promoted from the federal government to the state education agencies, questions arise from school district personnel who have never implemented the major features of the RTI or PBIS approach. For example, what are scientifically based practices at each tier of the model? How can districts ensure that teachers use the approaches? What types of professional development and structural changes need to occur to move the assessment process away from a school psychologist to a classroom teacher? What types of professional development are needed to ensure that teachers use scientifically based practices with fidelity? Who can lead the RTI initiative within districts, and how can resources be provided to ensure its success?

For those who do decide to implement RTI or PBIS, these questions are addressed through constant and relentless professional development activities. State departments have developed RTI task forces to assess their respective use of RTI procedures and to fund demonstration sites in school districts. Information on each state's approach to RTI is readily available on most state education agency web sites. Several states have incorporated their work into working papers that can be downloaded for review. A few quick examples of how states interpret and practice RTI may be useful at this point.

The Colorado Department of Education's (2008) *Response to Intervention (RtI): A Practitioner's Guide to Implementation* includes an overview of RTI, a discussion of the three-tiered model, and recommendations for putting RTI into practice. The document emphasizes that RTI should not be narrowly interpreted as merely an approach for identifying learning disabilities but instead should be broadly developed as an educational process that will improve the outcomes of all students. A full range of interventions and supports is recommended for all students, but the interventions and supports should be tailored and efficiently delivered through a collaborative process at the second and third tiers. Progress monitoring and problem solving are important features as school teams support both the academic work and behavioral performance of their students. The Colorado Department of Education document emphasizes six areas that relate to the effectiveness of RTI in practice: 1) leadership, 2) curriculum and instruction, 3) school climate and culture, 4) problem solving, 5) assessment, and 6) family and community involvement. The document pays close attention to describing how each of these areas should be addressed for successful RTI implementation. Notable in this document is the section on school climate and culture, which includes suggestions for the use of PBIS to create a caring school community that is based on improved use of socially productive behavior by students and staff. This integration of behavior and academic interventions is the current recommended approach to integrating PBIS and RTI in schools nationally.

A second state exemplar can be found in *A Tiered Instructional Approach to Support Achievement for All Students: Maryland's Response to Intervention Framework* (Maryland Department of Education, 2008). The document describes how Maryland approached the RTI initiative. In its statement of purpose, the Maryland Department of Education states that its tiered approach is intended to support the achievement and progress of all students in its system, but it emphasizes evidence-based approaches to reach and support students who are not demonstrating appropriate skill and content mastery. The document's guidelines present a description of the three-tiered approach to RTI, guidance for how districts can use the guide for identifying students with learning disabilities, and a recommended process developed by the expert team that wrote the framework. The essential components of Maryland's approach include 1) universal screening, 2) problem-solving/decision-making practices, 3) tiered levels of implementation of high-quality instruction/intervention, 4) progress monitoring, 5) fidelity of implementation, 6) family involvement, and 7) considerations for English language learning.

The three-tiered model promotes the use of prevention and support in both state models. Maryland, however, stays focused and targeted toward learning disabilities, whereas the Colorado model is broader and addresses behavior. Although Maryland includes some behavioral systems in its diagram of the three tiers, the document's descriptions of steps to take when implementing its recommended components are clearly focused on the academic domain.

## HISTORY AND CONTEXT OF THE THREE-TIERED MODEL IN BEHAVIOR

The PBIS Technical Assistance Center has been funded by the U.S. Department of Education's OSEP since 1997, and its mission is to promote the use of schoolwide positive behavior interventions and supports (SWPBIS) to improve students' social behavior. Three seminal pieces of information have been responsible for this focus on SWPBIS. The first came from Walker et al.'s (1996) description of a three-level approach for addressing student behavior. The first level, known as universal, addresses all students in the school and seeks to meet the social needs of all students by employing schoolwide social instruction. The second level uses targeted, specialized approaches to address the behavior of students who are at risk for school failure. The third level employs highly specialized approaches for students with chronic or intensive behavior problems. A critical feature of this three-tiered model is that school staff must work cohesively in a proactive, strategic manner across the school to enhance social behavior and reduce problem behavior of students.

The second major development, as previously noted, happened first in 1997 and was revised in 2004 with the reauthorization of IDEA, which stated that positive behavior supports should be used for any student whose behavior impedes his or her learning or the learning of others (20 U.S.C. §1414[d][3][B][i]). Positive behavior supports were intended to be integrated into behavior intervention plans to teach students effective social behavior related to educational achievement. Many suggestions and recommendations for developing schoolwide, classroom, and individualized positive behavior supports have since been described; leading this initiative have been George Sugai and Rob Horner. They, along with numerous colleagues, first developed and tested effective behavior support (EBS) in a number of schools. This work was developed and implemented to address some of the disappointing educational outcomes of students with emotional or behavioral problems (E/BPs) and disabilities, such as failing grades, high dropout rates, and disproportionate placement of minority students in special education services. EBS, the third major development, was touted as a more proactive, efficient early intervention approach that could improve the social development and academic performance of all students (Lewis & Sugai, 1999).

Lewis and Sugai (1999) described EBS as a system-based approach that enhanced the use of effective behavioral practices with all students. Problem-solving teams within schools were instrumental in identifying effective practices and teaching and sustaining their use throughout the school. Leadership teams worked to develop practices, assist with their implementation, and evaluate their use throughout the school. The goal of EBS was to have schools use the effective practices across four systems—the school, classroom, nonclassroom, and individual student—to improve the social climate and conditions for student learning. Strategies and recommendations were given for teaching and supporting student behavior for all four systems.

Drs. Horner and Sugai began the OSEP Center on PBIS at the University of Oregon with the goal of developing a national network of schools that would implement SWPBIS. The center's primary source of funding has been the U.S. Department of Education, and the center is working on scaling up PBIS in all 50 states. Each state has a coordinator (listed at http://www.pbis.org), and interested school staff can contact their state coordinator to become involved in this work. The evolution of the work from EBS to PBIS continued the earlier recommendations of Walker et al. (1996) to develop and implement the three-tiered approach to prevention and intervention. Drs. Horner and Sugai, codirectors of the center, have done an exemplary job of providing leadership, guidance, and information on the use of the PBIS approach in schools.

## THE FULL RESPONSE TO INTERVENTION MODEL: BRAIDING BEHAVIOR AND ACADEMICS

The RTI language in IDEA 2004 requires schools to assess students' academic performance, provide the students with necessary instruction, and evaluate the progress of students with learning difficulties prior to identifying the students as having a learning disability. These students would be considered to be receiving Tier 2 interventions, as their performance at Tier 1 was found to be lagging behind other students in the classroom. When students receive and are responsive to Tier 2 instructional approaches, according to the RTI model, they are more likely to be receptive to the ongoing academic instruction in their classroom. Tier 2 interventions are therefore able to thwart the development of further, more chronic academic problems that may require special education services.

The behavioral side of the RTI model is analogous to this instructional approach. In short, when a student in a general education classroom is displaying behavior that does not meet the social expectations and schoolwide behavior program (Tier 1), teachers can refer a student for Tier 2 supports and interventions in an attempt to ameliorate the behavior problem and teach the student more effective behavior for school success. The Tier 2 intervention should be an efficient and accessible approach that has a standard assessment approach and criteria for entering the intervention. The final tier (Tier 3) for behavior should be individualized and intensive, as it targets the improvement of productive behavior while effectively decreasing problem behavior. Whereas assessment and intervention approaches vary at present, it is generally agreed that the transition between tiers in the RTI model should be systematic and accessible to both teachers and students (see Hawken, Vincent, & Schumann, 2008).

School staff have been heavily influenced by the passage of state and federal laws to use the RTI approach for both behavior and academics since 2000. The model is multitiered and systemic, with an emphasis on the use of evidence-based practices to enhance the academic and behavioral performance of all students. When students are not meeting their educational goals in the general education curriculum, problem-solving teams in schools meet to discuss the next best steps to provide effective instruction and intervention. The model has typically been displayed as in Figure 1.1.

Figure 1.1 illustrates the three tiers of the model and displays the integrated nature of behavior and academics. It also shows that most students in a school will be expected to respond to the general education curriculum. For the approximately 20% of students in need of additional support, the second and third tier of the model provide targeted group interventions (e.g., group tutoring for academics or social-problem-solving groups for behavior). For a few students in any school, individualized programs—such as those that may be provided for students with significant learning or behavioral difficulties—may be developed and implemented with the support of school specialists, such as Title I reading instructors or special educators, or of counselors or school psychologists.

## SYSTEMIC NATURE OF RESPONSE TO INTERVENTION AND POSITIVE BEHAVIOR INTERVENTIONS AND SUPPORTS

The efficiency and effectiveness of the schoolwide RTI model depends on all staff working collaboratively to implement identified evidence-based practices. The overriding notion of this system's approach is that the agreed-on educational practices can be used with all students at Tier 1, with a targeted group of students at Tier 2, and with individual students at Tier 3. The

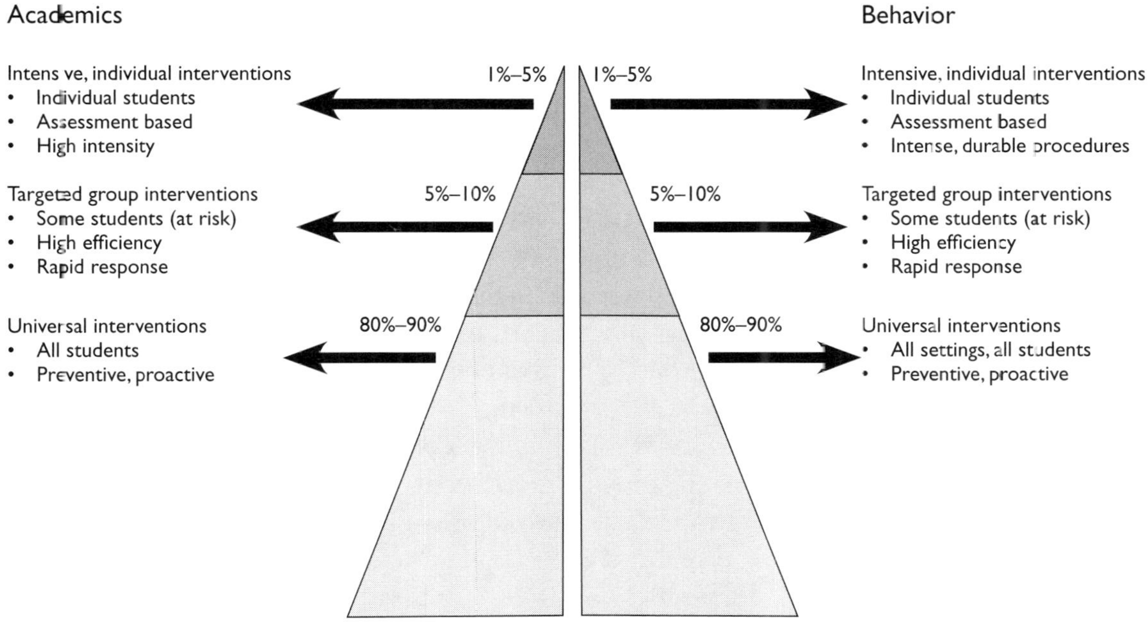


**Figure 1.1.** Visual representation of the positive behavior interventions and supports (PBIS)/response to intervention (RTI) model. (Adapted from OSEP Technical Assistance Center on PBIS. [2012]. *Response to Intervention [RTI] & PBIS*. Retrieved from http://www.pbis.org/school/rti.aspx; used by permission from OSEP TA–Center on PBIS.)

Technical Assistance Center on PBIS has noted that systemwide change is a process and that implementing schoolwide models takes up to 5 years. The center recently released its most current revision of its blueprint, which provides information for the assessment, planning, and implementation of SWPBIS for the implementation process (Sugai et al., 2010). The authors emphasize that SWPBIS is a framework or approach comprised of intervention strategies that enhance the schoolwide culture and influence students' academic and social outcomes. The blueprint promotes ideas to sustain durable outcomes for all students in schools. Implementation of SWPBIS is considered "interactive and informing" and necessarily involves multiple stakeholders (administrators, teachers, families, students) across school settings and into the community (Sugai et al., 2010, pp. 27–29). Implementation is therefore a team-based, action planning process lead by a school leadership team charged with: 1) assessing the PBIS priority needs from existing school data, 2) identifying and providing multiple professional development activities to enhance the use of evidence-based practices and interventions, 3) involving family and community members in the change process, and 4) using school data to regularly review their progress at monthly team and faculty meetings. To sustain any change in school, it is critical that this leadership group can translate the desired practices to the entire faculty so that the practices are used as intended across the school. The center blueprint is essential reading for any school/district that is interested in implementing SWPBIS.

In this context, it is important for school faculty and staff to keep in mind how deeply intertwined academic success is with social, emotional, and behavioral competence. For example, DiPerna and Elliott (1999) found five variables concerning student skills or behaviors that tended to predict overall success in school. They refer to these skills as "academic enablers," and they include prior academic achievement, prosocial skills, study skills, motivation, and levels of engagement. Their study found that students who have positively developed skills in all of these areas experienced the most school success, and those who had challenges in any of these areas had difficulties. Ray and Elliott (2006) later confirmed in a follow-up study that both self-concept and social skills are directly related to academic success for students.

These studies indicate that schools will not be effective if they focus solely on identifying and responding to student concerns in one area only, whether academic or social/behavioral. Instead, schools must recognize that student success is based on the interaction of *all* of these factors together. Knoff stated that the primary goals of the RTI and PBIS models should be to "maximize students' speed of academic and behavioral mastery, their academic achievement and independent learning capacity, and their social-emotional learning and behavioral self-management" (2009, p. 15). To that end, schools that use a proactive, systematic process for identifying and addressing student need across both academic and social/behavioral areas are better able to provide needed supports and skill development in the key areas *before* many students develop a more serious or prolonged problem that requires more intensive, formalized, and expensive supports to address. Schools today are faced with many students with a wide range of needs, and the practices outlined by the RTI and PBIS initiatives give schools the tools to more effectively and efficiently respond to these needs (Elliott, Huai, & Roach, 2007; Hawken et al., 2008; Knoff, 2009).

## CHARACTERISTICS OF HIGHLY EFFECTIVE SCHOOLS AND POSITIVE BEHAVIOR INTERVENTIONS AND SUPPORTS

The successful implementation of PBIS integrates important characteristics of effective schools across the three tiers of the model. For example, as a result of their research into the common characteristics of successful schools, Shannon and Bylsma identified nine common characteristics of schools that were consistently performing strongly or had dramatically improved their scores on required standardized testing, even when faced with the significant challenges of poverty, high mobility, and other variables. These characteristics include

> 1) a clear and shared focus; 2) high standards and expectations for all students; 3) effective school leadership; 4) high levels of collaboration and communication; 5) curriculum, instruction, and assessments aligned with state standards; 6) frequent monitoring of learning and teaching; 7) focused professional development; 8) a supportive learning environment; and 9) high levels of family and community involvement. (2007, p. 4)

These characteristics overlap significantly with the practices considered foundational for the effective implementation of PBIS (Knoff, 2009; Sugai et al., 2010).

Thinking of schools at their best as learning organizations (Senge, 2000) represents a step forward in the evolution of positive school environments. School staff have a clear understanding of their working realities, share this reality with one another, create new ways of dealing with old problems, and make positive movements in establishing effective practices. These schools become inquiry oriented and examine evidence around any practice before adopting it. In the end, they are better able to implement and sustain long-term improvements in their curriculum, collaborative practices, and student achievement and social interactions.

Another important characteristic of effective learning organizations, one that is strongly emphasized in PBIS, is the ability to identify evidence- (or scientifically) based practices that can be used as effective interventions, guidelines for program development, and ultimately as standards for success. Because both the No Child Left Behind Act of 2001 (PL 107-110) and IDEA 2004 require the use of evidence-based practices in schools, staff must consider how to integrate these practices into their daily work. In the context of program evaluation, this is often referred to as benchmarking. Benchmarking allows organizations to compare their growth against practices that are identified for essential change in their school, such as those listed previously. This becomes the means for a school to seek and maintain an optimum level of quality (Calabrese, 2000).

Several self-study approaches have been developed in the past 20 years to help schools measure their efforts to improve school climate by examining their level of functioning against benchmarks derived from school climate research. Examples include the Center for Prevention Research and Development's (2004) *School Improvement Self-Study*, the *Effective School Battery* (Gottfredson, 1991), and the *Organizational Health Survey* (Hoy & Feldman, 1999). The information from these surveys is analyzed and then returned to the school staff so that they can identify goals and objectives, address areas of concern, and measure progress. In the context of PBIS across the three-tier model a number of tools have been in development that utilize benchmarks to help school teams track progress in their implementation of recommended practices. Examples include the *Benchmarks of Quality* (Kincaid, Childs, & George, 2005, 2010), the *Team Implementation Checklist* (Sugai et al., 2011), and the *Effective Behavior Supports Self-Assessment Survey* (Sugai, Horner, & Todd, 2003). These tools are discussed further in Chapter 2.

The approach of deeply involving the individuals who will be responsible for implementing program change in the evaluation process itself is known as participatory evaluation (PE). Clancy (2010) summarizes PE as a theory-based program evaluation that provides a process for the direct involvement of key stakeholders, within the context of established evidence-based benchmarks, in a way that actually shapes the results of the evaluation. Involving stakeholders in the development and implementation of the evaluation process makes it more likely that the results will be understood and implemented with consistency. PE has proved an effective tool for organizational change, providing a structured process for evaluating the level of evidence-based practices currently in place while providing a framework for developing, implementing, and reviewing the status of key instructional practices over time. In addition, the consistent use of an assessment framework based on PE helps to develop a climate of ongoing organizational reflection and data-based decision making that also contributes to sustained improvement (Clancy, 2010; Fullan, 2007; Marino, 2007; Marzano, Waters, & McNulty, 2005).

Clancy (2010) suggested that PE can also be considered an empowerment process for teachers and staff because it acknowledges, respects, and utilizes the individual and shared knowledge of the stakeholders for the purpose of organizational learning and development, which is not typical of a more traditional top-down or external evaluation process (Owen, 2007; Patton, 2008; Wholey, Hatry, & Newcomer, 2004). As a result, PE helps educators bridge the research-to-practice gap by encouraging ongoing organizational and individual learning in the context of systematic data collection and analyses over time. PE facilitates a process of intentional change at the organizational and individual levels by creating learning environments and processes that carefully consider current instructional practices and then target training and support toward the development of needed new practices and skill sets. This leads to the improved implementation of evidence-based practices (Clancy, 2010; Owen, 2007; Patton, 2008; Wholey et al., 2004). The Self-Assessment and Program Review for Positive Behavior Interventions and Supports (SAPR-PBIS™) process we developed utilizes the principles of PE in a way that strengthens and empowers the school's PBIS leadership team while providing a tool for data-based decision making and program planning in order to support the implementation of an effective and sustained PBIS action plan.

SAPRpbis™ 2

# The SAPR-PBIS™ and How It Supports School Improvement

In 1998, we were funded by the U.S. Department of Education OSEP to evaluate a model demonstration project known as the Behavior, Emotional, and Academic Curriculum on the Needs of Students, or BEACONS, at four schools in Washington State (Cheney, 1998). One of the major goals of BEACONS was to evaluate the use of PBIS practices across the three-tiered model. In 2003, the BEACONS Project was awarded a second federal grant (Cheney, 2003) to expand the implementation of this project throughout the state, in an effort to increase the capacity of local school districts to establish and sustain PBIS programs. The focus of this project was to support schools in developing comprehensive SWPBIS systems to meet the needs of all students in the school, including those with or at risk of developing E/BPs. The project emphasized systematic school improvement efforts across all three levels of the PBIS model. In its first year, the BEACONS Outreach Project worked with 13 elementary schools in 7 school districts throughout Washington State. In the second year of the project, participating schools increased to 23 schools in 10 school districts. After the grant ended in 2008, a network of trainers in PBIS was established as the Washington PBIS network and has continued in more than 200 schools throughout the state.

BEACONS focused on using the PE process discussed in Chapter 1 to identify activities for schools as they addressed three training goals, which corresponded to the three-level model of PBIS. The first training goal focused on the foundations of PBIS and helped schools develop and enhance their schoolwide systems (Horner, Sugai, Todd, & Lewis-Palmer, 2004; Lewis & Sugai, 1999; Sugai et al., 2010). It included the development of a leadership team that was representative of the school community to guide the school through the process, establish the various features of PBIS, and introduce schools to using PBIS tools to inform their decision making. The second training goal focused on developing systematic supports for students at-risk of academic failure due to behavioral problems. The emphasis of this training goal was to expand the school's capacity to provide targeted interventions for students with behavioral problems (Hawken & Horner, 2003; Hawken et al., 2008; Walker, Cheney, Stage, & Blum, 2005). The third training goal focused on helping school teams learn how to effectively complete an FBA and use that information to develop a behavior intervention plan (BIP) for students with intensive or chronic behavior problems. These strategies help schools learn to understand the function of a child's behavior and to develop a system of supports and interventions that builds the child's prosocial skills and promotes social and behavioral success (Crone & Horner, 2003; O'Neill et al., 1997; Quinn, Gable, Rutherford, Nelson, & Howell, 1998).

Leadership teams at each of the schools also enhanced their approaches for supporting teachers, monitoring student progress, and involving parents more effectively in the school improvement process. Project staff met monthly with school leadership teams and faculty to provide coaching and technical assistance as the schools began to implement new strategies and systems supports. BEACONS emphasized systemic changes and strategies that were sustainable long after the project ended (Scott & Martinek, 2006). Participating school teams also had site visits with one another to observe and share strategies, approaches, and ideas for the implementation of PBIS.

To provide schools with a practical measure for assessing their progress in implementing evidence-based practices that are relevant to all three levels of PBIS supports, the BEACONS Project developed and piloted a self-assessment survey called the SAPR-PBIS™ evaluation tool (Cheney, Blum, & Walker, 2004). The SAPR-PBIS provides a tool for PBIS leadership teams to assess their progress on evidence-based practices that support the universal, secondary, and tertiary levels of the PBIS model. The evidence-based practices included in the SAPR-PBIS emphasize prevention and early intervention systems and supports for students with or at risk of developing E/BPs. Members of the school's leadership team completed the SAPR-PBIS annually or semiannually to provide a progress measure in areas that had been identified by each school's leadership team as priorities for improvement as part of its PBIS initiative. The leadership team was chosen as the focus for the process because it was capable of using the PE process to guide and implement critical PBIS school reform (Adelman & Taylor, 2001, 2007; Dwyer, 2002; Handler et al., 2007; Knoff, 2002; Sugai, Horner, & Gresham, 2002; Sugai et al., 2010).

It is important to note that, since 2000, a number of tools have been developed in the area of PBIS that integrate these principles of effective organizational learning with systematic feedback to schools, specifically with a PBIS focus. Three of these tools were developed by the National Technical Assistance Center on PBIS and were involved in the standardization process of the SAPR-PBIS. These tools include the School-wide Evaluation Tool (SET; Sugai, Lewis-Palmer, Todd, & Horner, 2001), which measures schools' progress across seven SWPBIS features at the universal level; the School-Wide Information System (SWIS; May et al., 2000), a web-based data collection and analysis system for tracking office discipline referrals; and the EBS Survey (Sugai, Horner, & Todd, 2003), which assists schools in annually evaluating their behavior support systems across four dimensions: schoolwide, nonclassroom, classroom, and individual student. Initially, the EBS Survey only addressed the schoolwide or primary dimension. Over subsequent years, features across the other dimensions of secondary and tertiary were added. The EBS Survey is given to each staff member, who reviews the items, then rates whether he or she feels the feature is either *in place*, *partially in place*, or *not in place* in the school. Staff also indicate what they believe the priority for improvement is for each feature. The leadership team then reviews the results and sets its action plan based on this feedback. Studies have been underway to establish its reliability and validity (Hagan-Burke et al., 2005; Safran, 2006). In addition, the Team Implementation Checklist (TIC; Sugai, Horner, & Lewis-Palmer, 2002) was developed to help leadership teams track their progress, on a quarterly basis, in implementing key aspects of universal SWPBIS. Specific steps related to the implementation of SWPBIS are outlined, and teams rate a practice as *achieved*, *in progress*, or *not started*. Space is provided for teams to set specific timelines and goals as part of ongoing action planning. The TIC has gone through three versions of development since 2001. It focuses primarily on Tier 1 universal implementation of SWPBIS but also includes some information regarding Tiers 2 and 3 (Sugai et al., 2001; Sugai, Horner, Lewis-Palmer, & Rossetto Dickey, 2011; Tobin, 2006). The TIC is useful for progress monitoring and formative evaluation of PBIS in schools and is intended to help school leadership teams make effective decisions that can influence all school staff to cooperate with their action plans

More recently developed, the Benchmarks of Quality (BOQ; Kincaid, Childs, & George, 2005) was also created for school teams to assess the level of implementation of schoolwide or primary-level practices. Designed as an alternative to the SET, which requires an external rater and several hours of training and time to administer, BOQ was developed for schools to complete themselves. It includes three components, a Coach Scoring Form, a Scoring Guide, and a Team Member Rating Form. The coach and members of the leadership team use the scale of *not in place*, *needs improvement*, or *in place* to rate their level of implementation of universal practices, and compare ratings and results until a final comprehensive rating is established. The BOQ has been found to have good reliability and validity, and serves as an effective alternative to the SET (Cohen, Kincaid, & Childs, 2007).

The Implementation Phases Inventory (IPI; Bradshaw, Barrett, & McKenna, 2008) was developed by PBIS Maryland to help track schools' progress in implementing 44 key practices across the three levels of SWPBIS. The tool is organized across four categories: preparation, initiation, implementation, and maintenance. Twice yearly, schools rate themselves using a three-point scale of *not in place*, *partially in place*, and *fully in place* for each practice. Every fall, teams rate their overall implementation along a seven-point scale that ranges from *preparation* to *maintenance of practices*.

## KEY FEATURES OF THE SAPR-PBIS PROCESS

The SAPR-PBIS is unlike many assessments of school progress in PBIS described previously, such as the EBS (Sugai, Horner, & Todd, 2003), which have staff members vote on items and then prioritize actions based on the majority of votes, or simply track progress toward the implementation of established practices or benchmarks over time. The SAPR-PBIS process is more like that of the BOQ, as it emphasizes the importance of discussion between a coach and team members about how 53 SWPBIS items are rated and decisions are made on priorities for schoolwide improvement. Not only does the SAPR-PBIS provide a tool to measure school improvement efforts over time using the principles of PE, but it also provides a structure for building and strengthening the leadership team itself, improving its capacity for facilitating and sustaining improved practices over time. When the leadership team has a team score as data, it provides them a reference point from year to year so that they can evaluate progress. Reviewing yearly data points has been used effectively in several studies that have targeted the improvement of school climate ratings (Griffith, 2000; Lindell & Brandt, 2000; Van Horn, 2003).

This team-based self-assessment approach has been well established for many years. In their discussion of the validity of self and team ratings when clinical psychologists rated their progress, Kelly and Fiske, as described in a classic article on the assessment validation process by Campbell and Fiske (1959), found what they called "a distinct trend for the staff-teammate block to show the greatest agreement. Both represent the external point of view. Both are averaged over three judges, minimizing individual biases and undoubtedly increasing reliabilities" (1959, p. 99). Kelly and Fiske concluded that self and teammate ratings "represent entirely separate methods and can be given the major emphasis in evaluating the data to be presented" (p. 95). James agreed that a rating built first from the perspective of its individual members, then by a meeting to establish a team rating, is an effective measure of organizational functioning, stating, "perceptual agreement implies a shared assignment of psychological meaning, from which it follows that an aggregate (mean) climate score provides the opportunity to describe the environment in psychological terms" (1982, p. 221). Of course, it is critical that team members consistently review data related to various aspects of the PBIS initiative so that their perspectives are also anchored in the daily reality of the school (Lewis & Sugai, 1999; Sugai et al., 2010).

Analysis of SAPR-PBIS data indicates that membership on a school team is a better predictor of the final team self-assessment results than any individual's professional role (Walker, Cheney, & Stage, 2009). This suggests that the group self-assessment ratings accurately represent a "shared psychological meaning" for the leadership teams in each of the schools. Therefore, the team scores can be considered accurate measures of organizational function.

Pilot testing occurred in 23 schools. In each school, a leadership team managed the completion of the SAPR-PBIS. Teams typically included the school administrator, special educator, school counselor or psychologist, general educators from both the primary and intermediate grade levels, as well as paraprofessionals. A total of 23 school leadership teams participated in the study, with 150 individual staff members. The average leadership team in this study included seven members.

The individual and team ratings process has three steps. First, individuals are given a copy of the SAPR-PBIS Individual Form. They look at all items that are organized under 10 evidence-based practices and individually rate the related indicators. For example, one practice that is important in the PBIS approach is the development of behavioral expectations. In the SAPR-PBIS, an individual would therefore rate how well the school is doing on defining and teaching behavioral expectations. He or she would rate items in this evidence-based practice on a five-point Likert scale, as shown in Figure 2.1. The ratings range from an item being *not in place* (1) to *fully in place* (5), and after rating all indicators, a total score is computed for the evidence-based practice.

After individuals rate all of the indicators representing the 10 practices, the next major step is for the team to meet and discuss its ratings. One member of the team, such as the School PBIS Coordinator, serves as the facilitator for the meeting. The facilitator asks the members for their scores and records the final ratings of the team on the SAPR-PBIS Team Meeting Form, along with relevant comments and questions for each evidence-based practice and/or indicator. For each practice, the facilitator asks each team member to share his or her total

| | |
|---|---|
| **Behavioral expectations are written and posted in classroom and nonclassroom settings.** | 1 2 3 4 5 |
| **Behavioral expectations are taught, monitored, and reinforced systematically in classroom and nonclassroom settings.** | 1 2 3 4 5 |

**Figure 2.1.** Example of two items in an evidence-based practice rated on a five-point Likert scale. (From Walker, B., & Cheney, D. [2012]. *The Self-Assessment and Program Review for Positive Behavior Interventions and Supports [SAPR-PBIS™]*. Baltimore, MD: Paul H. Brookes Publishing Co. Copyright © 2012 by University of Washington; adapted by permission.)

score and records that along the scoring bar located under each item. The team then determines an overall score for each of the 10 practices.

The final major step is for the team to identify schoolwide priorities for improvement. The team reviews its results and identifies at least three evidence-based practices to work on during the next school year. The practices and their related indicators are recorded as measurable objectives for improvement, and activities are generated to address each one. Throughout the year, the leadership team should revisit these objectives to determine the progress being made toward achieving them. This process is described in more detail in Chapters 3 and 4.

## THE TEN EVIDENCE-BASED PRACTICES IN THE SAPR-PBIS

Ten practices serve as the major domains for the SAPR-PBIS process. These practices were identified through a literature review, pilot testing in schools, and feedback from national leaders in the PBIS approach. Staff working on the BEACONS Project conducted an extensive literature review that included reviewing the tables of contents from journals that report on research related to school improvement, special education, prevention and early intervention, and behavioral issues. Journals reviewed included *Behavior Disorders*, *Prevention Science*, *Journal of Positive Behavior Supports*, *Exceptional Children*, *Journal of Emotional and Behavior Disorders*, and *Journal of School Psychology* between the years of 1997 and 2006. Once relevant articles were identified, staff reviewed their reference lists to locate other articles. In addition, a search of computer databases such as ERIC or PsychINFO under search terms such as *school improvement*, *positive behavior supports*, *school discipline*, *effective interventions*, and *school failure* resulted in identifying other relevant literature. These articles were reviewed, and key practices were identified for inclusion in the SAPR-PBIS. The literature review also included a content analysis of established school climate surveys as well as the existing PBIS evaluation tools, such as SET (Sugai, Lewis-Palmer, et al., 2001), the Positive Behavior Support Implementation and Planning Self-Assessment (Center on Positive Behavioral Interventions and Supports, 2002) and the EBS Survey (Sugai et al., 2003).

The results of this literature review were distilled into the content of the SAPR-PBIS. Because many of the identified practices permeate or support effective practices across the three levels of the PBIS model, the structure of the SAPR-PBIS was built on 10 core practices that

**Table 2.1.** Self-Assessment and Program Review for Positive Behavior Interventions and Supports (SAPR-PBIS™) subscales

1. Policies and procedures
2. Prevention and screening
3. Staff development
4. Behavioral expectations
5. Response to discipline referrals
6. Academic and social supports provided
7. Functional behavioral assessment as needed
8. Data collected and analyzed
9. Families as partners
10. Comprehensive plans for intensive needs

could be applied throughout the school improvement process rather than specifically organized around the three levels of the PBIS model. These 10 evidence-based practices formed the structure for what then became 10 subscales, which are referred to as *practices* throughout this manual. These subscales include what are referred to as *indicators*, which can provide benchmarks toward the implementation of the broader practice. The subscales also serve as a scaffold for schools to reference and use for planning throughout their PBIS work. Table 2.1 lists the names of the 10 evidence-based practices, or subscales, of the SAPR-PBIS.

Forty national leaders were included as participants in investigating the content validity of the SAPR-PBIS. Of the 40 who were identified, 21 individuals agreed to participate and 18 completed and returned surveys. The mean years of experience with PBIS was 10, with a range from 2 to 25 years. A descriptive analysis of levels of education found that half the respondents were at the Ph.D. level, slightly less than half at the master's level, and one at the bachelor's level.

Chapter 5 describes each of these practices in depth along with the related indicators that suggest at what level the practice is actually being implemented in the school. The information in Chapter 5 is intended to provide the empirical basis for each practice so that schools can be confident they are using evidence-based practices while they improve their SWPBIS methods.

SAPRpbis™ 3

# Beginning the SAPR-PBIS™ Process

Because the leadership team is a crucial part of the school improvement process, and central to the SAPR-PBIS™ process, it is important to take the time to establish an effective foundation from which the team can develop and function. This foundation is discussed throughout this chapter and includes strategically identifying members for the team, establishing group norms, and taking the time needed to address differences of opinion and experience. When teams take the time to address these dynamics proactively, they are more likely to be effective and are better prepared when challenges arise.

## SETTING UP THE LEADERSHIP TEAM FOR SUCCESS

The foundation of a school's approach to the effective implementation of PBIS or RTI rests on the behavioral expertise of its school leadership team. Members of the leadership team play a key role in facilitating and sustaining the change inherent in any school reform initiative (Dwyer, 2002; George & Martinez, 2007; Knoff, 2002; Sugai et al., 2010; Sugai et al., 2002). As part of his work on organizational change in schools, Knoff defined an effective team as "a highly communicative group of people with different backgrounds, skills, and abilities with a common purpose who are working together to achieve clearly defined goals" (2000, p. 30). Knoff added that effective teams include members who are "interdependent, motivated, unafraid of risks and failure, and thrive on challenge" (p. 30).

Effective leadership teams are made up of representatives of the stakeholders within the school and community that guide and shape the implementation of the PBIS initiative for the school. Typically, a leadership team includes an administrator, school psychologist, counselor, special education teacher, cross-grade general education teachers, and a paraprofessional, representing key areas of student supervision and support. Experienced leadership teams may expand to include parent and community representatives and, in secondary schools, a representative from the student body. To be most efficient and effective, leadership teams should be no larger than 8 to 10 people. In order for this team to have the time, resources, and energy to implement PBIS effectively, it is recommended that the PBIS initiative be one of the top three priorities in a school's strategic plan (Todd, Horner, Sugai, & Sprague, 1999).

Each year, the leadership team is charged with developing, evaluating, and updating the school's PBIS implementation plan, as well as leading the school community through the process of bringing the components of PBIS to life. This annual plan contains specific, measurable goals, activities, and timelines for the effective implementation of PBIS for the school. Since 2000, there has been a great deal of research to establish the key building blocks of effective PBIS systems; exactly how those indicators are implemented varies from school to school. One reason that PBIS has been effective for so many schools in a wide range of communities and grade levels is that, although the building blocks of effective PBIS are now well defined, the development and implementation process is shaped by the members of the school community to reflect the individual needs, strengths, and culture of each school.

The practices outlined in the SAPR-PBIS represent the key building blocks mentioned above, and the leadership team uses the process to begin crafting a plan for developing and implementing PBIS in a way that best meets the needs of its school. To be implemented effectively, the plan is shared regularly with staff, students, and families; monitored frequently; and adjusted as necessary to maximize the effectiveness and efficiency of the PBIS system (Cheney, Blum, & Walker, 2004; Sugai et al., 2010; Sugai et al., 2002). The SAPR-PBIS provides a process for the leadership team to develop and monitor systematic plans for school improvement using evidence-based benchmarks of effective practices. It serves as a first step for schools beginning the process and as a process for established teams to track ongoing efforts for school improvement and the implementation of PBIS in their schools.

## SETTING NORMS AND EXPECTATIONS FOR THE LEADERSHIP TEAM

Because the work of the leadership team is so important, it can be most effective when the members have first taken time to establish norms and procedures for their work together. This process lays the foundation for how the group will make decisions, establish priorities, communicate, and problem-solve throughout its work together. In their study of group and individual behaviors in work groups, Ehrhart and Naumann (2004) found that the more clearly developed group norms were, the better functioning and more productive the group was. In addition, they found that the individual members in such groups tended to be more productive and positive. In the context of PBIS, taking the time to craft a clear set of expectations and procedures for the leadership team sets an example for the entire school staff when they are asked during the school year to teach social expectations and procedures to their students. The leadership team is therefore modeling the skills and components of effective PBIS.

In this context, for the SAPR-PBIS process to be most effective, it is important that the team include input from staff that represent a range of perspectives and experiences throughout the school community. Therefore, it is critical that each team member know that his or her unique perspective on school functioning is a valued and necessary part of the self-assessment process, even when it may differ from that of other team members. For example, paraprofessionals are often charged with a great deal of supervision during unstructured times of the day (e.g., recess, lunchtime, before- and after-school transitions). They may observe and experience different types of student behavior and interaction that are not as evident when a teacher or an administrator is also present. When discussing their ratings during the team assessment process, it can be uncomfortable for paraprofessionals to share what may be a lower rating on a practice than an administrator or teacher. It is critical that everyone on the team recognize that *all* information is critical for gaining an accurate picture of the issues the school encounters; therefore, each individual must be supported in reporting his or her individual perspective, even if it varies from other members of the team. To support this process, it is very important for the team to first establish operating norms that clearly state the value of each individual's perspective on the team and that keep the content of the discussions professional, honest, and objective. A sample of one school leadership team's operating norms included the following:

Use professional, descriptive comments and feedback (not personal criticisms)
Begin and end meetings on time
Communicate regularly and directly with one another
Be data based whenever possible

In the spirit of PBIS, as these norms were established, the team discussed in detail what each meant in terms of practical daily behavior, and the norms were posted during all leadership team meetings.

Establishing roles and specific responsibilities is another procedure to improve the effectiveness of team meetings as well as the overall functioning of the leadership team. Establishing a facilitator for the SAPR-PBIS process and subsequent meetings is particularly important. In some schools, that role often seems to fall naturally to the building administrator. However, our experience suggests that giving the role of facilitator to another member of the team can be a powerful gesture. It signals that this truly is a collaborative team process wherein every member of the team has equal input and involvement. Another role that can be established is that of reporter. This individual is responsible for periodically updating staff on the leadership team activities and SAPR-PBIS results during faculty and staff meetings. In addition, establishing a notetaker or recorder who will take and distribute meeting minutes, a timekeeper to keep the group focused, and a data manager to prepare and share relevant data reports will also help teams function more efficiently. These roles can be rotated periodically based on the needs of individuals and the team.

Sharing responsibilities helps to cultivate investment and ownership in the school improvement process throughout the team while providing opportunities for distributing leadership experience and, with it, confidence. It also creates an opportunity for all members of the team to learn to support and coach one another throughout the PBIS initiative, rather than relying on building administrators to make sure things "get done" (Higgins, Young, Weiner, & Wlodarczyk, 2009). Involving multiple members in actively supporting the team process increases the likelihood that a sustainable structure for school improvement takes hold and that the PBIS process is perceived as a school-based initiative, requiring the support and involvement of the school community as a whole.

Teams that develop healthy group cohesion are more likely to be effective and are better able to address the inevitable types of conflict faced by working teams in a productive manner. In their research on measuring team effectiveness, Singh and Muncherji found that in a healthy, productive team, each person is "valued for his individuality as well as his unique competence and contribution" (2007, p. 130). Teams that cultivate mutual respect and high levels of trust are not only more productive, but they also provide greater satisfaction to participants.

## BEGINNING THE SAPR-PBIS PROCESS

The SAPR-PBIS is completed in two steps. First, each member of a school's PBIS leadership team completes the SAPR-PBIS Individual Form independently. Second, the team members meet and compile their individual scores using the SAPR-PBIS Team Meeting Form in order to develop a summary of the team's perceptions. The self-assessment includes the 10 evidence-based practices related to implementing PBIS systems and supports across all three levels of the PBIS model. Included within each practice is a list of indicators that further define and operationalize these practices. Once the leadership team is established and norms and operating procedures have been set up, the facilitator orients the team to the SAPR-PBIS process. After the team has discussed the process and reviewed the scoring instructions, team members are then given time (usually a week or two prior to the next leadership team meeting) to complete the Individual Form. Team members assess areas of strength and potential areas for further development when compared with the evidence-based practices. Details on the team aspect of the process are outlined in Chapter 4.

The references to data and documentation throughout the scale refer to existing practices, school documents, or data (e.g., discipline referrals, student or staff handbooks) available in the school. The team members should consider their unique perspectives and experience, along with the information available to them, to establish ratings on each of the practices. The ratings of each indicator within the practices are then added up, providing a total rating for each practice. It is important to note that, during the process of filling out the Individual Forms, leadership team members should *not* compare notes and ratings. That process will occur during the team meeting, when each team member brings a completed Individual Form to use as part of the team rating process on the scheduled date. This helps to preserve the unique perspective and understanding of the practices of each team member.

Occasionally a team member will feel that he or she does not know enough about a particular practice to establish a rating. This lack of knowledge alone is important information for the team, because in order for the leadership team to be effective, every member should have a basic understanding and awareness of how each of the 10 key PBIS practices are implemented in the school. In this case, the team member should rate that practice a 1 and make a note on the form that he or she has no awareness of the practice. That information should then be shared with the rest of the team during the team rating discussion and noted on the Team Meeting Form. As a part of the first team discussion, priority should be given to discussing how to ensure that all leadership team members are kept up to date on activities related to the PBIS initiative.

The SAPR-PBIS rating scales use the following Likert-type scale for each indicator, from which a total score is obtained for each practice throughout the process.

5 = This indicator of the evidence-based practice is *fully in place.* Data and documentation indicate that it is functioning well and implemented with a high degree of consistency. The practice requires only maintenance of effort at this time.
4 = This indicator of the evidence-based practice is *mostly in place.* Data and documentation indicate that it is consistently implemented in school practice. However, there may be some issues with the consistency of implementation that suggest it requires additional work to be fully in place.
3 = This indicator of the evidence-based practice is *moderately in place.* Data and documentation indicate that it may only be implemented with consistency about half the time. It is clearly in need of additional work to be fully in place.
2 = This indicator of the evidence-based practice is only *partially in place.* Data and documentation indicate that it is inconsistently implemented and needs much more work to be fully in place.
1 = This indicator of the evidence-based practice is *not yet in place.* Data and documentation indicate that it is rarely implemented with any consistency and will require extensive work before it can be fully in place. (*Note:* This rating may also mean that an individual does not know enough about a practice to establish a rating, in which case this reason for indicating a 1 should be noted; see Row 5.3 in Figure 3.1.)

Team members should familiarize themselves with the scale and discuss any questions as a group before completing the individual forms. Figure 3.1 provides a sample of a completed individual section with written comments for reference.

## TRANSFORMING DIFFICULT CONVERSATIONS INTO LEARNING CONVERSATIONS

One important aspect of an effective leadership team is how members approach conflict resolution (Singh & Muncherji, 2007). The most effective teams approach conflict resolution proactively as a part of their norm-building process, predicting where they are likely to run into challenges and establishing norms and procedures to address them (Behar, Peterson, Mannix, & Trochim, 2008). In their study comparing high-functioning to low-functioning teams, Behar and colleagues found that highly effective teams approached their tasks using a discuss or debate approach to communication, with the focus of reaching compromise and consensus that represented the input of all team members. These teams used nonemotional, fact-driven discussions that helped all the team members understand how and why the group came to consensus on issues. These high-functioning teams established norms and expectations that applied to all team members and framed the team's approach to interaction with one another and to their assigned task, with the goal of strengthening and enhancing the team's ability to work together in the future. When conflicting perspectives existed, these were explored carefully, and group members were able to use evidence to persuade one another and make

| 5 | School procedures for responding to discipline referrals and emergency situations are implemented consistently and effectively. | | |
|---|---|---|---|
| 5.1 | **The discipline process includes criteria for office referrals, addressing the behavior of concern, and returning the student to the classroom.**<br>Does a clear, consistently implemented process exist? Is it written down? Are all students, faculty, staff, and families aware of the process? Is it followed consistently? | *Notes*<br>Some of this is in place, and some is partially written down. See start of year notes to parents also. | 1 2 (3) 4 5 |
| 5.2 | **Discipline and suspension policies are clearly stated in the handbook and effectively communicated to parents, students, and staff.**<br>Does a written statement of the policies exist? Are the consequences for certain behaviors clearly defined? Is the statement available in all the languages of the student community? Does everyone understand and follow the written process? | *Notes* | 1 (2) 3 4 5 |
| 5.3 | **Discipline procedures meet state and federal regulatory requirements (e.g., use functional behavioral assessments [FBAs] and behavior intervention plans [BIPs] when appropriate, employ documentation and parent contact as required).**<br>Are all of the policies and procedures related to discipline aligned with regulations? Do students who qualify for special education due to behavioral problems have an effective FBA and BIP in place? Does everyone involved in discipline understand federal and state laws related to reporting and implementing discipline? | *Notes*<br>Not sure what this means | (1) 2 3 4 5 |
| 5.4 | **Staff with specialized training are available to help resolve students' social-emotional conflicts.**<br>Have some or all of your staff members been formally trained to respond to and help students who are having difficulties, and are they available to help such students calm down and/or talk about their problems? Does the method used align with PBIS? | *Notes* | 1 2 3 (4) 5 |
| 5.5 | **A designated area is available in the office, hallway, or a classroom to resolve students' social-emotional problems (e.g., a problem-solving area, think time area, cool-off spot, buddy room).** *Note:* This is *not* a reference to a time-out room.<br>Are there supervised places where students can be sent when a problem is starting, where they can refocus, calm down, and make a plan to get back on track? Is this system used consistently and effectively? | *Notes*<br>Have to meet with students in middle of busy office | (1) 2 3 4 5 |
| 5.6 | **A team of teachers and staff is trained to use a crisis prevention and intervention program for emergency situations.**<br>Have some staff members been specifically trained in responding to crisis situations and helping students de-escalate in a way that protects student and staff safety if needed? Is the approach used in alignment with PBIS? | *Notes* | 1 2 3 (4) 5 |

Comments or questions for the team:

Total your score for this practice: 15

**Figure 3.1.** Sample from a completed Individual Form. (From Walker, B., & Cheney, D. [2012]. *The Self-Assessment and Program Review for Positive Behavior Interventions and Supports [SAPR-PBIS™]*. Baltimore, MD: Paul H. Brookes Publishing Co. Copyright © 2012 by University of Washington; adapted by permission.)

final decisions. When team members were discussing difficult issues or differences of opinion, the team members purposefully focused on the content of what was being said rather than on the delivery style of the person speaking. In contrast, lower functioning teams often attempted to overlook conflict and interpersonal tension when they arose, or reacted to conflict by attempting to create rules in an effort to contain it when it occurred.

In their book *Difficult Conversations: How to Discuss What Matters Most*, Stone, Patton, and Heen (1999) suggested three key skills that can help team members "inquire to learn" during the more difficult aspects of conversations. First, ask open-ended questions. This gives speakers more flexibility regarding how to answer, directing their response to share what is most important to them—for example, "Help me better understand what you are saying." Second, ask for more concrete information. This helps all team members to better understand an individual's position regarding school practice. Examples include

- Can you describe an example of that situation?
- Can you say a little more about how you see things?
- How do you see it differently?
- What information do you have that others might not?
- Can you describe how this occurs from your perspective?

Finally, the authors suggest that the other team members paraphrase what the previous team member has said for clarity, before moving on to sharing their own feelings and perspectives. This allows team members to check their understanding of what their colleague has shared, demonstrates that they have listened carefully to the speaker, and acknowledges their contribution to the conversation.

Using these skills—and having the courage to work through some of the difficult conversations that arise when team members from varying perspectives work closely together on school reform—strengthens the team and the self-assessment process. Taking the time to build a shared understanding of the current status of practices within the school is the foundation for creating the unified vision for an even better future. As the leadership team grows more comfortable with these skills and with addressing more challenging topics, it may also find it helpful to share these same strategies during faculty and staff meetings focusing on the PBIS initiative.

SAPRpbis™ 4

# Conducting the SAPR-PBIS™ Team Meeting

One of the most important aspects of the SAPR-PBIS™ process occurs when the team discusses and completes the SAPR-PBIS Team Meeting Form together. Leadership team members come together with their completed Individual Forms to share their ratings and perspectives on how the school is doing across the 10 key PBIS practices. Because the leadership team plays such a crucial role in the implementation of a school's PBIS initiative, this opportunity to develop a group consensus on the status of existing practices and goals for improvement is a critical aspect of the SAPR-PBIS process. The process moves the leadership team beyond a simple benchmarking routine in which data on the activities of the school's PBIS initiative are recorded, toward an opportunity for the leadership team to transform into a powerful change agent in the school improvement process.

There is a powerful effect on the leadership team dynamic when colleagues have an ongoing conversation and focus their collective energy on the self-assessment process. The team discussion provides the opportunity for members to share their learning and insight with one another, and ultimately with the whole school community as a part of the school's PBIS initiative (Dwyer, 2002; Knoff, 2002, 2009; Sugai et al., 2010; Sugai et al., 2002) When a leadership team has a unified understanding of the strengths and needs of a school that is based on data along with a clearly defined plan for improvement, it is going to be more influential with the school community and better able to implement and sustain systemic change than a team that has not taken the time to establish a shared understanding and collective vision (Bruce, 1993; Knoff, 2000; Sugai et al., 2002). Because the SAPR-PBIS utilizes the principles of PE described in Chapter 1, it provides an evaluation structure intentionally designed to improve the utilization of findings for PBIS improvement by the leadership team, which will be responsible for directly implementing and supporting the recommended improvements based on the program evaluation. As a result, the SAPR-PBIS can be used as a tool for the facilitation of an organizational learning process that encourages intentional, lasting changes (Clancy, 2010; Suarez-Herrera, Springett, & Kagan, 2009). By involving stakeholders in the development and implementation of the program evaluation, utilization of results is likely to increase. Through this process, an environment of ongoing organizational reflection and data-based decision making emerges, including the development of systems that support sustained and ongoing improvement (Clancy, 2010; Fullan, 2007; Marzano et al., 2005).

## THE SAPR-PBIS TEAM MEETING

The first step of the team meeting is for the facilitator to review the norms and procedures previously established by the team, underscoring the importance and value of each team member's individual perspective and ratings, then summarizing the team scoring process. Then, the facilitator begins the process of gathering the individual team members' ratings across the 10 key PBIS practices, using the Team Meeting Form. This aspect of the process takes approximately 90 minutes. Because providing an opportunity for each member of the team to share his or her perspective is a vital part of the process, this is not a time to hurry the team discussion. Instead, schedule additional time to finish the process if it appears to be needed. As team members become more experienced in working together and with the SAPR-PBIS process overall, they will become more comfortable and efficient in the process. Details of how this process unfolds are described in the following sections.

### Scoring Each Practice

Beginning with the first PBIS practice, Policies and Procedures, the facilitator asks each individual team member for his or her total score for this practice and for any comments or questions related to this practice. As each team member reports his or her score for the practice, the facilitator places a tally mark on the corresponding section of the scoring bar representing the practice and other members of the team listen carefully. If any member of the team has a question about what is being discussed, clarifying questions should be asked as needed. After all individual scores are marked, the facilitator circles the implementation level that contains the majority of the individuals' scores. This will indicate the level at which the team perceives this practice to be in place. The facilitator also records the questions or comments made by team members in the area provided below the scoring bar. It is important for the team to take some time to discuss these questions before moving on to the next item. This direct, detailed discussion of the practices is a very important aspect of the process. It helps the team build a shared understanding related to the PBIS practices in the school as well as trust in one another.

### The Appearance of a Clear Consensus

At times there will be fairly consistent scores among the team members for a specific practice. In this case, it is tempting to assume that consistent total scores indicate that all team members have a shared perspective on the practice, and then move quickly on to the next item. That may not, however, be the case. Before moving to another practice, the facilitator should ask team members to review their ratings on specific practice indicators. Did any stand out to the various team members as functioning much higher or lower than the others?

If so, does agreement exist among the team members about those indicators? The facilitator then marks the indicator(s) that have been highlighted for further discussion when setting goals. If there is a true consensus, team members will have rated the indicators in a similar way. If there is some variation within the ratings of the indicators, the team should take some time to explore and discuss members' varying perspectives in order to come to consensus about what aspects of the practice stand out as a priority for improvement. See the scoring example in Figure 4.1 for details of how this can be recorded.

| 5 | **School procedures for responding to discipline referrals and emergency situations are implemented consistently and effectively.** |
|---|---|
| 5.1 | The discipline process includes criteria for office referrals, addressing the behavior of concern, and returning the student to the classroom.* *See action plan for details.* |
| 5.2 | Discipline and suspension policies are clearly stated in the handbook and effectively communicated to parents, students, and staff. |
| 5.3 | Discipline procedures meet state and federal regulatory requirements (e.g., use functional behavioral assessments [FBAs] and behavior intervention plans [BIPs] when appropriate, employ documentation and parent contact as required). |
| 5.4 | Staff with specialized training are available to help resolve students' social-emotional conflicts. |
| 5.5 | A designated area is available in the office, hallway, or a classroom to resolve students' social-emotional problems (e.g., a problem-solving area, think time area, cool-off spot, buddy room). *Note:* This is *not* a reference to a time-out room. |
| 5.6 | A team of teachers and staff is trained to use a crisis prevention and intervention program for emergency situations.* *See action plan for details.* |

Outliers

Tally marks represent scores from team members. Circle the range with the most scores. You may circle the overlap between two boxes if applicable.

| ✓ ✓ | ✓ | ✓✓✓✓ | ✓ | |
|---|---|---|---|---|
| **6–10**<br>1 = Not yet in place | **11–15**<br>2 = Partially in place | **16–20**<br>3 = Moderately in place | **21–25**<br>4 = Mostly in place | **27–30**<br>5 = Fully in place |

*Note:* The top numbers in bold represent the range of total scores from the Individual Form (e.g., 6 questions with 1–5 possible points equals a range of 6–30). The bottom numbers correspond with the rating scale, allowing the team to see where its total scores fall along that scale.

Place a tally mark above the box that includes the total score reported for the practice. If there is a significant discrepancy between ratings, or a low overall score, discuss the individual scores for each of the indicators in order to come to a consensus on the team rating and to identify priorities for improvement. In addition, record any specific questions, ideas, or comments that emerge from the discussion that the team would like to be able to reference in the future. See *The SAPR-PBIS™ Manual* for more suggestions about facilitating this discussion.

**Figure 4.1.** Example of team scoring process. (From Walker, B., & Cheney, D. [2012]. *The Self-Assessment and Program Review for Positive Behavior Interventions and Supports [SAPR-PBIS™]*. Baltimore, MD: Paul H. Brookes Publishing Co. Copyright © 2012 by University of Washington; adapted by permission.)

## The Importance and Value of Outliers

When a team member, or more than one member, reports a score that is outside the range reported by the majority of the team, it is very important for the facilitator to ask for more information about that team member's reasoning and experiences related to the score. In Figure 4.1, for example, the facilitator would want to ask whether there are particular indicators within the practice that received a low score, or if the low ratings were across all of the practice indicators, and then ask for examples or particular questions or issues that affect the rating(s). Then the team can compare and contrast the various team members' experience and understanding of the practice, which often leads to valuable insights related to its implementation. This same discussion might also happen when one or more team members rated the practice 1 or more points higher than the rest of the team. In that case, the facilitator would want to discuss the members' perceptions of strength for the practice. Although it can feel frustrating to stop and discuss a practice in depth based on one team member's experience, these outlier situations are very valuable to the team because they point to potential areas of improvement and signal to the team which practices are not as fully developed as some may have thought, while emphasizing the importance of each individual member's experience and perspectives.

For example, Practice 5 of the SAPR-PBIS focuses on how the school responds to discipline referrals. The administrator and team members working in the office may rate several of the indicators related to this practice as strongly in place due to their daily experience with discipline. Practices and procedures that they implement every day are likely to seem very clear to them. Other members of the team, such as teachers and paraprofessionals, who are not regularly part of implementing disciplinary actions, may not think the disciplinary code is consistently or systematically delivered. These team members may believe some policies and procedures are unclear or inconsistent and as a result may end up rating the item lower than the administrator. Rather than interpreting this difference of opinion as a lack of support or a negative judgment on the efforts of those team members more closely involved in responding to discipline who scored the practice highly, the team must recognize that this is a valuable opportunity to clarify practices, share experiences, and identify ways to improve the practice across perspectives. It is highly likely that what is being shared within the leadership team represents similar issues and/or confusion that exists in the school.

During these more difficult discussions, it is important for the facilitator to remind the team to uphold the established norms and keep the conversation focused on objective descriptions of experiences and based on data whenever possible. The challenge for the team is to use these opportunities to acknowledge that this difference of experience and perspective is valuable, helping the team to recognize areas of growth for the leadership team and the school as a whole. The section on transforming difficult conversations in Chapter 3 provides more detailed strategies for the team and facilitators concerned with this aspect of the process.

## TEAM SCORING EXAMPLE

This section explores how a team has evaluated its present performance in responding to discipline concerns, using Practice 5 as an example. As each team member reports on ratings of the six indicators within Practice 5, the other members of the team listen as the facilitator asks for the overall score for the practice. The facilitator then places tally marks over the scoring box corresponding to the total given by each team member. In the example in Figure 4.1, four team members reported and gave scores ranging from 16 to 20, yet two members of the group scored the practice much lower overall. They are identified as outliers in Figure 4.1. In the group discussion that followed the team reporting, the group determined that Indicators 5.1 and 5.6 were consistently the lowest rated by the individual team members, and they identified those as possible items for improvement by starring them.

## DETERMINING PRIORITIES FOR IMPROVEMENT

Once the facilitator has recorded the scores for each of the practices, the team begins to identify which practices and/or indicators it wants to focus on as priorities for improvement in the coming year. Singh and Muncherji (2007) found the following attributes helpful for identifying effective team objectives: 1) they are specific, measurable, challenging, and scheduled, 2) they are linked to the broader organizational strategy, 3) all team members participate in their development, and 4) they include regular presentation of team performance and decisions to the larger faculty and district leadership. With these attributes in mind, we recommend that team members complete these steps to determine their primary priorities for improvement:

1. Review the results of the team evaluation and identify three evidence-based practices to focus on improving in the schoolwide PBIS system initiative. If the team wants to identify more than three objectives for improvement, we suggest that it carefully determines whether it has the resources to be successful in more priorities. We have learned that it is better for a team to identify fewer priorities for improvement and successfully address them, than to identify many and be unable to address them adequately.

2. Review the indicators of these practices to help develop specific, measurable objectives in an action plan for improvement as shown in Figure 4.2. An additional example of an action plan is included in Appendix A.

3. In the space provided on the Action Plan page of the Team Meeting Form, record these objectives, briefly summarize the specific activities or strategies related to addressing each objective, and summarize a plan for tracking and measuring progress. Throughout the year, the leadership team periodically reviews progress made toward fully implementing these objectives.

| Objective 1 | Activities | Evaluation |
|---|---|---|
| Continue to improve our response to discipline concerns by enhancing the following:<br>5.1. The discipline process includes criteria for office referrals, addressing the behavior of concern, and returning the student to the classroom.<br>5.6. A team of teachers and staff is trained to use a crisis prevention and intervention program for emergency situations. | 5.1. During a full staff meeting, discuss the parameters of behaviors to be addressed directly by teachers and/or supervising staff versus what should be an office discipline referral. Leadership team will process input to develop clearer, more detailed language for the handbooks.<br>5.6. Develop a team, including representatives from administration, general education, and supervising paraprofessionals, to receive full training in crisis prevention and intervention.<br>During a full staff meeting, share key ideas and early warning signs and discuss strategies for seeking out a trained team member in a crisis situation. | 5.1a. Track the number of office discipline referrals and the number of incidents addressed by the teacher or supervising staff (via use of buddy rooms as well as minor discipline forms submitted monthly).<br>5.6a. Track the number of incident reports and office referrals documenting "crisis" response events.<br>5.6b. Obtain staff feedback on understanding and ability to apply strategies after basic training on crisis prevention and early response. |

**Figure 4.2.** Sample Action Plan for improvement based on scoring example. (From Walker, B., & Cheney, D. [2012]. *The Self-Assessment and Program Review for Positive Behavior Interventions and Supports [SAPR-PBIS™]*. Baltimore, MD: Paul H. Brookes Publishing Co. Copyright © 2012 by University of Washington; adapted by permission.)

## MONITORING POSITIVE BEHAVIOR INTERVENTIONS AND SUPPORTS PRACTICES OVER TIME

In order to visually display changes in the scores of each of the evidence-based practices across time, the leadership team can enter the team score for each PBIS practice into a spreadsheet such as Microsoft's Excel program. Because the number of indicators, and thus the total score possible, varies with each practice, the range of scores within each segment of the bar varies across practices. However, each segment of the scoring bar is anchored with the numbers 1–5 from the SAPR-PBIS rating scale. This feature will allow the team to generate line or bar graphs that display changes in scores over time. The graphs provide an "at a glance" summary of the team's ratings of each practice over time that can be easily shared with stakeholders.

Figure 4.3 displays a graph of 2 years of SAPR-PBIS scores for a school using this process to guide its implementation of PBIS. As indicated by the rating scale, scores of 4 indicate that the practice is mostly established in the school. However, further work is needed to ensure that all the indicators in the practice are implemented consistently and with fidelity. In relation to other data in PBIS measures, a rating of 4 on the SAPR-PBIS is somewhat equivalent to a practice functioning at the 80% level, a level that is considered optimal for key practices in measures such as the School-wide Evaluation Tool (SET; Sugai, Lewis-Palmer, et al., 2001). The practices in which the team has rated a 5, or fully in place, suggest that data and documentation within the school show that all the indicators in the practice are implemented with fidelity and are well established in the school. To identify priorities for improvement for a school year, team members should target practices scored at or below a rating of 4 and establish a plan of action for addressing them, with the exception of plans the team might make to move a practice to full implementation (from 4 to 5 on the rating scale). Figure 4.4 provides a sample action plan for improvement for a school that addresses three practices. The leadership team should keep in mind that it often takes 2–5

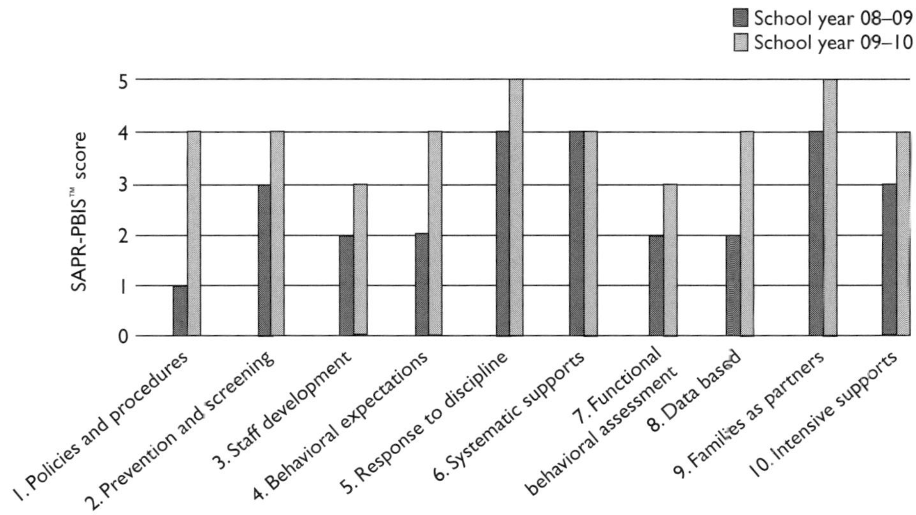


**Figure 4.3.** Sample progress chart for Apple Center School 2008–2010 showing Self-Assessment and Program Review for Positive Behavior Interventions and Supports (SAPR-PBIS™) scores.

years for schools to fully master PBIS practices (Lewis & Sugai, 1999; Sugai et al., 2010). Once a practice is established at the 4- to 5-point level, it is important to continue to monitor progress to be certain that the school maintains and updates the practice as needed.

It is also very important that the leadership team has access to clearly reported and organized sources of data to inform its decision making. This allows for better planning and problem solving. Therefore, data from the SAPR-PBIS is designed to be integrated with data from other common measures of PBIS such as the SET (Sugai, Lewis-Palmer, et al., 2001), and the PBIS Blueprint (Sugai et al., 2010), along with other related tools available from the national Technical Assistance Center on Positive Behavior Interventions and Supports (http://www.pbis.org). Another tool that can be very helpful to schools using the SAPR-PBIS process is the School-Wide Information System (SWIS; May et al., 2000). SWIS is an electronic database that tracks and reports office discipline referrals in a very easy to use yet detailed manner (http://www.swis.org). Any other detailed spreadsheet tracking of discipline referrals can also be useful. The team may also want to reference other data summaries that the school can provide (e.g., attendance and tardy rates, graduation and dropout statistics, academic assessments). When the leadership team strategically identifies the type of data and assessments that will best provide the information and guidance it needs to develop and monitor the PBIS implementation plan, it provides a firmer foundation for ongoing decision making and implementation.

## TROUBLESHOOTING STALLED PRACTICES AND PLANS

On occasion, a leadership team finds that despite well-written plans and interventions, it has not found evidence that a targeted practice is trending in the hoped-for direction. Such stalled progress suggests two potential issues, explained in the following sections.

| Objective 1 | Activities | Evaluation |
| --- | --- | --- |
| Improve staff response to emerging discipline issues (Practice 5) | Establish an interpersonal problem-solving approach and train all supervising staff in facilitating it with students. | a. Review office discipline data for increase or decrease in major referrals.<br>b. Collect problem-solving forms to review the number of students and staff using them.<br>c. Staff complete social validity questionnaire at year end. |
| **Objective 2** | **Activities** | **Evaluation** |
| Continue efforts to get a well functioning functional behavioral assessment (FBA) team in place so that we can provide better individualized interventions for students with significant emotional or behavioral problems (Practice 7). | 1. Continue training behavior support team (BST) on using FBA as needed.<br>2. Expand the number of students supported by FBA.<br>3. Provide all staff an introduction to FBA and behavior pathway model. | a. Count BST FBA case notes and behavior intervention plans (BIP) to determine the number of students supported.<br>b. Survey staff for interest, understanding levels of FBA at completion of orientation.<br>c. Track referrals to determine whether there is an increase in teachers requesting supports at this level. |
| **Objective 3** | **Activities** | **Evaluation** |
| Continue positive behavior intervention and support efforts in order to bring scores up in policy and procedures, expectations, and data-based decision making to a level that suggests ongoing fidelity of implementations (Practice 1). | 1. Revise and complete school policy manual and teacher/staff procedure manuals.<br>2. Develop and count skill lessons and strategies for teaching schoolwide expectations and share with teachers.<br>3. Provide incentives for teachers to review periodically.<br>4. Increase use of School-Wide Information System (SWIS) and School-wide Evaluation Tool (SET) data for reviewing schoolwide and student interventions. | a. Review content of school policy and teacher/staff policy manual to make sure all material is up to date and accurate.<br>b. Hold fun pop quizzes with students and staff to check their knowledge of policies.<br>c. Review SET and SWIS data at all leadership team meetings to identify areas for emphasis.<br>d. Review SWIS reports at related student support meetings. |

**Figure 4.4.** Sample Action Plan for improvement at Apple Center Elementary for the 2008–2009 school year. (From Walker, B., & Cheney, D. [2012]. *The Self-Assessment and Program Review for Positive Behavior Interventions and Supports [SAPR-PBIS™]*. Baltimore, MD: Paul H. Brookes Publishing Co. Copyright © 2012 by University of Washington; adapted by permission.)

## The Recess Rush

The first possible cause of stalled progress is that the data being used to monitor the practice are not detailed enough or collected with the frequency needed for the leadership team to see patterns and information at the level needed to problem solve. For example, one large, diverse elementary school found that even with well-established cafeteria and playground social expectations, implemented along with the regular reteaching of expectations, it experienced high levels of office discipline referrals for aggression during the lunch recess. The leadership team began exploring options for restructuring recess entirely in order to change the climate on the playground. After learning about the issues, the PBIS project coordinator working with the school prompted the team to look more closely at its office discipline referral data for even more details on when and where the problems occurred. Because the school had already been effectively using a comprehensive discipline database, SWIS, it was able to efficiently generate a detailed report, which included time periods for the referrals. The team learned that the incidents of aggressive behavior were primarily occurring at the very end of the primary grades' recess, as opposed to on the playground during recess, as it had thought. This time period happened to overlap with the time in which the intermediate students were leaving the lunchroom to go outside for their recess. Members of the leadership team observed the next lunch recess at that time and learned that the primary grade teachers were often late to pick up their students, who were lining up to come in. This left a bottleneck of active and excited students for the intermediate students to move through in order to get onto the playground. This ultimately created an invitation for impatient students to begin pushing and shoving.

When the leadership team presented these data-based findings and description of the observations to the staff at the next faculty meeting, the primary teachers realized that they were accountable for creating this situation and pledged to pick up their classes on time. The lunchroom supervisors also adjusted their procedures for allowing the intermediate students to go outside, to reduce the student overlap by just a few minutes. In neither case did the administration or leadership team have to take the position of the "heavy" and threaten or plead with faculty and staff members to change their behaviors. Because these data and observations were reviewed by the faculty and staff, the faculty and staff were able to bring forward solutions that they could own and implement. With these relatively small changes in staff behavior, the problem was eliminated. Had the leadership team not been prompted to look carefully at the details of the data provided by the SWIS system, it would have moved forward with larger, more substantial, and costly changes that still might not have addressed the problem. Clearly, one of the first questions a leadership team should ask when progress has not occurred in a targeted area is, "Are we getting the level of detailed information that we need to understand the problem and to make sound decisions?"

## Too Many Items on the Plate

The second common problem is that too many other issues or initiatives are going on, or directly competing with, the targeted practice, and the faculty and staff are unable to allocate the time and attention required to make sustainable changes. A large high school practicing PBIS ran into this challenge when trying to improve the consistent implementation of teacher supervision during passing periods to reduce hallway noise levels and behavior problems. The leadership team found that every time they held a discussion of the situation with the faculty and staff, the problem in a few hallways would improve but would return to previous problem levels within a week or two thereafter. This occurred three times in two months before members of the leadership team decided to talk more in depth with teachers in that part of the building. The leadership team learned that, although the teachers had every intention of supporting the PBIS practices, they were also faced with a significant district-mandated curriculum change that was affecting their department. Because the teachers were trying to become more familiar with their curriculum, they found themselves ignoring hallway supervision during passing periods so they could make quick adjustments in their lessons for the next class. As a result, teachers were unable to consistently be present in the hallways for supervision and noise levels and behavior problems persisted.

The leadership team had to work closely with the administration and the teachers from that department to address this problem. They decided to establish a rotating schedule of passing period supervision, which honored the need for the teachers to work on lessons in the new curriculum while also providing consistent adult presence in the hallways during passing periods. It was important that the leadership team discussed these challenges with the teachers, problem solved a solution, and maintained everyone's mutual respect and investment in the PBIS initiative. It would have been easy for the leadership team to make the assumption that those teachers were just "not committed" to PBIS work and therefore take a more heavy-handed approach to addressing the problem. However, that sort of approach would likely have led to divisions within the faculty that could undermine the school improvement efforts in the long term. Instead, the leadership team worked with the rest of the faculty to come up with a win–win solution that strengthened its relationships with teachers in this department and, with it, the rest of the faculty. Taking the time to ask careful questions and listen deeply to the faculty, staff, students, and parents involved is an important aspect of problem solving a stalled practice improvement plan.

# Practices and Resources

One of the necessary activities that the leadership team must accomplish is the identification of objectives, activities, and measures for the implementation of their action plan. In Chapter 4, we described how a team might develop these three areas for the practice related to discipline policies and practices. In this chapter, ideas for activities and resources to implement each of the 10 practices are provided. We first provide the rationale and short literature review for each practice, then provide further details for how to rate the practice on the SAPR-PBIS™, and after that describe how the team can make plans to improve the practice. Finally, for each practice, resources are provided that include web sites and published literature to further assist the leadership team in determining how they will make program improvements. The chapter is intended to position both the leadership team and the school staff in a positive stance to improve each of the practices they designated as a priority in their action plan.

## PRACTICE ONE

### Administrative policies and procedures support the education of all students, including those with or at risk of developing E/BPs

The foundation of a school's approach to the effective implementation of SWPBIS lies in its ability to establish clear policies and procedures that guide the implementation of the related practices. A school leadership team, which includes the school administrator and representative stakeholders from the school and community, is charged with establishing these SWPBIS policies and procedures and facilitating the process of bringing them to life with the rest of the school staff. This team is a keystone to effective school reform, as it oversees the development and implementation of the SWPBIS initiative. Members of the leadership team play a key role in facilitating and sustaining the change inherent in any school reform initiative (Dwyer, 2002; Knoff, 2002; Learning First Alliance, 2001; Sugai et al., 2010; Sugai, Horner, et al., 2002; Todd et al., 1999).

As noted in Chapter 3, Knoff defined an effective leadership team as "a highly communicative group of people with different backgrounds, skills, and abilities with a common purpose who are working together to achieve clearly defined goals" (2000, p. 30). Effective teams include members who are "interdependent, motivated, unafraid of risks and failure, and thrive on challenge" (p. 30). In order for this team to have the time, resources, and energy to implement PBIS effectively, it is recommended that the PBIS initiative be one of the top three goals in a school's strategic plan (Todd et al., 1999). It is important to keep in mind that many other initiatives can be readily integrated into the PBIS agenda. For example, initiatives such as school safety and parent communication fit naturally within the overall framework of PBIS. Time and resources spent on those important topics can be folded into the PBIS initiative and addressed through that work.

The leadership team is responsible for establishing a strategic plan that outlines goals and objectives related to PBIS. The team then meets at least monthly to monitor and evaluate progress toward the goals and objectives outlined in the strategic plan. This includes reviewing discipline data and teacher and parent feedback, assessing progress on the annual plan, and planning implementation and dissemination activities for the school community (Knoff, 2000; Sugai et al., 2010). Chapter 3 provides more information on creating and maintaining effective leadership teams.

An important first step of the leadership team is to articulate a purpose or mission statement with the school staff that 1) is related to the implementation of PBIS or RTI and 2) clearly supports students with or at risk of developing E/BPs as well as students with academic challenges in the school (Center for Mental Health in Schools, 2010; Knoff, 2002, 2007; Learning First Alliance, 2001). This statement defines the rationale, beliefs, and purpose for the PBIS efforts and guides staff, students, and parents through activities and plans being implemented throughout the school. An effective mission or vision statement helps to provide the school with a unifying vision and clear focus on established goals and objectives. Once articulated, the mission statement is found in written school materials as well as actively referenced during planning and decision making throughout the school reform initiative. This helps the school keep its reform efforts focused and coherent over time (Center for Mental Health in School, 2010; Cheney & Barringer, 1999; Shannon & Bylsma, 2007; Sugai et al., 2010). An example of a meaningful mission statement might be as follows:

> The mission of Apple Center School is to create a school environment in which all students can excel academically and socially. To this end, we commit to respecting one another, being responsible for our actions, and ensuring a safe school to support our collective work and well-being.

Another example is as follows:

> Albany Heights is a school where all students can learn to their highest potential. We create collaboration and respect in a safe environment and encourage communication between home and school. Our goal is to help each student grow up to be a lifelong learner.

As the school develops and implements various aspects of PBIS practices, such as a plan for teaching and reteaching the schoolwide expectations and guidelines for office discipline referrals (ODRs), the leadership team should begin to articulate clear policies about these practices and include them in all school policy manuals, such as the parent and staff handbooks and the school's discipline policies (Sugai et al., 2010; Sugai et al., 2002). School and district policies are therefore constantly guiding, informing, and refining practice.

Each year, the leadership team evaluates progress on the PBIS action plan. The action plan contains a series of goals, activities, and timelines for the effective implementation of PBIS in the school. The goal of the SAPR process is to help teams develop and track their progress on an action plan, but it may also include data and input from district improvement plans as well. The overall action plan and progress toward the listed annual goals is shared regularly with staff, students, and families; monitored frequently; and adjusted as necessary to maximize the effectiveness and efficiency of the PBIS system. In particular, student progress is of greatest concern as an outcome and should be assessed regularly to evaluate trends and determine instructional decisions (Cheney et al., 2004; Sugai et al., 2010; Sugai, Horner, et al., 2002).

## Rating This Practice

A school that is *fully implementing* this practice will have a well-established team that meets at least once a month to establish and review policies and procedures based on data collected throughout the year. This school has a student manual that clearly articulates the philosophy of the school, its commitment to the success of all learners, and the systems and supports available to make that happen. The annual goals and objectives set by the team are regularly shared with the full school staff for input and accountability. The rating for each of the indicators would be a 5 using the scale. The primary focus for a school fully implementing this practice is to celebrate and maintain the work that is already being done.

A school that is *moderately implementing* this practice may have a team that meets less than monthly and may not yet have clearly established policies and procedures related to student support. Plans are discussed but may not be written down and regularly shared with the full faculty. The plan may not be evaluated and adjusted based on data and input. The faculty and the student handbook may make some reference to supports for all students but may not include the school's philosophy and systems for supporting students and preventing the emergence of more significant problems. Some or all of the indicators are rated around 3 using the rating scale. Schools operating at this level should identify indicators to focus on while moving toward full implementation.

If all or most of the indicators are rated at 2 or below, the school is currently *not implementing* the practice. The team should discuss how it wants to prioritize its efforts to begin addressing the indicators listed.

## Setting Goals for Improvement of This Practice

In order to strengthen this practice, the team should discuss its ratings for the indicators listed. Which indicators represent relative strengths (i.e., may be scored a 3 or 4)? Are there relatively small steps that can be taken to move them toward full implementation? For example, if the school has a philosophy regarding SWPBIS but it is not clearly stated in the faculty and student handbooks, the team may decide to make that one goal because it can be completed fairly quickly and moves the school toward full implementation of that indicator. The team may also choose to address an indicator or indicators that the team consistently rated quite low. However, in this case it may take more time and effort to develop implementation. For example, if the leadership team is not yet meeting consistently and using data to monitor progress toward annual goals and objectives for school improvement, the team would discuss what steps need to be taken to put these components in place. Whenever teams address goal setting and improvement planning, it is important that they not attempt to do too much too quickly. What steps need to happen first in order to support the development of other indicators? Which indicators do team members feel are most critical to the development of the school?

Once the team has focused on an indicator for improvement, it needs to discuss concrete ways to collect data that will determine when it has made progress toward the goals. Following is an example of how the team might use the Action Plan on the last page of the Team Meeting Form to record its plan.

**Practice 1: Administrative policies and procedures support the education of all students, including those with or at risk of developing E/BPs.**

| Objective 1 | Activities | Evaluation |
|---|---|---|
| *The school's leadership team develops annual goals and objectives to improve schoolwide positive behavior supports and annually evaluates progress on goals and objectives.* | *1. Present the full plan at a faculty meeting within 3 weeks of developing the plan. Ask for input and discussion.*<br>*2. Once a month, a member of the leadership team will present an update on progress and issues related to the plan at a full staff meeting.* | *a. Leadership team revisits the team goals monthly to determine what progress is being met.*<br>*b. Each trimester, distribute an informal e-survey to faculty and staff asking them to rate how well the leadership team is addressing our goals.* |

(From Walker, B., & Cheney, D. [2012]. *The Self-Assessment and Program Review for Positive Behavior Interventions and Supports [SAPR-PBIS™]*. Baltimore, MD: Paul H. Brookes Publishing Co. Copyright © 2012 by University of Washington; adapted by permission.)

## Resources for Further Learning

Many resources related to implementing PBIS effectively, such as presentations and readings for faculty, staff, and families, are available at no cost at the following web sites:

Center for Mental Health in Schools, http://smhp.psych.ucla.edu/

National Technical Assistance Center on Positive Behavioral Interventions and Supports, http://www.pbis.org

Other references that provide detailed information on this practice include the following:

Adelman, H., & Taylor, L. (2001). *Organization facilitators: A change agent for systemic school and community changes*. Los Angeles, CA: Center for Mental Health in Schools. Retrieved from http://smhp.psych.ucla.edu/

Adelman, H., & Taylor, L. (2007). Systemic change for school improvement. *Journal of Educational & Psychological Consultation, 17*(1), 55–77.

Center for Mental Health in Schools. (2010). *School improvement planning: What is missing?* Los Angeles, CA: Author. Retrieved from http://smhp.psych.ucla.edu/whatsmissing.htm

Knoff, H.M. (2007). Best practices in strategic planning, organizational assessment, and school effectiveness. In A. Thomas & J. Grimes (Eds.), *Best practices in school psychology* (Vol. 5, pp. 903–916). Bethesda, MD: National Association of School Psychologists.

Senge, P. (2000). *Schools that learn: A fifth discipline fieldbook for educators, parents, and everyone who cares about education.* New York, NY: Doubleday.

Shannon, G.S., & Bylsma, P. (2007). *The nine characteristics of high-performing schools: A research-based resource for schools and districts to assist with improving student learning* (2nd ed.). Olympia, WA: Office of the Superintendent of Public Instruction.

Sugai, G., Horner, R.H., Algozzine, R., Barrett, S., Lewis, T., Anderson, C., & Simonsen, B. (2010). *School-wide positive behavior support: Implementers' blueprint and self-assessment.* Eugene, OR: University of Oregon. Retrieved from http://www.pbis.org.

## PRACTICE TWO

### School policies and programs emphasize prevention and the early identification of students with or at risk of developing E/BPs

For a PBIS system to be most effective, it should include a plan for prevention and early intervention for students with emerging academic and/or behavioral problems as well as for students with more longstanding academic difficulties (Dwyer, 2002; Severson, Walker, Hope-Doolittle, Kratchowill, & Gresham, 2007; Walker et al., 1996). To have the greatest impact, schools need to develop systems for identifying students early in their school experience and providing systemic supports before a problem becomes well established. One validated approach for identifying students who are displaying E/BPs is the use of a systematic schoolwide screening process such as the Systematic Screening for Behavior Disorders (SSBD; Severson et al.; Walker, 2010; Walker & Severson, 1992). Similar to the process schools use regularly to identify students with emergent academic or health problems, schoolwide screening for students with or at risk of E/BPs can help schools more effectively focus existing resources and supports on these students before their problems become chronic and expensive to address (McKinney, Montague, & Hocutt, 1998; Sprague & Walker, 2000; Walker, 2010; Walker et al., 2005). The SSBD (Walker & Severson, 1992) has been used by school staff to identify students at risk for school failure due to their social and emotional problems. In addition to the SSBD, a number of other screening tools are available for a range of grade levels and types of social-emotional problems. Table 5.1 provides a summary of several screening tools that your leadership team should consider using to support this practice.

Once students with E/BPs are identified, they are matched to a continuum of academic, social, and/or behavioral supports that already exist within the school that promote the development of successful academic and prosocial skills, while attempting to reduce the impact of any risk factors that will have a negative effect on learning (Adelman & Taylor, 2001, 2007; Walker et al., 1996). These supports can be matched to students, coordinated, and then

**Table 5.1.** Sample of available screening tools that address social and behavioral domains

| Name | Grade levels | Description |
|---|---|---|
| Behavior Assessment Scale for Children Two (BASC-2): Behavior and Emotional Screening Scale (BESS; Kamphaus & Reynolds, 2007) | Preschool and Grades K–12; includes teacher, parent, and self-rating forms for Grades 3–12 | Based on the popular Behavioral Assessment Scale for Children, used by many schools to assess students for special education; intended to be a universal screener to identify students with needs in both the academic and social domains |
| Brief Academic Competence Evaluation Scales System (BACESS; Elliott, Huai, & Roach, 2007) | Grades K–12, with teacher forms and student forms available for Grades 3–12 | Was developed as a universal screener (covering all of the academic enablers) and has three phases to determine risk level |
| School-Wide Information System (SWIS; May et al., 2002) | Grades K–12 | Detailed, easy to use, secure database designed to help schools use data on office discipline referrals to inform decision-making at both schoolwide and individual student levels; can be used for screening |
| Social Skills Improvement System (SSIS; Elliott & Gresham, 2007) | Grades preschool and K–12, with teacher, parent, and self-rating forms | A universal screener to identify students with needs in both the academic and social domains |
| Student Risk Screening Scale (SRSS; Drummond, 1993) | Originally Grades K–6; now includes middle and high school norms (Lane, Kalberg, Parks, & Carter, 2008) | Classroom teacher evaluates and assigns a frequency-based, Likert rating to each student in a class on seven behavioral criteria (lies, cheats, and sneaks; steals; behavior problems; peer rejections; low achievement; negative attitude; and aggressive behavior) to determine risk level |
| Systematic Screening for Behavior Disorders (SSBD; Walker & Severson, 1992) | Originally Grades K–6; now includes middle school norms (Caldarella, Young, Richardson, Young, & Young, 2008) | Based on multiple gating procedure; used to identify students in both the internalizing or externalizing dimensions of behavior |

From Walker, B. (2010). Effective schoolwide screening to identify students at-risk for social and behavioral problems. *Intervention in School and Clinic, 46*(2), 104–110; reprinted by permission.

monitored for effectiveness by a teacher assistance or prereferral intervention team (Walker, 2010; Walker et al., 2005). These supports might include the direct instruction of prosocial skills, a specialized behavior management plan, small-group or individual counseling supports, academic accommodations, and/or tutoring (Conduct Problems Prevention Research Group, 2000; Greenberg, Domitrovich, & Bumbarger, 2001; Hawken & Horner, 2003; Tuesday-Heathfield & Clark, 2004).

Figure 5.1 illustrates how the screening process works. Using this process enhances the teacher assistance or prereferral team's competence for developing prevention approaches and early intervention strategies, which address student needs more efficiently. Instead of waiting until students fall behind their peers academically or behaviorally, the team uses the screening process to identify students and provide them support when indicated (Walker, 2010). The involvement of family members in selecting and evaluating services, as well as providing any needed direct support, is also a crucial aspect to this process (Dwyer, 2002; Friesen & Stephens, 1998; Sprague & Walker, 2000). See Practice 10 for strategies for working effectively with families.

A study comparing schools with comprehensive prevention and early intervention programs containing these components to schools that had more traditional referral programs in Baltimore, Maryland, found that only 8% of the teachers in schools with comprehensive prevention programs referred students to "special programs" in the schools, compared with 19% in the comparison schools. It also found that teachers rated their school climate more positively than the teachers in the comparison schools (Bruns, Walrath, Glass-Siegel, & Weist, 2004).

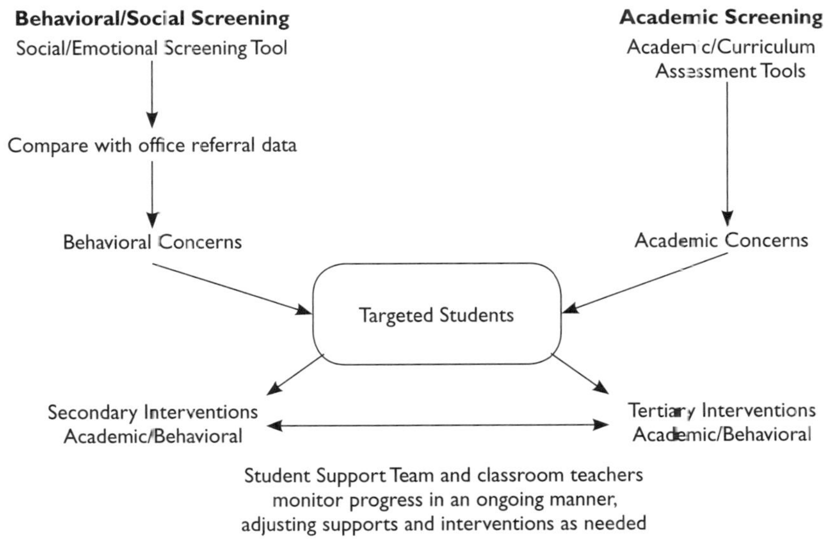


**Figure 5.1.** The schoolwide screening process. (From Walker, B. [2010]. Effective schoolwide screening to identify students at-risk for social and behavioral problems. *Intervention in School and Clinic, 46*[2], 104–110; reprinted by permission.)

Not only does this difference suggest important improvements in student learning, but it also represents a significant savings of instructional and leadership time and other related resources required when students are referred for special education. Effectively and efficiently identifying student needs and providing corresponding supports when issues are emerging has become even more essential during these times of limited resources.

## Rating This Practice

A school that is *fully implementing* this practice would integrate the screening process into its RTI and PBIS approaches. It would have screening tools in place to identify students who are having difficulties with both academic and behavioral or social domains. Teachers would receive in-service training on how to complete the screening with accuracy and fidelity. Possible tools for behavioral screening include the Systematic Screening for Behavior Disorders (Walker & Severson, 1992); the Student Risk Screening Scale (Drummond, 1993); or rating scales such as Teacher Report Form (Achenbach, 2001), the Behavior and Emotional Screening System (Kamphaus & Reynolds, 2007), and the Social Skills Improvement Scale (Elliott & Gresham, 2007). The school would also have in place a system for monitoring disciplinary referrals due to behavior problems (e.g., SWIS). The screening process would occur on a scheduled basis every month or quarter of the year to identify students who need additional social intervention. The school would have a teacher assistance team (TAT), behavior support team, prereferral intervention team, or student support team (SST) that would be accountable for the screening process and would monitor and/or recommend interventions for those identified in the screening. Established interventions in the school such as problem solving would be taught to the school staff and used by the counseling staff to diffuse student behavioral problems and expand social skills of students. When the screening process is completed and when students receive guidance counseling or problem-solving sessions, families are informed and involved as necessary. The rating for each of the indicators would be a 5 using the scale. The primary focus for a school fully implementing this practice is to ensure that screening and intervention services are coordinated and diminish behavior problems in the school.

A school that is *moderately implementing* this practice may have a TAT, prereferral team, or SST that meets irregularly and that has not yet fully adopted and trained staff in a screening approach. These teams would also be more likely to focus more on special education referrals than on proactive interventions. Students are most likely nominated by teachers when behavior problems arise, and there is no systematic process or schedule for identifying students with social or academic problems. An intervention plan may be developed for some students, but is not likely to be carefully monitored or evaluated by the TAT/SST members. Social problem solving and guidance counseling is not always available to students, and family members are not likely to be involved in helping their student to improve social skills at school. Some or all of the indicators are rated around 3 using the rating scale. Schools operating at this level should identify indicators to focus on moving toward full implementation.

If all or most of the indicators are rated at 2 or below, the school is currently *not implementing* the practice. The team should discuss how it wants to prioritize its efforts to begin addressing the indicators listed.

## Setting Goals for Improvement of This Practice

In order to strengthen this practice, the team should discuss its ratings for the indicators listed. Which indicators represent relative strengths (i.e., may be scored a 3 or 4)? Are there relatively small steps that can be taken to move them toward full implementation? For example, if the school is typically reactive to student problems and has stopgap measures, such as short-term problem solving, for meeting the student needs but no long-range monitoring, it may choose to identify the screening and support process as a clear goal. The team could adopt a screening process, use it three times yearly, and monitor those who are deemed at risk of long-term social or behavioral problems. This would provide the team with some clear, attainable goals for the school year. It would also greatly improve the team's approach toward screening and monitoring a small group of students in need of support or intervention. Whenever teams address goal setting and improvement planning, it is important that they not attempt to do too much too quickly. What steps need to be taken first in order to support the development of other indicators? Which indicators do team members feel are most critical to the development of the school?

Once the team has focused on an indicator for improvement, it needs to discuss concrete ways it can collect data that will determine when it has made progress toward the goals. Following is an example of how the team might use the Action Plan on the last page of the Team Meeting Form to record its plan.

**Practice 2: School policies and programs emphasize prevention and the early identification of students with or at risk of developing E/BDs.**

| Objective 1 | Activities | Evaluation |
|---|---|---|
| *The school's student support team will meet regularly to screen and identify students in need of social support or intervention.* | *1. Present a schedule to the faculty.*<br>*2. Adopt a screening tool.*<br>*3. Teach faculty how to use the tool.*<br>*4. Meet three times yearly (October, January, March) to review screening results.*<br>*5. Provide ongoing social problem solving to those students identified in screening.* | *a. Identify a screening tool by August.*<br>*b. Use the tool two or three times yearly.*<br>*c. Identify students from the screening.*<br>*d. Match identified students with available services.*<br>*e. Use other progress monitoring tools bimonthly.* |

(From Walker, B., & Cheney, D. [2012]. *The Self-Assessment and Program Review for Positive Behavior Interventions and Supports [SAPR-PBIS™].* Baltimore, MD: Paul H. Brookes Publishing Co. Copyright © 2012 by University of Washington; adapted by permission.)

## Resources for Further Learning

For specific interventions used during the prereferral process that address issues of overrepresentation of culturally and linguistically diverse students in special education see

Council for Exceptional Children. (2002). *Addressing over-representation of African American students in special education: The prereferral intervention process. An administrator's guide.* Washington, DC: Council for Exceptional Children. Retrieved from http://www.eric.ed.gov/PDFS/ED466051.pdf

For more information on more fully implementing this practice, we recommend the following the resources:

Achenbach, T.A. (2001). *Achenbach's Empirical Behavioral Assessment manual for Teacher Report Form.* Burlington, VT: Achenbach System of Empirically Based Assessment.

Brown-Chidsey, R. (2007). No more "waiting to fail". *Educational Leadership, 65*(2), 40–46.

Bruns, E., Walrath, C., Glass-Siegel, M., & Weist, M. (2004). School-based mental health services in Baltimore: Association with school climate and special education referrals. *Behavior Modification, 28,* 491–512.

Elliot, S., & Gresham, F. (2007). *Social Skills Improvement System.* Upper Saddle River, NJ: Pearson.

Hawken, L., Vincent, C., & Schumann, B. (2008). Response to intervention for social behavior: Challenges and opportunities. *Journal of Emotional and Behavioral Disorders, 16,* 213–225.

Kamphaus, R., & Reynolds, C. (2007). *The Behavior Assessment Scale for Children–2: Behavior and Emotional Screening System.* Upper Saddle River, NJ: Pearson.

Lane, K., Kalberg, J., Parks, R., & Carter, E. (2007). Systematic screening at the middle school level: Score reliability and validity of the student risk screening scale. *Journal of Emotional and Behavioral Disorders, 15,* 209–222.

Lane, K., Kalberg, J., Parks, R., & Carter, E. (2008). The Student Risk Screening Scale: Initial evidence of score reliability and validity at the high school level. *Journal of Emotional and Behavioral Disorders, 16*, 178–190.

Severson, H., Walker, H., Hope-Doolittle, J., Kratchowill, T., & Gresham, F. (2007). Proactive, early screening to detect behaviorally at-risk students: Issues, approaches, emerging innovations, and professional practices. *Journal of School Psychology, 45*, 193–223.

Walker, B. (2010). Effective schoolwide screening to identify students at-risk for social and behavioral problems. *Intervention in School and Clinic, 46*, 104–110.

Walker, B., Cheney, D., & Stage, S. (2009). The validity and reliability of the Self-Assessment and Program Review survey: Assessing school progress in schoolwide positive behavior support. *Journal of Positive Behavior Interventions, 11*, 94–109.

Walker, B., Cheney, D., Stage, S., & Blum, C. (2005). Schoolwide screening and positive behavior supports: Identifying and supporting students at-risk for school failure. *Journal of Positive Behavior Interventions, 7*, 194–204.

Walker, H.M., & Severson, H.H. (1992). *Systematic Screening for Behavior Disorders (SSBD)*. Longmont, CO: Sopris West.

## PRACTICE THREE

### Staff development activities focus on methods to educate all students, including those with or at risk of developing E/BPs

For a school to be successful in supporting students with or at risk of developing academic problems and/or E/BPs, teachers and staff need to have an array of skills to proactively and responsibly manage students with challenging behavior. These include effective instructional strategies for diverse learners, evidence-based prosocial skills instruction, individual and group behavior management strategies, and an understanding of how risk and protective factors can influence a child's success in school (Adelman & Taylor, 2001; Conduct Problems Prevention Research Group, 2000; Learning First Alliance, 2001). In addition, school staff need ongoing training related to the systems, interventions, and other approaches directly related to PBIS, such as strategies for effective collaboration with families, function-based approaches to solving chronic and intensive behavior problems, and principles of data-based decision making (Dunlap et al., 2000; Sugai et al., 2010). Because our schools are becoming increasingly diverse, this includes training that helps school staff better understand the cultural perspectives of their students, families, and communities. As staff become more competent using culturally responsive teaching and management strategies, they are better able to meet the needs of the diversity of students at all three levels of the RTI and PBIS model (Cartledge & Lo, 2006; Cartledge & Loe, 2001; Cartledge, Singh, & Gibson, 2008). Fortunately, there are many resources that address these topics available to schools at little or no cost. See Resources for Further Learning for details.

Within the PBIS model, professional development should include both formalized instruction provided by trainers ("experts" in a given topic) that may need to be brought into the school or district, and day-to-day support provided by "coaches" or "organization facilitators" (Adelman & Taylor, 2001; Sugai et al., 2010). Often, within the context of PBIS, these coaches or facilitators are members of the leadership team. These change agents go beyond the traditional training format to provide ongoing implementation support, helping school staff successfully bring to life the systems, concepts, and strategies required to implement PBIS effectively. More and more often, schools and districts employ coaches to assist in literacy and mathematics instruction. PBIS coaches function in a similar way, with an emphasis on providing support on strategies for teaching and reinforcing behavioral and social skills at the individual student and full-group levels, as well as problem-solving specific students or settings with particular problems or issues. Another important aspect of PBIS coaches is that they are available to support faculty and staff in both classroom and nonclassroom settings (e.g., cafeteria, hallways, common areas, playgrounds).

Finally, as part of the overall evaluation of a school's PBIS efforts, participants must be able to provide feedback on the effectiveness and impact of training activities to ensure that they are providing the desired results for staff (Dunlap et al., 2000; Sugai et al., 2010). This means that, after all formal professional development opportunities, faculty and staff are able to provide confidential feedback on the effectiveness of the training, the relevance of the content to their individual professional work as well as to the goals of the school, and their confidence level in implementing these practices independently. This type of feedback allows the leadership team to ensure alignment between goals and training activities as well as to better tailor follow-up training and coaching supports to help teachers and staff apply and implement new skills effectively.

## Rating This Practice

A school that is *fully implementing* this practice has regularly scheduled formal professional development opportunities for all of the school staff in the strategies and topics described previously in this section. This can include a combination of online modules and face-to-face training as well as a combination of district and school-based sessions. A plan is in place to make training content available to new teachers and staff who join the school between scheduled training opportunities (e.g., through written summaries of content, professional libraries, online training modules). Each session of formal professional development includes a confidential opportunity to provide written feedback on its effectiveness and relevance, and on the teachers' perceived ability to implement the information and strategies shared in the training. In addition, coaches are available to teachers and staff to support them in implementing strategies, approaches, and practices related to implementing academic and social or behavioral supports effectively in both classroom and nonclassroom systems at a full-time capacity.

A school that is *moderately implementing* this practice may have periodic training opportunities available in some to most of the topics listed earlier in this section and/or does not have a well-organized system for providing content to new teachers and staff. Feedback on the trainings is collected but is not consistently used by the leadership team to guide further training and support plans. Coaches or mentors who are skilled in these strategies are available to support teachers and staff, but not at a full-time capacity. Some or all of the indicators are rated around 3 using the rating scale. Schools operating at this level should identify specific indicators to focus on moving toward full implementation.

If all or most of the indicators are rated at 2 or below, the school is currently *not implementing* the practice. The team should discuss how it wants to prioritize its efforts to begin addressing the indicators listed.

## Setting Goals for Improvement of This Practice

In order to strengthen this practice, the team should discuss its ratings for the indicators listed. Which indicators represent relative strengths (i.e., may be scored a 3 or 4)? Are there relatively small steps that can be taken to move them toward full implementation? For example, if the school has regularly scheduled professional development available but does not yet have a system for sharing that content with new teachers and staff, the team may decide to make implementing that system one goal because it can be completed fairly quickly and moves the school toward full implementation of that indicator. The team may also choose to address an indicator that the team consistently rated quite low. However, in this case it may take more time and effort to develop implementation. For example, if the primary emphasis of professional development is academic instruction only, and/or if paraprofessional staff who regularly supervise and support students directly are not included in scheduled trainings, the leadership team has to problem-solve how to create these opportunities. As with all goal setting, it is important not to do too much too quickly and to carefully analyze each step that leads to the prioritized goal. The task analysis will help a team identify and order the steps that need to be accomplished, in the effort to implement these best-practice indicators. The analysis will also help answer the question of which indicator or indicators the team believes are most critical for development in the school. Once the team has focused on an indicator for improvement, it needs to discuss concrete ways to collect data that will determine when it has made progress toward the goals. Following is an example of how the team might use the Action Plan on the last page of the Team Meeting Form to record its plan.

**Practice 3: Staff development activities focus on methods to educate all students, including those with or at risk of developing E/BPs.**

| Objective 1 | Activities | Evaluation |
|---|---|---|
| *Three of the monthly professional days will focus specifically on concepts related to positive behavior interventions and supports and supporting students with or at risk of developing emotional or behavioral problems.* | *1. Leadership team will review the annual plan to identify a list of specific topics for these sessions, and teachers and staff will be surveyed to determine their top three priorities.* | *a. Leadership team will send out a link for an electronic feedback survey to all faculty and staff within 1 week of training.* |

| Objective 2 | Activities | Evaluation |
| --- | --- | --- |
| *Develop a cadre of teachers and paraprofessional staff who can serve as mentors or informal coaches in specific areas related to positive behavior interventions and supports and social or behavioral learning.* | 1. *The leadership team will identify a process for identifying potential coaches or mentors and determining priority topics and locations for pilot implementation.*<br>2. *The principal will explore ways to provide some extra hourly classroom coverage or other forms of support to create opportunities for this cadre to be available to teachers and staff in these priority areas.* | a. *Teachers and staff who work with this cadre will be surveyed on their feedback on the process overall.*<br>b. *School or classroom data related to areas affected by involvement with the cadre will be reviewed to determine positive impact.*<br>c. *A first priority is the cafeteria, with the goal of reducing noise levels and reducing office referrals. Office discipline referrals and walk-throughs with noise ratings will be used to measure impact.* |

(From Walker, B., & Cheney, D. [2012]. *The Self-Assessment and Program Review for Positive Behavior Interventions and Supports [SAPR-PBIS™]*. Baltimore, MD: Paul H. Brookes Publishing Co. Copyright © 2012 by University of Washington; adapted by permission.)

## Resources for Further Learning

Numerous training materials related to professional development in PBIS and supporting success for all learners, such as presentations and readings for faculty, staff, and families, are available at no or low cost at the following web sites:

The Center for Mental Health in Schools, http://smhp.psych.ucla.edu/
The Technical Assistance Center on Positive Behavioral Interventions and Supports, http://www.pbis.org

Other resources to help in this area include the following:

Adelman, H., & Taylor, L. (2001). *Organization facilitators: A change agent for systemic school and community changes*. Los Angeles, CA: Center for Mental Health in Schools. Retrieved from http://smhp.psych.ucla.edu/

Cartledge, G., & Lo, Y. (2006). *Teaching urban learners: Culturally responsive strategies for developing academic and behavioral competence*. Champaign, IL: Research Press.

Cartledge, G., & Loe, S. (2001). Cultural diversity in social skills instruction. *Exceptionality*, 9 (1 & 2), 33–46.

Cartledge, G., Singh, A., & Gibson, L. (2008). Practical behavior-management techniques to close the accessibility gap for students who are culturally and linguistically diverse. *Preventing School Failure*, *52*(3), 29–38.

DuFour, R., & Eaker, R. (1998). *Professional learning communities at work: Best practices for enhancing student achievement*. Bloomington, IN: National Educational Service.

Dunlap, G., Heineman, M., Knoster, T., Fox, L., Anderson, J., & Albin, R. (2000). Essential elements of in-service training in positive behavior supports. *Journal of Positive Behavior Interventions*, *2*, 22–32.

Firestone, W., Mangin, M., Martinez, C., & Polovsky, T. (2005). Leading coherent professional development: A comparison of three districts. *Educational Administration Quarterly*, *41*(3), 413–448.

## PRACTICE FOUR

### Clear and consistent behavioral expectations are established for students across all school settings

Central to the PBIS approach is the importance of providing students with direct teaching of the behaviors necessary to be successful in school (Lewis & Sugai, 1999; Sugai et al., 2010). This requires schools implementing PBIS to identify up to five positively stated expectations that can be applied to both classroom and nonclassroom settings (e.g., the playground, common areas, hallways). Once these are agreed on, they are written in the school handbook and posted throughout the school. These expectations are then clearly defined for each setting and a plan or program is developed for all staff to actively teach the expectations to students. Once students have been taught the expectations, staff consistently monitor student behavior and provide frequent recognition or reinforcement to students behaving appropriately. In addition, the staff will review and/or develop clear and appropriate consequences for problem behaviors that are consistently implemented when needed. Together, these activities help to develop a safe, orderly, and caring learning community, which is so critical to successful student learning and achievement (Horner, Sugai, et al., 2004; Learning First Alliance, 2001; Lewis & Sugai; Safran & Oswald, 2003).

Lynass, Tsai, Richman, and Cheney (2011) completed a national survey, which examined the types and frequency of schools' social expectations and behavioral indicators for the expectations. Participants were from 155 schools practicing PBIS in 12 regionally representative states. Each participant was from the school's leadership team and provided a sample of the school's behavioral matrix, which contained the expectations and indicators. Analyses of the matrices showed that the three most commonly occurring social expectations nationally were respect, responsibility, and safety. These three expectations occurred in more than 60% of the schools sampled. Regional and state comparisons of the social expectation frequency suggested there is homogeneity of both expectations and behavioral indicators across these categories throughout the country. One can infer from this study that these three social expectations are most likely to be valued in elementary schools and that staff would be teaching specific behaviors that match the expectations.

As an example, one elementary school that the authors have worked with phrased their expectations as "We participate respectfully, act responsibly, follow directions, and behave safely." The school's leadership team also identified what these behaviors looked like, explicitly taught them, and regularly reinforced students for demonstrating them. Periodically throughout the year, or when concerns arose, the staff reviewed the expectations. Within 3 years of the consistent application of PBIS practices, major office referrals in this school dropped from 102 annually to 23. Suspensions went from 54 to 4, and the number of students referred for special education dropped by half. This school was the only elementary school in its district to achieve annual yearly progress across the 2008 and 2009 academic years, and the school was recognized as exemplary in five of the categories for high performing schools by the state education department (I. Olson, personal communication, September 10, 2010). This positive progress is representative of the results schools can experience when they truly commit to the implementation of their PBIS initiative. The process enables schools to create a significant change in the climate and tone of the school, allowing staff and students to focus on learning rather than deal with the ongoing distraction of large and small discipline issues.

In a survey of 400 teachers in Washington State, Knapp, Elfers, and Plecki (2004) found that 33% of the teachers surveyed thought that a positive school climate was an important reason for staying in the teaching profession and 60% thought it very important. They also found that, among teachers who agreed that their school had well-defined expectations for student learning, 45% of the teachers felt somewhat prepared to help students achieve standards and 30% felt very prepared. Clearly, well-established behavioral expectations are an important factor in creating a teaching environment where teachers can teach effectively and students can learn.

As described in Chapter 1, the OSEP Center on PBIS has developed a tool for measuring the fidelity with which a school is implementing these aspects of PBIS, called the SET. The SET is a 28-item research tool that is completed on site by an external evaluator. It examines and documents the implementation of the PBIS systems discussed previously (Sugai, Lewis-Palmer, et al., 2001). In 2004, the reliability and validity of the SET were examined and found to be acceptable in all areas (Horner, Todd, et al., 2004). Findings indicate that schools scoring more than 80% on the teaching behavioral expectations subscale and on the total score are considered to be implementing the primary level of PBIS with fidelity. In a study of 140 elementary schools, Horner et al. (2004) found that those schools that met the SET criteria had 25% fewer ODRs. This finding suggests that these components of PBIS, when implemented with fidelity, remain important in positively affecting school culture.

Along with directly teaching and reinforcing the schoolwide expectations, it can be very helpful toward creating a positive classroom environment and improving the interpersonal skills of all students when teachers provide direct instruction from an evidence-based prosocial skills program. For example, the Fast Track Project, a national longitudinal project that examined the effects of systematic interventions across school, classroom, and family for young children at high risk for the development of long-term antisocial behavior, trained teachers to use the Promoting Alternative Thinking Strategies (PATHS) curriculum as part of its elementary level, school-based intervention component. Classroom teachers taught the PATHS social skills curriculum two or three times a week. The social skills curriculum includes teaching students strategies for increasing self-control, emotional self-awareness, positive peer interactions, and social problem solving. Several studies have demonstrated that PATHS can significantly improve the social-emotional competence of students (Conduct Problems Prevention Research Group, 2000, 2002; Greenberg et al., 2001). The Fast Track Project found that, by including this prosocial skills development program in the school curriculum and integrating it into a comprehensive system of supports within the school and the home, these high-risk students had lower overall levels of aggression than students who were not involved in the project, and participating teachers had higher ratings on the quality of the classroom atmosphere (Conduct Problems Prevention Research Group, 2002; U.S. Department of Health and Human Services, 2001).

Several other respected longitudinal studies included the use of an evidence-based social skills development curriculum as a part of their integrated interventions. The Seattle Social Development Project included the Interpersonal Cognitive Problem Solving program (Hawkins et al., 2003) in first-grade classrooms. The Linking the Interests of Families and Teachers (LIFT) project included a 20-session program designed to increase student social and problem-solving skills as well as the ability to resist negative peer groups (Greenberg et al., 2001; Reid, Eddy, Fetrow, & Stoolmiller, 1999). The Incredible Years Series is a curriculum used in early elementary and preschool classrooms, as well as in parent training, to build social competence and prevent, reduce, or treat emerging conduct problems in young children (Webster-Stratton, Reid, & Hammond, 2004; Webster-Stratton & Taylor, 2001). Although many teachers state that they do not have enough time in their instructional day to add "another curriculum or subject," these studies indicate that time spent in providing students with prosocial skill instruction is regained in the form of a more positive classroom environment and improved student behavior. This, in turn, contributes to more effective student learning.

Since 1997, there has been increasing interest at the school, district, and state level in exploring the implications of a focused approach to prosocial skill development, referring to these skills collectively as social-emotional learning. Studies on the effects of a focused, schoolwide approach to social-emotional learning indicate that students performed better academically in this context than students in schools with a more traditional discipline program (Zins & Elias, 2006; Zins, Payton, Weissberg, & O'Brien, 2007). Some states, such as Illinois, New Jersey, and Wisconsin, have enacted social-emotional learning standards for all students in an effort to improve school climate and student academic learning in all schools (Collaborative for Academic, Social, and Emotional Learning, 2010). It is important that schools approach prosocial skills development from a culturally relevant perspective, assuring that the strategies are taught in a way that has relevance and meaning to students from culturally and linguistically diverse perspectives. When implemented effectively, "culturally relevant social skills instruction is intended to affirm students and empower them to achieve maximally within their own subculture as well as the mainstreamed school environment" (Cartledge & Loe, 2001, p. 41).

## Rating This Practice

A school that is *fully implementing* this practice has taken the time to discuss the major social expectations in the school, has had the faculty and staff agree to these, and conducts frequent teaching activities for the social expectations. A visitor or family enrolling a child in the school would be able to read about these expectations in the school handbook and would see posters throughout the building that highlight the major three to five social expectations. The school principal or behavior support team reminds or prompts teachers to reteach the social expectations throughout the year. In addition, the school staff have adopted approaches to diminish problem behavior, such as increased supervision in areas where problems might arise (e.g., hallways, playground, cafeteria); prompting, cueing, and reminding students about meeting the social expectations; and using a problem-solving approach when problems are observed. Family members are fully advised of the social expectations and agree to support the social expectations in the community. The leadership team members also review data to let the school faculty know that the skills are being used properly or if there are discipline problems related to the social expectations. Professional development opportunities are available to new faculty and staff in the school so that they will know the social expectations and how and when to teach them.

A school that is *moderately implementing* this practice may have developed some schoolwide social expectations but may not be systematically teaching, monitoring, or evaluating the use of the expectations by their students. There may be evidence of the social expectations in the school handbook, but staff would not report that it is a priority to teach and reinforce social expectations in the school. Likewise, the staff or the students would probably not be able to tell a visitor what are the three to five expectations in the school when asked. Staff would also not be likely to say that they have systematic approaches for correcting behavior and therefore are not actively working to diminish problem behavior. Whereas staff may discuss behavior in meetings, they are not likely to review data or discuss active teaching approaches for the school's social expectations.

If all or most of the indicators are rated at 2 or below, the school is currently *not implementing* the practice. The team should discuss how it wants to prioritize its efforts to begin addressing the indicators listed.

## Setting Goals for Improvement of This Practice

In order to strengthen this practice, the team should discuss its ratings for the indicators listed. Which indicators represent relative strengths (i.e., may be scored a 3 or 4)? Are there relatively small steps that can be taken to move them toward full implementation? For example, when schools first attempt to identify a consistent set of schoolwide expectations, it is helpful to designate a behavior support team that represents the school's administrators, specialists, paraprofessionals, and teachers. This group is often composed of 8–12 people. That team may discuss and develop the social expectations and then recommend them to the full staff. The full staff can then discuss any modifications to the expectations or vote to adopt them. Once there is an adopted set of expectations, the behavior support team can make a recommendation to the faculty on how to implement a plan of action to teach and supervise the social expectations throughout the school year. As with all goal setting, it is important to try not to do too much too quickly and to carefully analyze each step that leads to the prioritized goal. What steps need to happen first in order to support the development of other indicators? Which indicators do team members feel are most critical to the development of the school? Once the team has focused on an indicator for improvement, it needs to discuss concrete ways to collect data that will determine when it has made progress toward the goals. Following is an example of how the team might use the Action Plan on the last page of the Team Meeting Form to record its plan.

**Practice 4: Clear and consistent behavioral expectations are established for students across all school settings.**

| Objective 1 | Activities | Evaluation |
|---|---|---|
| Identify and teach three to five schoolwide social expectations. | 1. Leadership team members identified.<br>2. Team meets and identifies three to five expectations.<br>3. Team recommends to faculty in August.<br>4. Faculty discusses how to teach the practices.<br>5. Social expectations are taught in September and retaught after breaks and whenever necessary. | a. The leadership develops and recommends the expectations in August.<br>b. All teachers and staff teach the expectations in September.<br>c. Expectations are retaught during the year as necessary. |

(From Walker, B., & Cheney, D. [2012]. *The Self-Assessment and Program Review for Positive Behavior Interventions and Supports [SAPR-PBIS™]*. Baltimore, MD: Paul H. Brookes Publishing Co. Copyright © 2012 by University of Washington; adapted by permission.)

## Resources for Further Learning

For numerous free resources and materials for establishing schoolwide expectations as well as the SET, see the web site of the Technical Assistance Center on Positive Behavioral Interventions and Supports at http://www.pbis.org. See also the following:

Sugai, G., Horner, R.H., Algozzine, R., Barrett, S., Lewis, T., Anderson, C., & Simonsen, B. (2010). *School-wide positive behavior support: Implementers' blueprint and self-assessment.* Eugene, OR: University of Oregon. Retrieved from http://www.pbis.org/pbis_resource_detail_page.aspx?Type=3&PBIS_ResourceID=216

A number of free and low-cost resources on effective programs and approaches to promote social and emotional learning in schools are available from the Collaborative for Academic, Social, and Emotional Learning (CASEL) at http://www.casel.org.

For information on evidence-based programs to systematically teach prosocial skills, see the following web sites:

Behavior Institute for Children and Adolescents, http://www.behavioralinstitute.org/Resources/Resources.htm

Committee for Children (Second Step and Steps for Success), http://www.cfchildren.org/programs/ssp/overview/

Prevention Research Center (the PATHS curriculum), http://www.prevention.psu.edu/projects/PATHS.html

Project Achieve (The Stop and Think Program), http://www.projectachieve.info

Other resources to help in this area include the following:

Bloomquist, M.L. (2006). *Skills training for children with behavior problems: A parent and practitioner guide* (Rev. ed.). New York, NY: The Guilford Press.

Brown, W.H., Odom, S.L., & McConnell, S.R. (2008). *Social competence of young children: Risk, disability, and intervention.* Baltimore, MD: Paul H. Brooks Publishing Co.

Cartledge, G., & Kleefeld, J. (2009). *Taking part: Introducing social skills to children PreK–grade 3.* Champaign, IL: Research Press.

Cartledge, G., & Lo, Y. (2006). *Teaching urban learners: Culturally responsive strategies for developing academic and behavioral competence.* Champaign, IL: Research Press.

Cartledge, G., & Loe, S. (2001). Cultural diversity in social skills instruction. *Exceptionality*, 9 (1 & 2), 33–46.

Cartledge, G., & Milburn, J.F. (1996). *Cultural diversity and social skills instruction: Understanding ethnic and gender differences.* Champaign, IL: Research Press.

Hensely, M., Dillon, J.C., Pratt, D., Ford, J., & Burke, R. (2005). *Tools for teaching social skills in school.* Boys Town, NE: The Boys Town Press.

Lynass, L., Tsai, S., Richman, T., & Cheney, D. (2011). Social expectations and behavioral indicators in schoolwide positive behavior supports: A nationwide behavior matrices study. *Journal of Positive Behavior Interventions.* (Advance online publication.) doi: 10.1177/1098300711412076

Mannix, D. (2009). *Social Skills Activities for Special Children* (2nd ed.) [K–5]. San Francisco, CA: Jossey-Bass.

Mannix, D. (2009). *Social Skills Activities for Secondary Students with Special Needs* (2nd ed.) [6–12]. San Francisco, CA: Jossey-Bass.

McGinnis, E. (2012). *Skillstreaming in early childhood: A guide for teaching prosocial skills. The Arnold P. Goldstein Approach* (3rd ed.). Champaign, IL: Research Press.

McGinnis, E. (2012). *Skillstreaming the adolescent: A guide for teaching prosocial skills. The Arnold P. Goldstein Approach* (3rd ed.). Champaign, IL: Research Press.

McGinnis, E. (2012). *Skillstreaming the elementary school child. A guide for teaching prosocial skills. The Arnold P. Goldstein Approach* (3rd ed.). Champaign, IL: Research Press.

Odermann-Mougey, M., Dillon, J.C., & Pratt, D. (2009). *More tools for teaching social skills in school: Grade 3–12.* Boys Town, NE: Boys Town Press.

Sheridan, S.M. (2010). *Social skills for the tough kid: Tips and tools for parents.* Eugene, OR: Pacific Northwest Publishing.

Sheridan, S.M. (2010). *The tough kid social skills book* (2nd ed.). Eugene, OR: Pacific Northwest Publishing.

## PRACTICE FIVE

### School procedures for responding to discipline referrals and emergency situations are implemented consistently and effectively

Even with a well-developed system of teaching and recognizing schoolwide expectations, problem behaviors will still occur. This reality requires schools to develop a system for responding to and tracking ODRs that is well integrated with the established schoolwide expectations. As in the case of establishing specific descriptions of the student behaviors faculty and staff want to teach and recognize, the school must clearly articulate how it will respond to problematic behaviors. In PBIS, corrective consequences are important to providing students with accountability for their behaviors while at the same time taking advantage of the discipline situation to problem-solve and reteach the desired behavior as necessary so that the student is less likely to repeat a disciplinary issue.

For example, it should be very clear to faculty and staff which types of discipline issues they are responsible for managing in their classroom or area of supervision (e.g., not following directions, noncompletion of homework) and which issues are automatically referred to administration for follow-up (e.g., bullying, harassment, aggression). These guidelines are then included in the faculty and staff handbook, summarized in the parent or family handbook, and revisited as needed based on the data the school collects on ODRs and school climate. These systems provide clear guidelines for students, families, and school staff, as well as promote the consistent use of corrective consequences where they are needed (Lewis & Sugai, 1999; Todd et al., 1999).

Most often, discipline situations can be managed through these systems of established consequences and procedures. However, some discipline issues involve students, and at times adults, escalating behavior to a level that significantly disrupts learning and/or may jeopardize safety. For these situations, it can be helpful for the school to establish an area where students can go to resolve issues and/or problem-solve with the support of a staff person. For example, if there is a conflict on the playground or in a common area, a student could come to the office and request assistance from an adult as an alternative to acting out the frustration directly. This would also be a designated area in the office, hallway, or a classroom where a student can be sent for a serious discipline issue to gain assistance in resolving the issue of concern rather than just to receive a consequence for the problematic behavior. The student is expected to calm down before discussing the issue with a supervising adult. Some schools approach this by assigning "buddy rooms" or "problem-solving areas" where a teacher or staff person can send a student to refocus and problem-solve using an established process. For example, Nelson and Carr (1999) developed the Think Time strategy, which provides teachers with a consistent strategy for addressing the initial phases of problem behavior by systematically prompting students to redirect their behavior. Students who do not respond to the teacher's cues are sent to another classroom where they complete a problem-solving process before being able to return to class. If a student receives Think Time four times within a day or week (depending on a school's criteria), the consequence becomes an office discipline referral.

It is also critical that schools are prepared to respond effectively to crisis situations so that a serious, escalating problem such as a very angry and defiant student or fight can be resolved safely and positively (Colvin, 2009; Walker, Ramsey, & Gresham, 2003). For this reason, the school should develop a team of faculty and staff who have been trained in effective crisis de-escalation and management, as well as have a clear, practiced procedure for responding to serious problems so that the disruption to the learning environment is minimized. Students should also be prepared to respond quickly to a potentially unsafe or a volatile situation (e.g., move away, call for help, lockdown). This preparation helps protect student and staff safety in a worse-case scenario and may keep volatile situations from further escalating (Colvin, 2009; Walker et al., 2003).

As a part of monitoring schoolwide discipline data, the leadership team establishes a process in which the discipline data are regularly reviewed at both a systems and individual student level. This allows the school team to identify students who are beginning to display an ongoing pattern of problem behaviors that may require a focused, more in-depth problem-solving approach. Students who are being evaluated for or are already qualified for special education have specific types of intervention planning mandated, such as functional behavior assessment and behavior intervention plans (see discussion on Practice 7 later in this chapter for more information on these strategies).

## Rating This Practice

A school that is *fully implementing* this practice has a well-defined system for responding to problem behaviors that is discussed with faculty and staff, published in staff and student handbooks, and reviewed periodically for effectiveness and consistency. Data on discipline issues are regularly collected and reviewed to inform problem solving and decision making in these areas. The school has an established procedure that provides a time and place for a student to calm down, problem-solve with the help of an adult, and refocus when needed. In addition, there is an established team that is trained in crisis prevention and de-escalation that can respond effectively to an escalating situation. All or most of the individual practices are rated at a level of 4 or 5.

A school that is *moderately implementing* this practice may have some of these practices in place, but they are not implemented consistently and/or have not been communicated well to faculty, staff, students, and parents. Decisions related to this process may not include data related to discipline issues. There may not be an established process for students to problem solve and refocus their behavior when needed, or a systematic process for providing a functional assessment and behavior plan for students who require it. Some or all of the indicators are rated around 3 using the rating scale. Schools operating at this level should identify specific indicators to focus on moving toward full implementation.

If all or most of the indicators are rated at 2 or below, the school is currently *not implementing* the practice. The team should discuss how it wants to prioritize its efforts to begin addressing the indicators listed.

## Setting Goals for Improvement of This Practice

In order to strengthen this practice, the team should discuss its ratings for the indicators listed. Which indicators represent relative strengths (i.e., may be scored a 3 or 4)? Are there relatively small steps that can be taken to move them toward full implementation? For example, if the school has a defined process for responding to problem behavior but it has not yet been published in the school handbooks, the team may want to begin there because it can be completed fairly quickly and moves the school toward full implementation of that indicator. The team may also choose to address an indicator that the team consistently rated quite low. Perhaps there is not currently a crisis intervention team in place. The team may make the training and development of this group a priority. However, in this case it may take more time and effort to develop implementation. For example, if there is a lack of consistency and coherence to how teachers, staff, and administrators respond to problem behaviors, the leadership team has to problem-solve how to begin that very important discussion and begin to move toward consensus in this area.

As with all goal setting, it is important not to try to do too much too quickly and to carefully analyze the initial steps that lead to addressing priority goals. What steps need to happen first in order to support the development of other indicators? Which indicators do team members feel are most critical to the development of the school? Once the team has focused on an indicator for improvement, it needs to discuss concrete ways to collect data that will determine when it has made progress toward the goals. Following is an example of how the team might use the Action Plan on the last page of the Team Meeting Form to record its plan.

**Practice 5: School procedures for responding to discipline referrals and emergency situations are implemented consistently and effectively.**

| Objective 1 | Activities | Evaluation |
|---|---|---|
| *Establish clearly defined guidelines describing which behaviors teachers and supervising staff are responsible for responding to, and options for doing so productively.* | *1. Leadership team will put together a one-page summary of current discipline data and initial recommendations on approaches to respond to problem behavior.* | *a. Leadership team will review office discipline referral data for the following month and share that with faculty and staff, as well as send out an electronic survey asking teachers and staff about level and types of behaviors they are now addressing themselves.* |
| **Objective 2** | **Activities** | **Evaluation** |
| *Conduct two trainings during professional development days on effective classroom and student area management strategies.* | *1. Leadership team will identify classroom management strategies and work with staff to use in classroom (e.g., increase differential reinforcement, prompt, cue, remind social expectations, problem-solve with students, or use think time).* | *a. Teachers and staff who attend these trainings will be surveyed on their feedback on the process overall.*<br>*b. School and classroom data related to discipline will be reviewed to determine impact.* |

(From Walker, B., & Cheney, D. [2012]. *The Self-Assessment and Program Review for Positive Behavior Interventions and Supports [SAPR-PBIS™]*. Baltimore, MD: Paul H. Brookes Publishing Co. Copyright © 2012 by University of Washington; adapted by permission.)

## Resources for Further Learning

For numerous free resources and materials for establishing schoolwide discipline procedures and for information about the SWIS system for tracking and monitoring school discipline data, see the following web sites:

School-Wide Information System, http://www.swis.org

Technical Assistance Center on Positive Behavioral Interventions and Supports, http://www.pbis.org

For further information on using the PBIS model to reduce disproportionate discipline issues and address the overrepresentation of culturally and linguistically diverse students, see the following:

Cregor, M. (2008, Fall). Building blocks of PBIS. *Teaching Tolerance, 34*, 18–20. Retrieved from http://www.tolerance.org/magazine/number-34-fall-2008/building-blocks-positive-behavior

Drakeford, W. (2006). *Racial disproportionality and school discipline practices.* Tempe, AZ: National Center for Culturally Responsive Educational Systems. Retrieved from http://www.nccrest.org/Briefs/School_Discipline_Brief.pdf

For tools on evaluating and strengthening the school's ability to respond to students with urgent needs or crisis situations, see the following:

Center for Mental Health in Schools at UCLA. (2008). *Responding to a crisis at a school.* Los Angeles, CA: Author. Retrieved from http://smhp.psych.ucla.edu/pdfdocs/crisis/crisis.pdf.

Other resources for further detailed information in this practice include the following:

Algozzine, R., Daunic, A., & Smith, S. (Eds.). (2010). *Preventing problem behaviors: School-wide programs and classroom practices* (2nd ed.). Thousand Oaks, CA: Corwin Press.

Colvin, G. (2007). *Seven steps for developing a proactive schoolwide discipline plan: A guide for principals and leadership teams.* Thousand Oaks, CA: Corwin Press.

Colvin, G. (2009). *Managing noncompliance and defiance in the classroom: A road map for teachers, specialists, and behavior support teams.* Thousand Oaks, CA: Corwin Press.

Nelson, R., & Carr, B. (1999). *The think time strategy for schools kit.* Frederick, CO: Sopris West.

Skiba, R., & Sprague, J. (2008). Safety without suspension. *Educational Leadership, 66*(1), 38–43.

Walker, H., Ramsey, E., & Gresham, F. (2003). *Antisocial behavior in school: Strategies and best practices* (2nd ed.). Pacific Grove, CA: Wadsworth.

## PRACTICE SIX

### Systematic supports are developed to address the academic and social needs of students with E/BPs

Although PBIS can be extremely effective in promoting positive behavior for most students, there will still remain a group of students with ongoing behavioral concerns. PBIS research since 2002 has found that approximately 10%–15% of the students in a school will require some type of more intensive supports beyond the schoolwide system, and another 5% will require a comprehensive, individualized behavior support program (Horner, Sugai, et al., 2004; Sugai & Horner, 2002; Walker et al., 1996). This means that teachers need additional support from other professionals with more specialized behavioral and instructional expertise to provide suggestions and strategies for these students. This type of support is critical for both teacher and student success (Knapp et al., 2004).

One important way to provide this support is for schools to develop an SST made up of professionals with the necessary expertise in academic and behavioral supports for students, who can meet regularly with staff to ensure that interventions are in place for students with or at risk of E/BP (Knoff, 2009; Sugai & Horner, 2002). Some of the key elements of effective behavior support teams include clear policies and procedures outlining the roles and function of the team, a process for the early identification of at-risk students, an efficient referral process that is responsive to emergent needs, adequate behavioral and instructional expertise, team-based problem solving, and active administrative support. This team works with the teacher and family to develop a student intervention and support plan and to monitor its efficacy over time (Sugai & Horner, 2002; Todd et al., 1999).

By matching academic and behavioral supports to students in a proactive manner as issues emerge, it may be possible to stabilize the functioning of some students before problems become even more intensive (Walker, 2010; Walker et al., 2005). For example, in a study on the implementation of PBIS in three schools in Washington State, Walker et al. (2005) found that within a group of 72 students who were identified as at risk for E/BPs through the SSBD (Walker & Severson, 1992), nearly half of the students were able to maintain their academic progress by accessing the schools' existing student supports (e.g., counseling, tutoring, peer tutors). Of the remaining students, one third were referred to a specialized academic support team, 11 to a FBA team, and only 7 qualified for special education. These results suggest that a systematic student support process, within the context of a comprehensive PBIS program, can provide the necessary interventions to assist students who are struggling academically or behaviorally and keep referrals to special education to a minimum.

Between 2004 and 2011, the RTI process has relied on the SST to address both social and academic problems and to develop what are referred to as Tier 2 or 3 interventions for students. Walker (2010) stated that academic success is linked with competence in social and behavior skills. In one study, researchers identified five predictor variables concerning student skills or behaviors related to overall success in school. These variables are referred to as *academic enablers* and include academic achievement, interpersonal and study skills, motivation, and school engagement, and they predict a student's ultimate school success (DiPerna & Elliott, 1999). Knoff (2009) also identified the importance of addressing both academic and social or behavior skills within the RTI model in a manner that supports mastery of learning and behavioral goals for all students. Recognizing that school success is based on the interaction of all of these factors, the use of a proactive, systematic process for identifying student need across both areas allows schools to provide needed support and skill development before a student develops a more serious or prolonged problem (Center for Mental Health in Schools, 2007; Elliott et al., 2007; Knoff, 2009).

To address this interaction of factors, Walker (2010) recommended that the school's SST address both social and academic functioning of students in an integrated fashion. The team would be responsible for reviewing a student's academic and social functioning and then developing intervention plans to assist general educators in enhancing students' academic or social performance. The team's responsibility, therefore, extends to assisting a teacher by coaching him or her in using the suggested interventions and providing the necessary materials or training to implement the intervention. Existing interventions found throughout many schools include volunteer tutors, focused academic skill instruction, peer-mediated instruction, social skills groups, individual behavior contracting, buddy systems, and peer mentors. Matching students identified in the screening process to specific supports *before* they begin to have difficulty is the hallmark of this practice. This process is discussed in more depth in Practice 2.

In schools that are fully implementing PBIS, teachers will often be called on to implement Tier 2 behavioral interventions. The most fully researched approaches at this time include the Behavior Education Program (Crone, Hawken, & Horner, 2010; Hawken, MacLeod, & Rawlings, 2007; Simonsen, Myers, & Brier, 2011), Check, Connect, and Expect (Cheney et al., 2009), and the check-in and check-out process (Anderson, Christenson, Sinclair, & Lehr, 2004; Fairbanks, Sugai, Guardino, & Lathrop, 2007; McIntosh, Campbell, Carter, & Dickey, 2009; Sinclair, Christenson, & Thurlow, 2005). All of these programs use daily progress reports to monitor and give students feedback on how they are meeting the school's social expectations. The programs rely on positive, caring adults who have daily social interactions and structured supervision of students with behavior problems. These positive, caring adults are referred to as coaches or mentors. They "check in" with students frequently and provide them with feedback on their academic and social progress. Coaches or mentors help students set daily social goals for success and provide students with reinforcement when goals are met.

Teachers in a Tier 2 intervention are often asked to increase their rates of social interaction and feedback to target students. Feedback pertains to the school's social expectations, and teachers are asked to rate the student's behavior on the daily progress report or every 60–90 minutes. Enhancing a teacher's positive attitude toward students, giving positive social feedback, and increasing supervision and monitoring are all important aspects of successfully implementing positive behavior management systems in classrooms. Figure 5.2 provides an example of a daily progress report that we used with staff and students in a local elementary school.

## Rating This Practice

A school that is *fully implementing* this practice has a well-defined system for integrating and using data from the academic and behavioral screening process into Tier 2 additional support for students. To have these practices available, the school has devoted time and resources into developing its RTI process. Academic and social interventions are adopted, reviewed, practiced, and implemented with fidelity in classrooms. General educators, therefore, have an array of Tier 2 academic and behavioral interventions to use once a student is demonstrating problems in the classroom. These include, but are not limited to, academic tutoring; isolated skill instruction; modified academic materials; social skills groups; coaching; and mentoring on behavioral interventions such as the Behavior Education Program or Check, Connect, and Expect. These interventions are accessible, efficient to implement, and effective with struggling students. Progress monitoring data are collected for any student in a Tier 2 intervention, and the SST monitors the effectiveness of the intervention with the participating teacher. All or most of the individual practices are rated at a level of 4 or 5.

A school that is *moderately implementing* this practice may have some of these practices in place, but they are not implemented consistently and/or have not been communicated well to faculty, staff, students, and parents. Teachers may not be trained in the interventions and may not find that there is sufficient support to implement the interventions. Implementation of interventions may not include progress-monitoring data to evaluate the instruction or

**Excel at Apple Center**

Our expectations: Be respectful. Be responsible.
Be safe. Be a hard worker.

| Checked in | Yes | No |
|---|---|---|
| Checked out | Yes | No |
| Parent Signature | Yes | No |

Student: ______________ Date: __________ Goal: ______________

| | Reading | | | | Math | | | | Afternoon subjects | | | | |
|---|---|---|---|---|---|---|---|---|---|---|---|---|---|
| Expectations | Tough time | Okay | Good | Way to go! | Tough time | Okay | Good | Way to go! | Tough time | Okay | Good | Way to go! | Totals |
| Be respectful. | 1 | 2 | 3 | 4 | 1 | 2 | 3 | 4 | 1 | 2 | 3 | 4 | |
| Be responsible. | 1 | 2 | 3 | 4 | 1 | 2 | 3 | 4 | 1 | 2 | 3 | 4 | |
| Be safe. | 1 | 2 | 3 | 4 | 1 | 2 | 3 | 4 | 1 | 2 | 3 | 4 | |
| Be a hard worker. | 1 | 2 | 3 | 4 | 1 | 2 | 3 | 4 | 1 | 2 | 3 | 4 | |
| | | | | | | | | | | | | Daily total: | |

Way to Go! (4): Met expectations with positive behavior; worked independently, no reminders or corrections.
Good (3): Met expectations with only 1 reminder or correction.
Okay (2): Needed 2–3 reminders or corrections.
Tough time (1): Needed 4 or more reminders or corrections.

Parent signature: ______________

Comments:

**Figure 5.2.** Example of a Tier 2 daily progress report.

behavioral intervention. Some or all of the indicators are rated around 3 using the rating scale. Schools operating at this level should identify specific indicators to focus on moving toward full implementation.

If all or most of the indicators are rated at 2 or below, the school is currently *not implementing* the practice. The team should discuss how it wants to prioritize its efforts to begin addressing the indicators listed.

## Setting Goals for Improvement of This Practice

In order to strengthen this practice, the team should discuss its ratings for the indicators listed. Which indicators represent relative strengths (i.e., may be scored a 3 or 4)? Are there relatively small steps that can be taken to move them toward full implementation? For example, if the school has a screening approach for academic or social behavior, the team could begin by conducting an inventory of existing supports to implement with students once identified in the screening. The team may also choose to identify academic or social supports that would serve as Tier 2 interventions, identify an approach to professional development, and plan an action to use these approaches in the coming school year. Whichever indicator is addressed, the team should consider the linkage between academic and social intervention, the methods to address both, and the manner in which professional development can address the areas of concern.

As with all goal setting, it is important not to try to do too much too quickly and to carefully analyze the initial steps that will lead to accomplishing priority goals. What steps need to happen first in order to support the development of other indicators? Which indicators do team members feel are most critical to the development of the school? Once the team has focused on an indicator for improvement, it needs to discuss concrete ways to collect data that will determine when it has made progress toward the goals. Following is an example of how the team might use the Action Plan on the last page of the Team Meeting Form to record its plan.

**Practice 6: Systematic supports are developed to address the academic and social needs of students with emotional or behavioral problems.**

| Objective 1 | Activities | Evaluation |
|---|---|---|
| *Expand the academic and social supports that are used as Tier 2 interventions.* | *1. Student support team (SST) conducts inventory of existing academic and social supports.*<br>*2. SST and faculty discuss how students obtain supports once screened.*<br>*3. SST and faculty review effectiveness data for existing supports.*<br>*4. SST eliminates ineffective practices.*<br>*5. SST identifies one or two new approaches in academic or social intervention.*<br>*6. Administrator budgets for professional development and materials for new practice.* | *a. SST monitors and evaluates effectiveness of existing practices.*<br>*b. Administrator plans for professional development and buys new materials.*<br>*c. Professional development is completed.*<br>*d. Students in new interventions are evaluated through use of progress monitoring tools.* |

(From Walker, B., & Cheney, D. [2012]. *The Self-Assessment and Program Review for Positive Behavior Interventions and Supports [SAPR-PBIS™]*. Baltimore, MD: Paul H. Brookes Publishing Co. Copyright © 2012 by University of Washington; adapted by permission.)

## Resources for Further Learning

A number of free and low-cost resources on effective programs and approaches to promote social and emotional learning in schools are available from Collaborative for Academic, Social, and Emotional Learning (CASEL) at http://www.casel.org.

The Check and Connect program is an evidence-based practice for secondary schools that has been found to be effective in dropout prevention research; for more information, see http://ici.umn.edu/checkandconnect/.

Additional references for Practice 6 include the following:


Center for Mental Health in Schools. (2007). *A resource aid packet on screening/assessing students: Indicators and tools.* Los Angeles, CA: Author.

Cheney, D., Lynass, L., Flower, A., Waugh, M., & Iwaszuk, W. (2010). The Check, Connect, and Expect program: A targeted, tier two intervention in the school-wide positive behavior support model. *Preventing School Failure, 54*, 152–158.

Cheney, D., Stage, S., Hawken, L., Lynass, L., Mielenz, C., & Waugh, M. (2009). A two-year outcome study of the check, connect, and expect intervention for students at-risk of severe behavior problems. *Journal of Emotional and Behavioral Disorders, 17*, 226–243.

Crone, D., Hawken, L., & Horner, R. (2010). *Responding to problem behavior in schools: The behavior education program* (2nd ed.). New York, NY: Guilford.

Fairbanks, S., Sugai, G., Guardino, D., & Lathrop, M. (2007). Response to intervention: Examining classroom behavior support in second grade. *Exceptional Children, 73*, 288–310.

Hawken, L.S., & Horner, R.H. (2003). Evaluation of a targeted intervention within a school-wide system of behavior support. *Journal of Behavioral Education, 12*, 225–240.

Hawken, L.S., MacLeod, S.K., & Rawlings, L. (2007). Effects of the behavior education program (BEP) on office discipline referrals of elementary school students. *Journal of Positive Behavior Interventions, 9*, 94–101.

Hawken, L.S., Vincent, C.G., & Schumann, J. (2008). Response to intervention for social behavior: Challenges and opportunities. *Journal of Emotional and Behavioral Disorders, 16*, 213–225.

McIntosh, K., Campbell, A.L., Carter, D.R., & Dickey, C.R. (2009). Differential effects of a tier two behavior intervention based on function of problem behavior. *Journal of Positive Behavior Interventions, 11*, 68–81.

Simonsen, B., Myers, D., & Briere, D. (2011). Comparing a behavioral check-in/check-out intervention to standard practice in an urban middle school setting using an experimental group design. *Journal of Positive Behavior Interventions, 13*, 31–48.

Zins, J.E., & Elias, M.E. (2006). Social and emotional learning. In G.G. Bear & K.M. Minke (Eds.), *Children's needs III* (pp. 1–13). Bethesda, MD: National Association of School Psychologists.

## PRACTICE SEVEN

### FBAs are completed for students with significant behavior problems to develop intensive interventions

When some school team members see the phrase "functional behavioral assessment," they think of completing a legally required form for a special education student who has serious conduct problems and a behavior plan (IDEA, 2004). In daily educational practice, FBA can be more positively viewed as a problem-solving approach for students with chronic and/or intensive behavior problems, regardless of whether they have been identified as needing special education (Crone, Hawken, & Bergstrom, 2007; Scott & Caron, 2005; Walker et al., 2005). Through the use of direct or indirect data collection strategies such as observations and interviews, FBA helps to identify the underlying function for a student's behavior by determining what triggers and maintains the pattern of problem behavior. The goal of FBA is to determine the "pay-off" for the student when engaging in the problematic behavior. Frustrated administrators and teachers sometimes feel that students with serious behavior problems continue to act out to get back at the staff and/or other students. An FBA, on the other hand, might suggest the student is seeking to meet an important need and he or she does not know a more socially acceptable way to obtain the need (Sugai, Horner, et al., 2002). These important needs (e.g., to get away from something difficult or painful or to obtain something that is desired) are referred to as *functions*.

Any effective FBA includes clear problem identification and systematic problem analysis that inform the development of a BIP and are followed up in a manner that includes effective plan implementation and evaluation (Crone & Horner, 2003; O'Neill et al., 1997). FBA may be done in either an informal or formal manner to help schools problem-solve chronic behavior problems at both the whole school level and the individual student level. The informal or more simple FBA involves reviewing existing data, brief interviews with school staff or family members, and the development of a hypothesis related to the function of the problem behavior. This hypothesis helps the team identify a function-based intervention for the problem behavior that alters antecedent events, teaches productive behavior, or modifies consequences. For serious/chronic behavior problems, a more formal approach to FBA is implemented, involving more in-depth data collection and individualized interventions (Scott & Caron, 2005).

A formal FBA for a student with chronic/intensive behavior problems is often completed using what is called the *competing pathway analysis*. This approach examines the behavior on the basis of the following components (Crone & Horner, 2003; O'Neill et al., 1997; Sugai, Horner, et al., 2002):

1. *Setting events:* Those events that are not immediately involved in the problem behavior but tend to affect it (e.g., a bad night's sleep, difficulty on the bus, missed medication)

2. *Antecedent events:* Those events that occur immediately before the problem behavior and tend to predict or initiate it (e.g., difficult math lesson, sitting next to unfriendly peer)
3. *Specific description* of the problem behavior (e.g., yelling, shouting, arguing)
4. *Maintaining consequence*: Outcomes that occur immediately after the problem behavior that serve to reinforce it (e.g., teacher attention, move student to hallway, remove work).

Once the elements of the behavioral pathway are identified, a BIP can be developed that provides intervention options for each part of the pathway. Setting and antecedent events can be modified or changed to reduce the likelihood the behavior will occur. Prosocial skills instruction can be used to teach more appropriate replacement behaviors, which in turn makes the problem behavior less efficient. Maintaining consequences can be modified so that the problem behavior is no longer effective or relevant (Crone & Horner, 2003; O'Neill et al., 1997; Scott, Anderson, & Spaulding, 2008; Sugai, Horner, et al., 2002).

By having a range of intervention options for antecedents, behavior, and consequences, the team can develop a comprehensive, written BIP based on the function of the student's behavior and that includes strategies for monitoring and evaluating the effectiveness of the plan. One member of the team is then assigned the role of case manager, taking on the primary responsibility of tracking and monitoring the effects of the plan. The SST ensures that the teacher and other staff who will be responsible for the implementation of the plan have adequate training and support to do so effectively and with fidelity. The active involvement of family members and the staff responsible for implementing the interventions helps to ensure that the plan has good "contextual fit," which means that it is acceptable and doable from the perspective of those most closely involved with the child (Crone & Horner, 2003; Knoster & McCurdy, 2002; Sugai, Horner, et al., 2002).

When a student is identified as displaying chronic or intensive problem behavior, there is likely the need for a more in-depth form of problem solving that pinpoints the function or reason for the student's behaviors. Although federal and state mandates require FBA and BIP for all students with disabilities whose serious behavior has lead to frequent disciplinary actions and changes of placement due to their disability, it is a helpful strategy for any student with chronic behavior problems (Scott & Caron, 2005; Scott et al., 2008). The goal of FBA is to develop a comprehensive plan to teach students more effective, efficient, and relevant behavior in difficult social and academic situations. By using more positive and productive behavior, the student begins to experience increasing success in socially acceptable ways to get his or her needs met.

## Rating This Practice

A school that is *fully implementing* this practice has a well-defined system for tracking the progress of all students receiving Tier 2 interventions. Students who are not responding to these interventions are progress monitored and reviewed by an established SST to determine if an FBA is a needed. The SST is made up of professionals who have received some in-depth training on the various approaches to FBA and effective behavior intervention planning. They are adept at analyzing setting events, antecedents, problem behaviors, and consequences to formulate hypotheses regarding behavioral function and to develop function-based interventions. The team also provides formal training and informal coaching on use of function-based interventions for students with challenging behavior to the faculty and staff in the school. All or most of the individual practices are rated at a level of 4 or 5.

A school that is *moderately implementing* this practice may have some of these practices in place, but they are not implemented consistently and/or have not been communicated well to faculty, staff, students, and parents. Teachers may understand the role of function in student behavior and have an awareness of effective interventions, but they may not match behavioral function to interventions or have sufficient support to implement the interventions effectively. Implementation of interventions may not include progress-monitoring data to track student progress or a systematic way to collect data on student functioning. Some or all of the indicators are rated around 3 using the rating scale. Schools operating at this level should identify specific indicators to focus on moving toward full implementation.

If all or most of the indicators are rated at 2 or below, the school is currently *not implementing* the practice. The team should discuss how it wants to prioritize its efforts to begin addressing the indicators listed.

## Setting Goals for Improvement of This Practice

In order to strengthen this practice, the team should discuss its ratings for the indicators listed. Which indicators represent relative strengths (i.e., may be scored a 3 or 4)? Are there relatively small steps that can be taken to move them toward full implementation? For example, if the team has developed some consistently implemented Tier 2 interventions, the SST may explore ways to carefully monitor student progress and identify students who may be in need of an FBA and begin practicing the related strategies. The SST might provide the school faculty with an overview of the FBA approach and some effective intervention strategies for students with ongoing behavior challenges. The school should be shifting its approach from punishing students with ongoing behavior problems to one that involves problem solving and effective interventions, helping students to learn more effective, socially appropriate ways to meet their needs and experience academic and social success.

As with all goal setting, it is important not to try to do too much too quickly and to carefully analyze the initial steps that lead toward the priority goals. What steps need to happen first in order to support the development of other indicators? Which indicators do team members feel are most critical to the development of the school? Once the team has focused on an indicator for improvement, it needs to discuss concrete ways to collect data that will determine when it has made progress toward the goals. Following is an example of how the team might use the Action Plan on the last page of the Team Meeting Form to record its plan.

**Practice 7: FBAs are completed for students with significant behavior problems to develop intensive interventions.**

| Objective 1 | Activities | Evaluation |
|---|---|---|
| *Increase the skills and fluency in functional behavioral assessment (FBA) strategies for members of the student support team (SST).* | *1. Team will attend PBIS training on FBA and then present a summary of the content learned and a proposed pilot process to the faculty at a faculty meeting.*<br>*2. The SST will then outline a process for identifying and supporting students who would benefit from a proactive FBA process. The team will pilot this process with three to five students from the school.* | *a. Faculty will provide feedback on the content and process presented at the faculty meetings.*<br>*b. Pre and post data will be collected on the students involved in the pilot study, and parents and other involved staff will complete a short survey on their perceptions of the effectiveness of the FBA process and the related behavior intervention plans. These will be shared with the faculty at the end of the year.* |

(From Walker, B., & Cheney, D. [2012]. *The Self-Assessment and Program Review for Positive Behavior Interventions and Supports [SAPR-PBIS™]*. Baltimore, MD: Paul H. Brookes Publishing Co. Copyright © 2012 by University of Washington; adapted by permission.)

## Resources for Further Learning

For numerous free resources and materials related to students with intensive, individualized needs who may benefit from an FBA, see the following web sites:

Center for Effective Collaboration and Practice (CECP), http://cecp.air.org/fba/default.asp

Technical Assistance Center on Positive Behavioral Interventions and Supports, http://www.pbis.org

The New Mexico Public Education Technical Assistance Manual includes a fairly easy to use tool for teams learning to use FBA, http://www.ped.state.nm.us/RtI/behavior/4.fba.11.28.pdf, and the Virginia Department of Educations created a helpful monograph on using FBA, http://www.doe.virginia.gov/support/student_conduct/functional_behavioral_assessment.pdf.

The following are helpful books and articles:

Crone, D.A., & Horner, R.H. (2003). *Building positive behavior support systems in schools: Functional behavioral assessment.* New York, NY: Guilford Press.

Jordan, D. (2006). *Functional behavioral assessment and positive interventions: What parents need to know.* Minneapolis, MN: The Pacer Center.

Knoff, H.M. (2009). *Implementing response-to-intervention at the school, district, and state levels: Functional assessment, data-based problem solving, and evidence-based academic and behavioral interventions.* Little Rock, AR: Project ACHIEVE Press.

O'Neill, R., Horner, R., Albin, R., Sprague, J., Storey, K., & Newton, S.J. (1997). *Functional assessment and program development for problem behavior: A practical handbook.* Pacific Grove, CA: Brooks/Cole.

Scott, T., & Caron, D. (2005). Conceptualizing functional behavior assessment as prevention practice within positive behavior support systems. *Preventing School Failure, 50*(1), 13–20.

Scott, T., Nelson, C.M., & Zabala, J. (2003). Functional behavior assessment training in public schools: Facilitating systemic change. *Journal of Positive Behavior Interventions, 5*, 216–224.

Umbreit, J., Ferro, J., Liaupsin, C., & Lane, K. (2008). *Functional behavioral assessment and function-based intervention: An effective, practical approach.* Columbus, OH: Pearson Prentice Hall.

Walker, B., Cheney, D., Stage, S., & Blum, C. (2005). School-wide screening and positive behavior support: Identifying and supporting students at-risk for school failure. *Journal of Positive Behavior Interventions, 7,* 194–204.

## PRACTICE EIGHT

### Data are routinely collected and systematically analyzed by the leadership team for program-evaluation and decision-making purposes

A hallmark of PBIS implementation has been the collection of relevant data to identify school needs, establish priorities, select practices, make decisions, and evaluate actions during school improvement efforts (Lewis & Sugai, 1999; Sugai et al., 2010). Schools are quite familiar with the collection and evaluation of ongoing data related to academic issues but are less practiced in collecting, analyzing, and making decisions on practices related to discipline and behavior. Lewis and Sugai (1999) stated that school leadership teams must learn to establish data collection systems that help them determine what has happened in the past, what is currently happening, whether something is working, and what should happen next. However, because time is so limited in schools, this process needs to be both efficient and effective.

One readily available data source is the number of ODRs occurring in a school. These data can be consistently collected by a school team when it analyzes its ODR process and revises its referral forms to include important data regarding type of problem, location and time of problem, person who refers the problem, and possible function of the problem behavior. These data can be efficiently entered into an electronic database, such as the SWIS (May et al., 2000), which is currently used by several thousand schools. As introduced in Chapter 2, SWIS is a secure web-based data management system that allows schools to enter and monitor ODRs on a schoolwide and individual basis. SWIS can be used to create numerical reports or charts to reflect individual or schoolwide discipline reports. This information can be used for internal decision making on schoolwide discipline issues; to assist in the development of an individual behavior support plan; or to create school, district, or state discipline reports. In a review of several studies utilizing ODRs as measures of school and/or student change, Irvin and colleagues found it to be both a valid and a sensitive measure of school performance in relationship to PBIS (Irvin et al., 2006; Irvin, Tobin, Sprague, Sugai, & Vincent, 2004).

To be most effective, leadership teams should review data regularly (e.g., monthly, biweekly), summarize the data for the staff, and use the data for active decision making (Horner, Sugai, et al., 2004). For example, using SWIS to track the number of ODRs in its schools, the state of Maryland measured the time involved in responding to discipline issues in schools utilizing PBIS (Scott & Barrett, 2004). It was determined that school administrators spent an average of 10 minutes processing an ODR and that a student lost an average of 20 minutes of instructional time as well. Across the 2 years that PBIS was implemented in Maryland schools, administrators saved an average of 11.06 days, and students regained an average of 29.5 days as the result of reduced ODRs (Scott & Barrett, 2004). Because PBIS is an evolving process, schools that learn to use data to evaluate and monitor their efforts are likely to find the most success.

Data on individual students should be used to review the progress of students with BIP or who are receiving academic remediation. Through the analysis of school records, Tobin and Sugai (1999) found the frequency of ODRs to be a significant ($p < .001$) predictor of chronic discipline problems in middle schools, which also predicted the frequency of suspensions in ninth grade ($p < .001$). These findings suggest that providing supports for students with multiple ODRs through a behavior support team and an individualized plan may help to prevent an ongoing pattern of discipline problems for many students.

Teams that are monitoring individual students should also consider a monitoring approach using daily progress reports in Tier 2 interventions and individualized behavior report cards in Tier 3 interventions, as used in BEP and CCE (see Practice 6). We have described this process in Practice 6 (Cheney, Flower, & Templeton, 2008; Cheney et al., 2009; Crone, Hawken & Horner, 2010), but in brief, the percentage of points earned by students on a daily basis are recorded and charted. Goals are set for the student to consistently earn more than 75% or 80% of points daily, and students are expected to be successful in meeting this criterion for a period of 6–8 weeks. By charting these data, the team can monitor student growth or decline in Tier 2 or 3 interventions. The difference in the data collection between Tier 2 and 3 is typically that the school expectations (e.g., respect, responsibility) are on the daily progress report as student goals, whereas individualized behavior goals (e.g., take turns, listen to others, take care of own or others' property) are used at Tier 3.

Figure 5.3 is an example of how data from a daily progress report were charted in the CCE project. In the chart, the daily criterion for success was set at 75% of total points. This criteria was established because the scale for the daily report was based on 4 point scale like that shown in Figure 5.2. Earning on average a 3 on this scale would therefore show success for the student. The charting system in this project was built so that green showed successful days and red indicated days when the student did not meet criteria. (*Note:* Color is not reflected in Figure 5.3.) On successful days, we always suggest that verbal or social reinforcement is provided by the teacher and coach in a school. As students meet success across 2-week periods, the criteria is moved to 80% and 85%, and ultimately the student graduates from the program. Most studies completed on this work suggest that a student should be able to meet these criterion for success in an 8- to 12-week period (Cheney et al., 2009; Crone et al., 2010; McIntosh et al., 2009; Simonsen et al., 2011).

## Rating This Practice

A school that is *fully implementing* this practice has a well-defined system for integrating and using progress-monitoring data in both the academic and social domains. For example, curriculum-based measures such as the Dynamic Indicators of Basic Early Literacy Skills

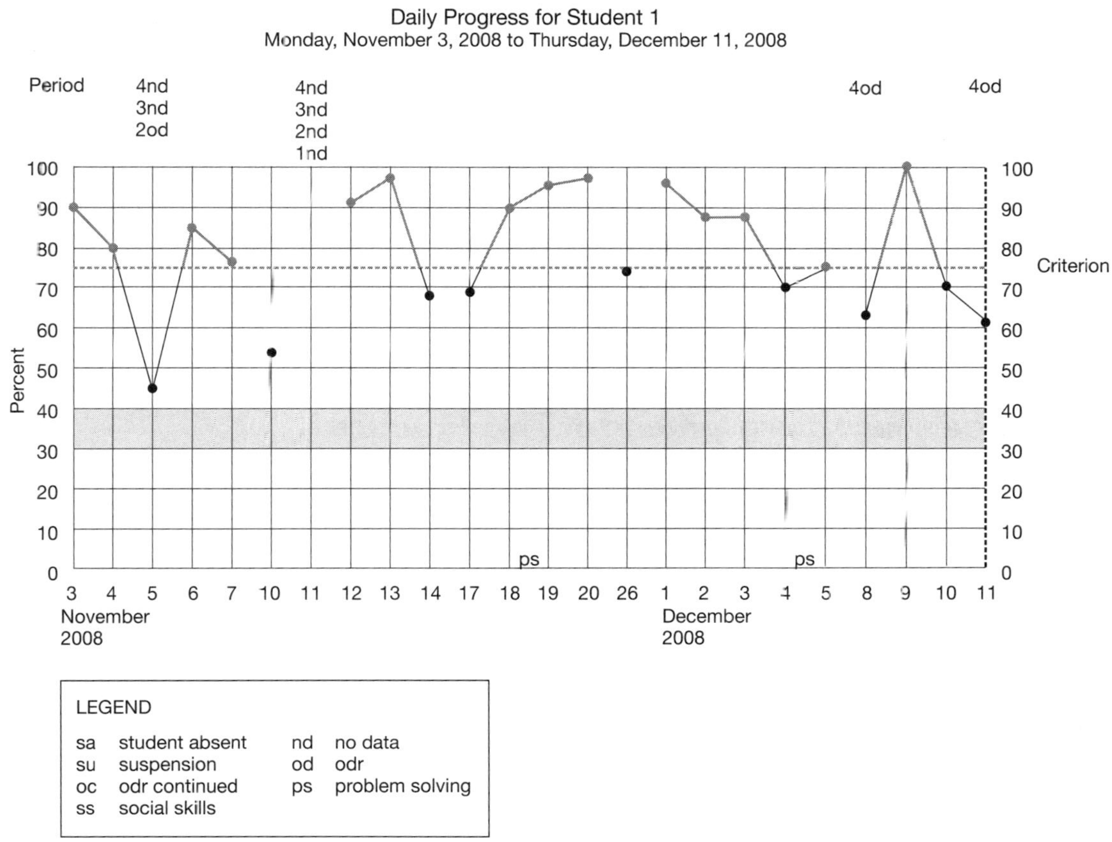


**Figure 5.3.** Charting Tier 2 progress report data. (*Note:* In this sample, the student received 45% of possible points on November 5; he received an office discipline referral in second period. No data were available for third and fourth period. The legend shows the range of possible codes. Color used in the original chart not reflected in this figure.) (*Key:* odr, office discipline referral.)

(DIBELS; Good & Kaminski, 2002) might be in use to analyze student progress in literacy. In the behavioral domain, SWIS might be in use to evaluate ODRs. In addition, a progress monitoring system might be in use for Tier 2 or 3 behavioral interventions that allows for charting of the student behavior or daily ratings. Once the system is in place, the SST would use the data in a systematic approach for monitoring students of concern. The team might include an administrator, school psychologist, counselors, and special and general education teachers. The team meets regularly (monthly at a minimum) throughout the year to review student data, review progress, and provide reports to the school faculty on how the school as a whole is doing with its PBIS implementation. In addition, the team would be conscious of issues relating to disproportionality in discipline and analyze the data to ensure that all students are being evaluated and supported in an equitable manner. SWIS, for example, provides these analyses by displaying bar graphs for ODRs by race/ethnicity, allowing schools to better determine if their discipline practices are fair and equitable toward all students. Using data to evaluate effectiveness of Tier 2 interventions can ultimately be beneficial in decreasing the disproportionate placement of students of color in special education.

A school that is *moderately implementing* this practice may have some of these practices in place, but they are not implemented consistently and/or have not been communicated well to faculty, staff, students, and parents. Data systems are not used systematically so that progress monitoring can be used to evaluate schoolwide approaches to PBIS. In particular, the Tier 2 interventions may not be effective because data systems such as SWIS or DIBELS are not in place. Some or all of the indicators are rated around 3 using the rating scale. Schools operating at this level should identify specific indicators to focus on moving toward full implementation.

If all or most of the indicators are rated at 2 or below, the school is currently *not implementing* the practice. The team should discuss how it wants to prioritize its efforts to begin addressing the indicators listed.

## Setting Goals for Improvement of This Practice

In order to strengthen this practice, the team should discuss its ratings for the indicators listed. Which indicators represent relative strengths (i.e., may be scored a 3 or 4)? Are there relatively small steps that can be taken to move them toward full implementation? For example, if the school has no systematic data collection procedure for ODRs, then this would serve as a very important goal for the team to address. If the school is not systematically monitoring the effects of Tier 2 interventions on students with emerging academic and/or behavioral needs, the team may want to explore ways to do so.

As with all goal setting, it is important not to try to do too much too quickly and to carefully analyze the initial steps that will lead toward priority goals. What steps need to happen first in order to support the development of other indicators? Which indicators do team members feel are most critical to the development of the school? Once the team has focused on an indicator for improvement, it needs to discuss concrete ways to collect data that will determine when it has made progress toward the goals. Following is an example of how the team might use the Action Plan on the last pages of the Team Meeting Form to record its plan.

**Practice 8: Data are routinely collected and systematically analyzed by the leadership team for program-evaluation and decision-making purposes.**

| Objective 1 | Activities | Evaluation |
|---|---|---|
| *Adopt and use a schoolwide system such as School-Wide Information System (SWIS) to evaluate office discipline referrals (ODRs).* | *1. Administrator budgets for purchase of SWIS.*<br>*2. Staff are trained in use of SWIS.*<br>*3. ODR system is reviewed for consistency with SWIS variables.*<br>*4. Staff are trained in new ODR process.*<br>*5. System is started and data are analyzed monthly.*<br>*6. Student support team reports results at faculty meetings.* | *a. Analysis SWIS ODR data conducted monthly*<br>*b. Effects of using ODR data at faculty meetings* |

## Resources for Further Learning

For numerous free resources and materials on effective data collection and data-based decision making, see the Technical Assistance Center on Positive Behavioral Interventions and Supports web site at http://www.pbis.org. For information on the SWIS database for managing ODRs and Tier 2 interventions, visit http://www.swis.org. The Success at the Core Project web site offers a free leadership team training module on "Using Data Effectively," http://www.successatthecore.com/leadership_development_module.aspx?module=2. The California Learning Resources Networks also provides free online resources and strategies on using data effectively, http://www.clrn.org/elar/dddm.cfm.

Other references for detailed information of this practice include the following:

Cheney, D., Flower, A., & Templeton, T. (2008). Applying response to intervention metrics in the social domain for students at risk of developing emotional or behavioral disorders. *Journal of Special Education, 42*, 108–126.

Cheney, D., Stage, S., Hawken, L., Lynass, L., Mielenz, C., & Waugh, M. (2009). A two-year outcome study of the check, connect, and expect intervention for students at-risk of severe behavior problems. *Journal of Emotional and Behavioral Disorders, 17*, 226–243.

Crone, D., Hawken, L., & Horner, R. (2010). *Responding to problem behavior in schools: The behavior education program* (2nd ed.). New York, NY: Guilford.

Freeman, R., Smith, C., & Tieghi-Benet, M. (2003). Promoting implementation success through the use of continuous systems-level assessment strategies. *Journal of Positive Behavior Interventions, 5*, 66–70.

McIntosh, K., Campbell, A.L., Carter, D.R., & Dickey, C.R. (2009). Differential effects of a tier two behavior intervention based on function of problem behavior. *Journal of Positive Behavior Interventions, 11*, 68–81.

Scott, T., & Martinek, G. (2006). Coaching positive behavior support in school settings: Tactics and data-based decision making. *Journal of Positive Behavior Interventions, 8*, 165–173.

Simonsen, B., Myers, D., & Briere, D. (2011). Comparing a behavioral check-in/check-out intervention to standard practice in an urban middle school setting using an experimental group design. *Journal of Positive Behavior Interventions, 13*, 31–48.

## PRACTICE NINE

## Families are seen as partners in the development of their child's program

Thoughtfully and intentionally engaging all families in developing and sustaining a positive school culture helps to build more inclusive and supportive learning environments (Elizalde-Utnick, 2002; Learning First Alliance, 2001). For PBIS, the goal is to develop a true partnership with parents, involving them as deeply as possible in the development and implementation of the school improvement process. In particular, family members are viewed as important stakeholders and should be recruited as members of schools/district's PBIS leadership teams to provide cultural perspectives on policies and practices. Parent advocates suggest that strategies for effectively engaging families and caregivers in their school include 1) regularly informing and involving parents in school activities and priorities, 2) providing a series of parenting workshops, 3) developing a library of resources for parents and families, 4) creating a climate in which teachers and administrators communicate frequently and directly with parents on positive issues as well as concerns, 5) linking families with community resources, and 6) developing a parent-to-parent network of support (Cheney & Osher, 1997; Elizalde-Utnick; Kohl, Lengua, & McMahon, 2000). Muscott et al. (2008) recommended that building trust between educators and family members should be central to the PBIS initiative and that each family should be respected for their individual and unique contributions. In particular, family members should have influence in the specific decisions about PBIS in local schools.

Ensuring that efforts to involve family members are performed in a manner that is responsive to cultural variables, socioeconomic status, and diverse perspectives is also of critical importance. For many schools, this means having key documents translated into several languages, observing and honoring holidays and traditions from many cultures, and using translators as needed for parent meetings. Schools mean many things to their families and community; therefore, it is important for school faculty and staff to create a climate that is welcoming for all families and community members (Cheney & Osher, 1997; Kohl et al., 2000).

When a student begins to struggle in school, involving families or caregivers in the development and implementation of the child's intervention and support plan is critical for several reasons. First, family members and caregivers have important insights and information about the student that is necessary for the development of a meaningful intervention and support plan. Second, once strategies have been identified to support a student, they are most effective when implemented and/or supported by both school staff and family members. Finally, a meaningful support plan also addresses the needs and issues that may occur in the family context in response to a student's academic concerns and/or challenging behaviors in school. This involvement empowers the family and caregivers to be part of the solution so that they are better able to work in partnership with the school in responding more effectively to the student's needs (Cheney & Osher, 1997; Fox & Dunlap, 2002; Kohl et al., 2000).

A number of studies have examined the impact of actively involving family members and teachers together in training on effective behavior management and student support strategies. Such a partnership allows both teachers and family members to respond more consistently to the needs of students as well as interact more frequently and positively with one another. Studies that have used this multimodal approach to supporting students have found improvements in student behavior at home and at school; improved academic performance; and reductions in violent behavior, drug and alcohol use, and other risky behaviors later in life. For example, the LIFT program included a classroom-based prosocial skills program, a playground-behavior training program, parent training, and strategies for enhanced parent–teacher communication. The researchers found that students had increased prosocial skills and decreased levels of aggression, particularly in fifth- and sixth-grade students (Reid et al., 1999). The First Step to Success project worked with schools to identify kindergarten students who were showing signs of antisocial behavior, then provided training on effective supports and interventions to both teachers and parents. The researchers found that students who were involved in the project decreased in aggressive behavior, improved in prosocial skills, and were more actively engaged in their learning than at-risk students who did not participate in the project. These changes continued across the 2 years the children were followed after the interventions (Walker et al., 1998).

Another long-term study, the Fast Track Project (Conduct Problems Prevention Research Group, 2000), provided a similar set of interventions and supports to schools and families in communities across the country. At the elementary school level, these included the classroom-based social skills curriculum PATHS, training for teachers on effective instructional and behavior management strategies, and parenting training for families. The research group found that, after 3 years of involvement in the Fast Track program, there were positive effects at school, home, and within the peer group. This included improving parenting strategies overall (Conduct Problems Prevention Research Group, 2000, 2002).

As students enter adolescence, it remains important for schools to work closely with families, particularly when a student begins to struggle academically and/or socially. The Check and Connect program has had success in supporting children and youth with learning and/or emotional or behavioral challenges to stay in school, increase academic engagement, and improve school completion. Check and Connect has been evaluated by the U.S. Department of Education's What Works Clearinghouse and has been determined to have positive effects on dropout prevention. Components of the Check and Connect model include relationship building, goal setting, prosocial skills training, family involvement, and partnerships with the community (Anderson et al., 2004; Sinclair et al., 2005).

## Rating This Practice

A school that is *fully implementing* this practice has a well-articulated process for including families in school activities and policy development. Parent representatives may sit on the leadership team and contribute to the planning and implementation of the school improvement process and school or family activities. When students begin to struggle academically and/or socially, parents are immediately involved in the discussion of needs and alternatives and are considered partners in supporting the student. Translators are used when needed, and a network of parents is available to provide support and give ideas to one another. The school has contacts and materials related to important community resources (e.g., housing assistance, the local food bank, public health, quality child care) that it can share with families who need it. All or most of the individual practices are rated at a level of 4 or 5.

A school that is *moderately implementing* this practice may have some of these practices in place, but they are not implemented consistently and/or have not been communicated well to faculty, staff, students, and parents. Parents may be involved in the planning and implementation of school activities and policies on an informal or inconsistent basis. There may be groups of parents and families that do not consistently participate in school meetings and activities or that may require a more individualized and intentional approach for engagement. Families of students with more intensive needs may not be consistently involved in intervention planning and implementation. Some or all of the indicators are rated around 3 using the rating scale. Schools operating at this level should identify specific indicators to focus on moving toward full implementation.

If all or most of the indicators are rated at 2 or below, the school is currently *not implementing* the practice. The team should discuss how it wants to prioritize its efforts to begin addressing the indicators listed.

## Setting Goals for Improvement of This Practice

In order to strengthen this practice, the team should discuss its ratings for the indicators listed. Which indicators represent relative strengths (i.e., may be scored a 3 or 4)? Are there relatively small steps that can be taken to move them toward full implementation? For example, if there is a subgroup of the school community that is not consistently involved in school activities and meetings, the leadership team explores potential reasons and makes a plan to intentionally engage that group more meaningfully. A member of the school team might reach out to a leader in that community to explore concerns and options. Perhaps materials such as the school handbook and other communications need to be translated into more languages.

As with all goal setting, it is important not to try to do too much too quickly and to carefully analyze the initial steps that lead toward priority goals. What steps need to happen first in order to support the development of other indicators? Which indicators do team members feel are most critical to the development of the school? Once the team has focused on an indicator for improvement, it needs to discuss concrete ways to collect data that will determine when it has made progress toward the goals. Following is an example of how the team might use the Action Plan on the last page of the Team Meeting Form to record its plan.

**Practice 9: Families are seen as partners in the development of their child's program.**

| Objective 1 | Activities | Evaluation |
|---|---|---|
| Develop a parent-to-parent network to welcome new families to the school and provide support and resources as needed. | 1. Work with the PTA to identify parents who are representative of the school community and who are willing to help develop this network.<br>2. Work with local parent or family advocacy groups to identify training and resources for members of the network.<br>3. Create materials and a plan to introduce the network and its roles and resources to the parent community. When a family enrolls in the school, a member of the network makes a follow-up telephone call to welcome the family and determine any needs. School staff refer families as needed. | a. Create short surveys for families who have used the parent network.<br>b. Track number of families contacted and types of resources used and needed.<br>c. Survey student support team members on their use of the parent network to support and encourage families who have students struggling in school. What are the results and effects? Is there any difference? |

(From Walker, B., & Cheney, D. [2012]. *The Self-Assessment and Program Review for Positive Behavior Interventions and Supports [SAPR-PBIS™]*. Baltimore, MD: Paul H. Brookes Publishing Co. Copyright © 2012 by University of Washington; adapted by permission.)

## Resources for Further Learning

For numerous free or low-cost resources and materials related to the meaningful involvement of parents, family members, and caregivers in school, as well as resources for families with students who may be having school difficulties, see the following web sites:

Beach Center on Disability, University of Kansas, http://www.beachcenter.org/families/default.aspx

Collaborative for Academic, Social, and Emotional Learning (CASEL), http://www.casel.org/home.php

Kansas School-Wide PBS, http://www.swpbs.org/schoolwide/families.html

National Federation of Families for Children's Mental Health, http://www.ffcmh.org/

PACER Center, Champions for Children with Disabilities, http://www.pacer.org/index.asp

Research and Training Center on Family Support and Children's Mental Health, http://www.rtc.pdx.edu/

Technical Assistance Center on Positive Behavioral Interventions and Supports, http://www.pbis.org

For information on the programs described in this section, see the following web sites:

Check and Connect program, http://www.ici.umn.edu/checkandconnect/default.html

Fast Track Project, http://sanford.duke.edu/centers/child/fasttrack/

First Step to Success, https://firststeptosuccess.sri.com/

Linking the Interests of Families and Teachers (LIFT) program, http://www.oslc.org/projects/popups-projects/link-family-teacher.html

The following are helpful materials to explain and involve family members in schoolwide positive behavior interventions, student support, and social and emotional learning:

Ballard-Krishnan, S.A., McClure, L., Schmatz, B., & Travnikar, B. (2003). The Michigan PBS initiative: Advancing the spirit of collaboration by including parents in the delivery of personnel development opportunities. *Journal of Positive Behavior Interventions, 5*(2), 122–126.

Fredericks, L., Weissberg, R., Resnik, H., Patrikakou, E., & Utne O'Brien, M. (2010). *Schools, families, and social and emotional learning: Ideas and tools for working with parents and families.* Retrieved from the Collaborative for Academic, Social, and Emotional Learning (CASEL) at http://casel.org/in-schools/tools-for-families/

Lewis, T.J. (2009). Increasing family participation through school wide positive behavior supports. In W. Sailor, G. Dunlap, G. Sugai, & R. Horner, *Handbook of positive behavior support* (pp. 353–373). New York, NY: Springer.

Morse, A.B., Christenson, S.L., & Lehr, C.A. (2004). School completion and student engagement: Information and strategies for parents. In A.S. Canter, L.Z. Paige, M.D. Roth, I. Romero, & S.A. Carroll (Eds.), *Helping children at home and at school II: Handouts for families and educators* (pp. S2-69–S2-71). Bethesda, MD: National Association of School Psychologists. Retrieved from http://www.naspcenter.org/principals/nassp_completion.html

Muscott, H.S., Szczesiul, S., Berk, B., Staub, K., Hoober, J., & Perry-Chisoholm, P. (2008). Creating home partnerships by engaging families in schoolwide positive behavior supports. *Teaching Exceptional Children, 40*(6), 6–14.

Patrikakou, E.N., & Weissberg, R.P. (2007). School–family partnerships and children's social, emotional, and academic learning. In R. Baron, J.G. Maree, & M.J. Elias (Eds.), *Educating people to be emotionally intelligent.* Rondebosch, South Africa: Heinemann Educational Publishers.

Ryan, A.K. (2001). *Strengthening the safety net: How schools can help youth with emotional and behavioral needs complete their high school education and prepare for life after school.* Burlington, VT: School Research Office, University of Vermont. Retrieved from http://cecp.air.org/safetynet/safetynetnoframe.html

Stansberry Brusnahan, L., & Neilsen Gatti, S. (2008). *School-wide positive behavior interventions and supports (SW-PBIS): What parents need to know.* Retrieved from the PACER Center at http://www.pacer.org/pbis/infoforparents.asp

## PRACTICE TEN

### Comprehensive plans are developed for students and families in need of intensive support

Even with the conscientious use of PBIS and the development of individual behavior intervention plans, some students need more resources than a school can provide in the general education program. In many cases, students with this level of need are then referred to special education with the goal of the development of an individualized education program. The child and/or family may also have needs that reach beyond those typically provided by the school. In these cases, schools must attempt to link with other agencies and service providers to integrate their support into a comprehensive plan for a student and family with intensive needs (Eber, Sugai, Smith, & Scott, 2002). To accomplish this integration, the school and/or the district may have or seek a formalized agreement with a community mental health provider, health clinic, and/or other social service agency to work in collaboration with the school to provide supports for families with significant needs (Woodruff et al., 1999).

Often this process is referred to as *wraparound* because it wraps services and supports around the unique needs of children and their families, rather than requiring them to comply with or fit into an existing set of services (Kutash & Duchnowski, 1997). Wraparound is typically family and person-centered and has a strength-based philosophy for planning services for students with emotional or behavioral problems and their families. A team composed of the child, family members, and professional providers develops all necessary supports and services for the child and family (Eber et al., 2002). The goal of these services is to enhance the educational and community goals of the child or youth in the least restrictive setting possible. Because children spend most of their day at school, integrating services and supports there can be both natural and beneficial. Families may find services coordinated through the school more accessible and less stigmatizing than those provided from more typical health or mental health centers (Eber et al., 2002). In several states and numerous cities around the country, a network of supports has been put into place to work with schools to provide comprehensive supports for children and youth with E/BPs. Eber and Keenan (2004) identified 10 key elements of a successful wraparound process: 1) community based, 2) individualized and strength based, 3) culturally competent, 4) families are full and active partners, 5) team based, 6) flexible in approach and funding, 7) balance both formal and informal family and community resources, 8) unconditional commitment, 9) development and implementation of an individualized plan (utilizing school, community, interagency collaboration), and 10) outcomes are determined and measured through a team process. In this approach, supports are implemented that expand on the traditional services available in schools. To maintain communication and consistency, these supports are organized by a case manager or family support liaison who may or may not be employed by the school (Eber & Keenan, 2004).

Another term used to describe a similar approach to service provision is *system of care* because supports are child and/or family centered rather than agency centered and services are coordinated across agencies in a manner that is more family friendly (Stroul & Freidman, 1986). As with wraparound services, the goal is to develop child-centered, community-based support plans. Cheney and Barringer (1999) identified several guiding principles of this approach to care. These include providing supports in the least restrictive, most normative setting possible, family participation in service delivery, coordinated services, and supports that are culturally sensitive and nondiscriminatory to the family's context.

Proponents of the wraparound process suggest that it is a very good fit for the three-tiered model of PBIS (Bruns & Suter, 2010; Eber et al., 2002; Scott & Eber, 2003; Sugai et al., 2010). The wraparound process is thought of as proactive, flexible, and having a continuum of possible services and supports to any individual student and family. Team members are asked to engage in conversations about the best way to meet student and family needs; hold meetings that are strength-based; focus on meeting student needs across life domains such as school, leisure, work, or community; and develop plans of action that enlist all agencies and natural supports to implement the plan. By including the family voice and addressing cultural competence and unconditional care, wraparound emphasizes positive values that enhance the quality of one's life, much like the person-centered approaches in PBIS (Carr et al., 2002; Eber et al., 2002). PBIS offers an opportunity to include the many positive features of the wraparound process into systemic change in school to benefit students with E/BP and their families.

## Rating This Practice

A school that is *fully implementing* this practice has identified the community agencies to attend the wraparound meetings and has allowed the student and family members to invite their closest friends and individuals that represent other supports to be part of the team. The team meets to identify the goals and actions it needs to take to meet the student's needs and enable him or her to be successful in the school and community. These goals, although not required in a student's individualized education program, could include medical, mental health, and community services in a wraparound plan of action. The team would therefore be advised of any medications the student is taking and how to best monitor the medications. An individual from one of the agencies becomes the wraparound case manager, facilitating meetings and serving as case manager for implementing actions. The team meets monthly or quarterly to discuss progress and modifications for the plan. The school district attempts to formalize all agreements with other agencies and develop and implement treatment plans that are family centered, strength based, and sensitive to cultural and linguistic differences.

A school that is *moderately implementing* this practice may have some interactions and attendance at meetings by family members or community agencies. It might also have some service provisions by some community agencies to assist the family and student. The overall plan, however, is not fully integrated, and there is not likely to be a case manager who is responsible for the implementation and monitoring of progress. The team is not likely to have formal agreements and may still be working on learning about how best to be strength and family based with culturally competent practices.

If all or most of the indicators are rated at 2 or below, the school is currently *not implementing* the practice. The team should discuss how it wants to prioritize its efforts to begin addressing the indicators listed.

## Setting Goals for Improvement of This Practice

In order to strengthen this practice, the team should discuss its ratings for the indicators listed. Which indicators represent relative strengths (i.e., may be scored a 3 or 4)? Are there relatively small steps that can be taken to move them toward full implementation? For example, if the school has connections with a mental health provider or social service agency, team members may wish to meet with representatives of those agencies and get formal commitments to being involved in the wraparound process. This action would move the school toward fuller implementation of that indicator. The team may also choose to address an indicator that the team consistently rated quite low. However, in this case it may take more time and effort to develop implementation. For example, if the primary emphasis of the planning process is to increase the coordination of services across agencies and family members and no agreements are established between families and agencies, the team will have to create these connections. As with all goal setting, it is important to try not to do too much too quickly and to carefully analyze the smaller steps that lead to the larger changes that are needed. The task analysis will help a team identify the steps that need to be accomplished, and their order, in the effort to implement these best-practice indicators. It will also help answer the question of which indicators team members believe are most critical for development in the school. Once the team has focused on an indicator for improvement, it needs to discuss concrete ways to collect data that will determine when it has made progress toward the goals. Following is an example of how the team might use the Action Plan on the last page of the Team Meeting Form to record its plan.

**Practice 10: Comprehensive plans are developed for students and families in need of intensive support.**

| Objective 1 | Activities | Evaluation |
|---|---|---|
| *Working with school district representatives, formalized agreements will be developed with community agencies providing services to Tier 2 and 3 students.* | *1. Leadership team will inventory local service providers through family and community surveys.*<br>*2. The team will invite representatives from the services to a meeting to discuss coordination.*<br>*3. Agreements for service provision will be discussed and developed.*<br>*4. A case manager will be identified to monitor progress of 5–10 students within the first year of agreements.* | *a. A list of participating agencies will be developed.*<br>*b. Agencies will attend and formalize agreements.*<br>*c. The case manager will report on student progress at meetings.* |

(From Walker, B., & Cheney, D. [2012]. *The Self-Assessment and Program Review for Positive Behavior Interventions and Supports [SAPR-PBIS™]*. Baltimore, MD: Paul H. Brookes Publishing Co. Copyright © 2012 by University of Washington; adapted by permission.)

## Resources for Further Learning

Numerous training materials related to professional development in PBIS and supporting success for all learners, such as presentations and readings for faculty, staff, and families, are available free or at low cost at the following web sites:

Center for Effective Collaboration and Practice (CECP) wraparound resources, http://cecp.air.org/wraparound/intro.html

Center for Mental Health in Schools, http://smhp.psych.ucla.edu/

Illinois PBIS Network, http://www.pbisillinois.org/

National Technical Assistance Center for Children's Mental Health, http://gucchd.georgetown.edu/67211.html

National Wraparound Initiative, http://www.nwi.pdx.edu/

Technical Assistance Center on Positive Behavioral Interventions and Supports, http://www.pbis.org

Web sites with helpful information for schools and families supporting students with significant needs include the following:

Pathways to Positive Futures, http://www.pathwaysrtc.pdx.edu/index.shtml

Research and Training Center on Family Support and Children's Mental Health, http://www.rtc.pdx.edu/index.php

Other resources that provide detailed information on this practice include the following:

Bruns, E.J., & Suter, J.C. (2010). Summary of the wraparound evidence base. In E.J. Bruns & J.S. Walker (Eds.), *The resource guide to wraparound.* Portland, OR: National Wraparound Initiative. Retrieved from http://www.nwi.pdx.edu/publications.shtml

Carr, E.G., Dunlap, G., Horner, R.H., Koegel, R.L., Turnbull A.P., Sailor, W., ...Fox, L. (2002). Positive behavior support: Evolution of an applied science. *Journal of Positive Behavior Interventions, 4,* 4–16.

Eber, L., Sugai, G., Smith, C., & Scott, T. (2002). Wraparound and positive behavioral interventions and supports in the schools. *Journal of Emotional and Behavioral Disorders, 10,* 171–180.

Scott, T., & Eber, L. (2003). Functional assessment and wraparound as systemic school processes: Primary, secondary, and tertiary systems examples. *Journal of Positive Behavior Intervention and Supports, 5,* 131–140.

Stroul, B.A., & Freidman, R. (1986). *A system of care for severely emotionally disturbed children and youth.* Washington, DC: Child and Adolescent Service System Program Technical Assistance Center.

SAPRpbis™ 6

# Building Action Plans for Sustainable Improvement

Once the leadership team has completed the SAPR-PBIS™ process and created an action plan for the upcoming year, there is a great deal to celebrate. After the celebration is over, it is time for the team members to roll up their sleeves and begin the task of bringing that plan to life. Committing and adhering to timelines on school reform activities may be one of the most difficult goals for a school to attain. Schools must consistently contend with issues such as staff stability, leadership changes, and funding shifts that compete for time, energy, and resources. The focus of this chapter is on strategies leadership teams can use to bring their action plan to fruition effectively.

## THE LEADERSHIP TEAM AND ASPECTS OF EARLY SCHOOLWIDE POSITIVE BEHAVIOR INTERVENTIONS AND SUPPORTS IMPLEMENTATION

In their research on school improvement and PBIS, Knoff (2002) and Sugai et al. (2010) have suggested that it takes 3–5 years for a school to fully implement a PBIS initiative with fidelity and sustain their identified practices. This length of time is required to fully complete system change goals and to take the necessary steps that guarantee sustainability. For example, Rogers (1995) proposed that there are four stages that a system, such as a school or district, moves through to take a new program from introduction to diffusion. These are adoption of the new program, actual implementation of the program (with fidelity), dissemination of the program throughout the school or system, and sustainability. The pace at which schools move through these stages varies, but it is ultimately determined by the length of time faculty need to implement PBIS practices with fidelity.

To begin the PBIS initiative on strong footing, it is necessary for the leadership team to identify a few key practices as their primary goals and clear steps for accomplishing those goals early in their action plans. Once those goals are established, the team must then focus the time, energy, and resources needed to ensure successful implementation. If the team initially attacks too many goals and objectives and if follow-up on the plan is inconsistent or unsuccessful, the school staff may become concerned about the overall effectiveness of the PBIS initiative. As a result, the team may lose the confidence and support of the school staff and any momentum they have built to date. This initial loss of support will likely make it harder to refocus later work.

This level of systems change is not an easy or quick process in schools. Teachers see many programs and initiatives come and go throughout their careers and can become somewhat cynical or even pessimistic about any new initiative. Newly emerging practices, however, remain the key factors in making substantive changes in schools. Dusenbury and Hansen (2004) suggested that, just as systems go through stages as they adapt to change, within any group of professionals, there is a predictable pattern for the diffusion of an innovation. The first people to embrace an initiative and move toward implementation are called *innovators*. In the context of PBIS, this group is likely to be the leadership team and those teachers and staff who immediately are willing to be involved in initial implementation. They are followed next by *early adopters* who are willing to take on a new program fairly quickly once they have a chance to understand how it works. As the program is implemented effectively for a short time, other teachers and staff observe the success and decide to become involved, creating the *early majority*. As the initiative begins to build momentum and increasing evidence indicates effectiveness, most of the remaining faculty and staff then buy in, establishing the *late majority*. The last few remaining faculty and staff members who continue to resist implementation are referred to as the *laggards*. They often require individualized support to engage in the program or initiative at all. Again, not until the faculty and staff as a whole are implementing an innovation fairly consistently can it be considered as fully in place. The ongoing challenge for leadership teams is to be aware of this dynamic and to strategize how to move all school members through this pattern of adoption to fully realize any reform initiative.

Because the leadership team plays such a critical part in guiding the school community through the implementation of a PBIS initiative, it is important for team members to stay in constant contact with the school community to address their questions, concerns, and issues regarding the PBIS initiative. A large part of the leadership team's role is to help educate the school staff and broader community on the principles of effective PBIS programs, present data related to the school's current functioning, and guide the school community through the implementation of the ongoing PBIS-related goals and objectives. This role requires the leadership team to be well ahead of the full faculty and staff in awareness, understanding, and planning. One challenge that emerges early for a leadership team that is "ahead of the curve" is that their scores on SAPR-PBIS ratings of practices may be higher than other school staff due to their understanding and planning for the specific practice. The school staff, on the other hand, may feel as if implementation is going slower and rate their functioning on a practice lower. It is important that, as much as possible, the leadership team checks their perspective with school staff to gain a broader schoolwide understanding about the implementation of the these practices.

In their studies of effective educational leadership and school improvement, Spillane, Hunt, and Healey (2009) described two important components of a school's reality. The first is the "formal or designed" aspect of the school. This represents how the school operates, as defined by its handbooks, organizational charts, annual plans, committee membership, operating procedures, and so forth. The second aspect of a school's identity is referred to as "informal or lived." This refers to how the school really operates on a daily basis as it is actually experienced by the members of the school community. This experience may occur very differently from what has been written down in documents or is discussed or intended by leadership. When there is a significant misalignment or discrepancy between the formal and informal realities in a school, any school improvement activity will struggle to be effective (Spillane et al., 2009). School leadership may not be fully aware that such a discrepancy exists until they use a process such as the SAPR-PBIS because it is specifically designed to identify strengths and weaknesses in a PBIS initiative. Once weaknesses or discrepancies are identified, a plan of action can be made to correct discrepancies while also strengthening the depth and effectiveness of its formal reality. PBIS has been most successful in schools that are able to build a robust, well-articulated formal identity that is well aligned with the daily reality experienced by students, staff, faculty, and families.

Although the goal of the SAPR-PBIS process is to minimize the discrepancies between the leadership team's perspective and the realities of daily practice, it is likely that such discrepancies will be identified, particularly at the early stages of the school improvement initiative. The leadership team should be aware that identifying and addressing these issues are important work early in the school reform process. Members of the leadership team must continue to regularly reach out to the faculty, staff, and community to keep the understanding of the PBIS initiative steadily growing and ensure the momentum needed to implement it is in place. As a result, we have found that it is very effective if, early in the initiative process, the leadership team establishes some foundational routines for communicating with the school community.

First, PBIS should become a standing item on the faculty and staff meeting agenda on at least a monthly basis. A member of the leadership team can give a short update on the various goals and objectives underway, as well as any related data or key information. These do not need to be lengthy reports but should include discrete information to keep the PBIS work fresh in the minds of the faculty and staff as well as to demonstrate the progress that is underway. When the group encounters challenges or issues, it is best to be up front about it. This keeps the efforts of the leadership team realistic and honest, and often faculty and staff can have great suggestions. When larger issues are raised or more in-depth information is needed, more time may need to be dedicated during specific meetings.

To build the faculty and staff understanding of PBIS strategies and practices, regular, formal professional development should be planned throughout the year as well. Workshops can be led by members of the leadership team, district PBIS coaches, and/or local PBIS experts. There are many resources available free or at low cost to support schools in this process, and many are listed in Chapter 5. As these aspects of the PBIS initiative get underway, it is also important to provide overviews of the information to parents via newsletters, the school web site, and parent or family events. This dissemination of information helps to further formalize and diffuse emerging practices and helps orient families to the school's efforts.

Finally, the leadership team should keep in mind how powerful its informal interactions with the school community can be when modeling and otherwise sharing the principles and practices of PBIS. Studies of school improvement have found that professional practice improves whenever faculty and staff are talking together about new practices and policies, sharing strategies for effective instruction and management, working together to share expertise, and pushing one another to implement new initiatives (Parise & Spillane, 2010). Taking advantage of these "informal" teachable moments that come with this type of school improvement work is important in schools. When the faculty, staff, and community see the strategies in action or receive a few helpful tips shared by a member of the leadership team, the initiative gains momentum and credibility.

## Anything but Bus Duty!

Early in the launch of its PBIS initiative, the leadership team of one middle school decided to address two parts of the day that had a large negative impact on the entire school community: the arrival of students on buses at the beginning of the day and the departure routine as students left for home at the end of the day. Because of the large size of the school and the many discipline problems that occurred during these times, all faculty and staff were required to assist with supervision of these routines. Even with all "hands on deck," it was a chaotic and unpleasant part of the day for all concerned.

The leadership team asked for one full staff meeting to be dedicated to addressing this issue. It carefully collected some discipline data related to those times of day, crafted an agenda for structuring the meeting, and even did a few informal observations of the bus routines to share at the meeting. During the meeting, the team defined the problem carefully, shared the data it had collected, and provided suggestions of effective practices for supervising transitions and common areas that they had learned at a recent PBIS training. The team gave the faculty and staff time to brainstorm additional solutions to the issue, and then the leadership team and the faculty and staff crafted a potential solution together. At the beginning of the meeting, the team had asked the faculty and staff to commit to whatever solution the group identified for 3 weeks, after which the group would review the data to determine whether the solution was effective. With this agreement in place, most of the group were willing to make an immediate commitment to supporting changes.

The solution the group finally agreed on involved four elements: 1) creating bus signs that would be held by student safety volunteers to help students locate their buses more readily, 2) teaching students an orderly routine for lining up and moving on and off the buses, 3) designing a system for recognizing students for following through on the new routines, and 4) determining strategic placement of school faculty and staff for effective supervision. An assembly was held a few days later, at which all four elements were demonstrated and taught (in a fun and humorous way—the students loved watching their teachers behave as middle school students!), and reinforcement for student involvement was provided. That afternoon, the system was implemented.

Of course, over the first few days there had to be some correction and reteaching of the new expectations and routines, but the faculty and staff also emphasized recognizing students who were following through on the routine. Soon, even the students appreciated starting and ending the school day in a calmer and more predictable way. When the faculty and staff reviewed the data 3 weeks later, it reinforced what they were already experiencing: fewer behavior problems and a much more efficient and orderly approach during the bus transitions. The group voted to continue implementing the new system, and within a few more weeks, things had calmed down to the point that the school no longer needed every member of the faculty and staff to assist in supervision. A rotation schedule was developed to spread the responsibility across faculty and staff members on a weekly basis throughout the year, providing more time for faculty and staff to focus on other aspects of their jobs. This plan was win–win for the adults and students in the school. In addition, because the leadership team really focused on setting this process up for success and recognizing the faculty and staff for their efforts, it was a tremendous positive public relations statement for the PBIS initiative as a whole and provided much-needed positive energy and momentum for later work.

## Addressing the Challenging Issues

Particular practices and topics of discussion can be much more challenging for the faculty and staff to work through than others. For example, developing a systematic response to discipline problems is one challenging example that schools face within their PBIS initiatives, and it requires quite a bit of time and dedication to make consistent discipline an effective practice. To systematically respond to discipline problems, the leadership team works with the faculty and staff to identify exactly which behaviors warrant an ODR (e.g., severe disruption, aggression, harassment) and those that should be handled directly by the classroom teacher or area supervisor (e.g., not following directions, uncompleted homework, low levels of disruption). This categorizing of behaviors often results in an increase in the types of behavior that are now to be managed in the classroom, on the playground, and in other common areas. This is an easier change for some faculty and staff to accept responsibility for than others. Therefore, addressing concerns and questions often requires a series of faculty and staff meetings, regular professional development on effective behavior and classroom management strategies to provide skills and strategies to everyone, and an ongoing analysis of ODRs and other related data before this practice is consistently implemented and well established in the school and classroom cultures (Dwyer, 2002; Horner, Sugai, et al., 2004; Sugai et al., 2002). During these times, the leadership team may have to call on the skills outlined in Chapter 3 related to facilitating difficult conversations and addressing conflicting opinions in order to help the staff work through these difficult topics. The team will also need to rely on the faculty and staff who are the early adopters to assist in the initial implementation of new procedures and strategies. These faculty and staff can then serve as models and informal coaches to other faculty and staff, building skills and positive momentum related to new or different practices.

## "Sorry, I Just Can't Buy into This"

At an elementary school staff meeting, a discussion occurred to establish effective discipline practices for all students, and then teachers were asked to use the common practices for behavior management in their classrooms. Midway through the meeting it was clear that one veteran sixth-grade teacher was disagreeing with the ideas being discussed. When he was asked to share his thoughts, he honestly expressed that he would not buy in to filling out the new ODR form and sending kids to the office for certain specific behaviors because for many years he had "never seen anything helpful come from that process." Rather than become defensive, the members of the leadership team (including the administrator) responded supportively, saying that they appreciated his honesty and understood that use of ODRs had previously led to unknown or inconsistent consequences for students. The team asked him to give the process some time, stating that they would review data to look at outcomes and have all staff review the new approach throughout the year.

It is important to note that, at the beginning of their PBIS initiative, the faculty and staff of this school had agreed on a series of group norms for their meetings (as is discussed for leadership teams in Chapter 3). One of those norms stated that, even if a few group members did not agree with some of the decisions related to moving forward with the initiative (decisions were made by majority in this school), they agreed not to "torpedo" or sabotage (directly or indirectly) the efforts and work of those who did choose to move forward. In this case, the teacher agreed to keep an open mind on the new ODR process and looked forward to future meetings to review data on outcomes. Such an agreement is important for the faculty and staff to develop because it protects the early adopters and early majority as they begin to implement practices in the PBIS initiative. It is their work that develops the momentum and the initial results, which ultimately may sway the position of those who are not ready to buy in to the changes early in the process.

Meanwhile, as the school year unfolded, the leadership team continued to regularly report ODR data and patterns to the school faculty and staff (it was using the SWIS system to track school discipline), post this data in the faculty and staff lunchroom for reference, and use the data to problem-solve difficult situations with the faculty and staff. The administrators worked very carefully to respond to discipline issues in a manner that was consistent with the faculty and staff agreement as well. Throughout the year, this sixth-grade teacher participated in the group discussions but did not participate in this aspect of the schoolwide discipline plan. Then, during one faculty meeting later in the year, as the members of the team were providing a brief overview of the discipline data patterns for the spring and discussing the changes across the year, this sixth-grade teacher raised his hand and announced that he wanted to make a statement. The teacher went on to say that he had seen how the leadership team and faculty were using the discipline data across the school and with individual students to make good decisions. He thought the administrative team was working consistently to address ODRs in the way agreed on by the faculty and staff, and he felt there was new meaning to the process. It was clear to him that the ODR form was not just busy work for teachers and staff, as he had thought previously. Therefore, he shared that he was ready to buy in to the process and implement it.

The teacher then asked for a member of the leadership team to meet with him to discuss how he should best integrate the school's ODR process with his own classroom management approach. A member of the leadership team immediately agreed to provide some coaching and support to this teacher. Over the next 2 years, this teacher became one of the school's most vocal PBIS supporters. What allowed this issue to be resolved positively was that the team acknowledged the perspective of the teacher from the beginning (because it is likely he was voicing concerns others had but did not state), gave the teacher time to reflect on the work that was underway, and let the actual practice and data-based decision-making process change the teacher's mind. This is in contrast to some administrative decisions that personalize or intensify an issue in an effort to force compliance. Because using discipline data for decision making is often new to schools, adding the dimension of focused group discussions can depersonalize issues and "hot topics," allowing the staff to be part of the problem-solving process and the implementation of positive solutions.

## GROWING THE INITIATIVE AND SPREADING THE SKILLS

Because there is so much to accomplish in a PBIS or RTI initiative, it is easy for the leadership team to become overwhelmed if they have too many actions or goals. When added to the many responsibilities each team member has as a part of his or her daily teaching and supervision responsibilities, it can be hard to know where to begin. The SAPR-PBIS process recommends that the team identify and focus on 2–3 initial practices and steps that, over time, will begin to build positive momentum and interest across the school. As the school community experiences success with the early goals of the initiative and becomes more competent with effective PBIS practices, the school staff will move into the early majority stage described previously in this chapter. In this stage, most of the school community is involved with supporting the initiative at some level. At this time, the leadership team can begin to involve more and more members of the school community in guiding and implementing the next steps of the process. In this way, the leadership team helps the school community increase its capacity for implementing and sustaining PBIS practices. This is an approach often referred to as *distributed leadership* in school improvement circles.

Rather than structuring leadership responsibilities through a hierarchy of roles and committees, distributed leadership recognizes that there is more to do in school improvement than can be managed by a formal leadership structure. As a result, it "concentrates on engaging expertise wherever it exists within the organization, rather than seeking this only through formal position or role" (Harris, 2004, p. 13). It has also been described as an organic, emergent process wherein teachers and staff pool their energy and skills in order to accomplish a shared goal or vision, such as a school improvement or reform initiative. As a result, teachers and staff work closely together, collaborating, sharing skills and knowledge, and developing into natural "teacher/staff leaders." Since leadership is viewed as a behavior rather than a role, implementing and sustaining the PBIS initiative moves beyond being the sole responsibility of an administrator to being promoted by the leadership team and then finally, becoming a system that is owned and maintained by the entire school staff. Thus, all school members are formally and informally monitoring and supporting implementation of the school improvement plan (Spillane et al., 2009).

Studies have found that when teachers and staff have the opportunity to work closely together in this form of distributed leadership, they develop a shared vision of school and instructional improvement, improve their teaching quality and, ultimately, attain improvement in student achievement (Leithwood et al., 2007; Leithwood, Seashore-Louis, Anderson, & Wahlstrom, 2004; Lieberman, 2000). For this to occur, the formal leadership structure must intentionally create the space and opportunity for these teacher and staff leaders to emerge. In the context of the PBIS plan, this might include the development of subcommittees or teams involving faculty, staff, and community members that focus on guiding the implementation of specific practices and goals within the action plan. These teams must coordinate their work within the established PBIS action plan developed by the leadership team, and include other members of the school community in achieving these goals. The responsibility for PBIS implementation is shared and an opportunity for natural leaders to emerge is created.

For example, one practice that is critical to success in a PBIS initiative is developing a system for teaching schoolwide social expectations to all students. One or two members of the leadership team might coordinate a group of other members from the school community to develop strategies for accomplishing this goal. This team would create a schedule for implementation, develop teaching guidelines and routines for the entire faculty to use, and facilitate an array of teaching opportunities. Meanwhile, other members of the leadership team might coordinate a group that is focused on setting up a dependable, efficient system for tracking and monitoring the school's ODRs. They might review various electronic systems, evaluate and revise their current referral form and system, and begin drafting guidelines for discipline decisions on a schoolwide level. By distributing the responsibility, knowledge, and skills needed to implement these objectives, the components of PBIS begin to permeate the culture of the school, enhancing implementation and sustainability. Because the PBIS initiative belongs to the school community as a whole, the vision and practices established by school team and community is more likely to continue, even if there is a change of administration at the school.

In recruiting potential members of these subcommittees, the leadership team should clearly define their scope and function and be honest about the time commitments involved. Staff members can then choose which PBIS goals and activities they wish to address based on their particular interests, needs, and skills. As broader involvement in PBIS takes place in the school, the leadership team is charged with coordinating the subcommittees and provides the overarching structures to analyze progress based on data generated from the subcommittees. Without this guidance and evaluation, the initiative runs the risk of falling into a *misguided delegation* wherein the focus and unifying vision of the group is lost and the efforts begin to fragment and lose effectiveness, which is why so many school reform initiatives tend to fall short of their potential (Harris, 2004).

It is important for the leadership team to review the many tools and resources they can use to help inform and guide its efforts. We referenced many of the most helpful resources throughout Chapter 5, along with examples of effective goals and objectives for teams to consider.

Developing and guiding a PBIS initiative is challenging work, but thousands of schools in diverse settings, both nationally and internationally, have demonstrated how to effectively implement PBIS. Since 2000, research on PBIS in these schools has shown how hard work really does pay off in school and classroom climate improvements and in students' social and academic success. Focused, determined work on the part of the leadership team is the first step in bringing this positive change to a school. Congratulations to all those schools that take the first step and initiate, implement, and evaluate PBIS!

## Tracking the Fidelity of Implementation of Positive Behavior Interventions and Supports Practices

Being able to measure the fidelity with which key PBIS practices are being implemented is a crucial aspect of sustainability. This is one reason the SET, discussed in Chapter 2, is useful in conjunction with the SAPR-PBIS. Available from the Technical Assistance Center on PBIS (http://www.pbis.org), the SET helps to measure how well the universal level practices of PBIS are being implemented by the faculty, staff, and students. The SET is completed by an external evaluator, usually within a half-day school visit. It involves short interviews of students and staff, a walk through of the building, and a review of written products related to aspects of SWPBIS. The results rate the fidelity of implementation across a school's universal level of PBIS across seven subscales, such as Teaching Expectations, Appropriate Behavior Is Recognized, and Discipline Data Is Used for Decision Making. These data, in conjunction with SAPR-PBIS results, can help leadership teams get another perspective on how well established their schoolwide systems have become (Appendix B discusses the relationship between the SET and SAPR-PBIS in more detail).

The challenge with using the SET for additional data is that it requires a trained external evaluator to complete it, an option not affordable or available to all schools. In addition, a 2010 study of SET results across more than 100 K–12 schools implementing SWPBIS conducted by Vincent, Spaulding, and Tobin (2010) found that while the SET is highly cohesive in its content, it has limited variability in its scores, particularly among elementary and middle schools. As a result, it was found to be most useful to early adopters, providing broad feedback to schools as they initially establish their universal level practices. This suggests that its ability to provide more detailed, nuanced data related to refinements in practices as schools move further into their implementation of PBIS can be limited. This limitation can be minimized when the SAPR-PBIS is used because it offers a wider range of scores across key PBIS practices across all three levels of the model. Because the SAPR-PBIS also allows teams to track progress on the indicators of all the key practices, the results can give teams a more detailed report of where adjustments need to be made to develop or further strengthen any practice. This level of data supports the development and maintenance of practices over time. Since the initial development of the SAPR-PBIS, there are a number of other tools that have been developed that also address the fidelity of implementation of key practices. These include the tools introduced in Chapter 2, such as the BOQ and the IPI.

## SCALING UP: IF A SCHOOL CAN DO IT, HOW ABOUT A SCHOOL DISTRICT?

Once one school in a district has been successful with assessing, planning, and implementing the features of PBIS, it is time for school district administrators to weigh the benefits of the process and consider expanding the approach to other schools. In much of the PBIS literature, this is known as *scaling up* the approach. If one initial school, such as Apple Center in the example from Chapter 4, began the PBIS approach and demonstrated progress, it could be considered the district's demonstration site. Other schools in the district could send representatives to see the PBIS process in action and to discuss its potential in their own buildings.

Sadler (2000) gave one of the earliest reports on how a district-level approach was developed in PBIS. An initial cohort of eight schools started the work in PBIS and was led by a district coordinator. Leadership teams within each school were composed of six to eight representatives and guided the work of the school staff. One measure used to evaluate progress was ODRs, and the schools reported decreases in both ODRs and suspensions and expulsions. The school board found these results promising and expanded the program to all of its 14 schools in the succeeding years.

Sadler and Sugai (2008) later reported on how this district progressed after scaling up to the district level. Within 5 years of beginning the PBIS approach, the district expanded the effort to an RTI approach that addressed both behavior and academics. The authors emphasized the importance of a leadership structure and team development to accomplish the goals of PBIS and RTI. For example, in this district a school-level PBIS leadership team was established, along with grade-level teams that monitored instruction and intervention implementation, and a behavior support team met monthly to lead, coordinate, and maintain schoolwide behavior prevention activities and supports. These teams evaluated a set of data to note which students were being responsive to interventions and which were in need of further Tier 2 support. They also evaluated the types of curriculum and behavioral interventions. The district established an evidence-based practice and was successful in showing the positive trends of PBIS progress using the SET.

### School Cohorts and Recruitment—Establishing a District Coach

One important feature of scaling-up PBIS efforts from the school to the district level is to identify and support a district coordinator. In our district work with the SAPR-PBIS, the district coordinator has had the responsibility for assisting or leading professional development, maintaining effort in schools, collecting and evaluating data, and disseminating progress. The district coordinator also is in charge of conveying the knowledge and skills to school staff and informing district administrators of progress in schools. This coordinator is typically a school psychologist, school counselor, or special educator who is funded full time to work with all school coordinators and teams in the district. The example in the following section from a district that we worked with may be instructive to the reader.

## Getting the Work Started in the District

In 1998, we began working with a school district in the Seattle area of Washington. The district had about 20,000 students, 18 elementary schools, 4 middle schools, and 4 comprehensive and 2 alternative high schools. The district identified one school to serve as a demonstration site for the implementation and within 3 years had an additional four schools join in the PBIS implementation. All of the schools in this first cohort were elementary schools, Grades K–6, and were supported with grant funding from the authors' research project. These five schools were closely watched for 7 school years before the district agreed to scale up to the other elementary, middle, and high schools. In the next 5-year period, however, an additional 14 schools joined the effort. The district made plans to have PBIS in all schools by 2012.

As we began this scaling-up effort with the schools, there were several roles to fill. These roles were all important so that the critical features of PBIS would be assessed, developed, and sustained. The roles included a district coordinator, school coordinators, and building administrators (principal or vice principal). The authors initially supported the district with grant funds and provided the necessary professional development that assisted those in leadership roles to disseminate information to each school. The district coordinator, building administrator, and school coordinator then led the implementation of all efforts at the school.

The school coordinators recruited a building PBIS team to coordinate implementation across the school. They served a critical role in influencing and supporting staff to implement the PBIS effort to assess features and begin teaching the school's social expectations. The initial assessment of school features was when we introduced the SAPR-PBIS. Staff learned how the SAPR-PBIS would be used to monitor progress and how individuals and the team would complete it to set priorities for the school. This process followed the steps discussed previously in this chapter and in Chapter 4 for the Apple Center school.

Organizing important data and findings to present to critical consumers such as administrators, school board members, and family members is an important task to attend to when scaling up in a district. For example, once the cohort of five schools in this district completed the SAPR-PBIS, began completing the SWIS, and started teaching and supporting social expectations, the district coordinator needed to organize their results. These results served as baseline information for the districts and needed to be translated to the important leadership and consumers.

It is recommended that district-level results be reported in a chart covering the 10 practices of the SAPR-PBIS. This chart provides a visual display regarding how well the practices are in place in the school or district. In this case, the district coordinator aggregated the information from across the schools to display the district data. It might also be helpful to give district administrators each school's chart to show variation across schools. The chart in Figure 6.1 shows aggregated results from one district as it completed work in eight schools.

The data in the chart show the district's relative strengths and weaknesses as assessed on the SAPR-PBIS. As it was the first year of expansion to additional schools, several of the

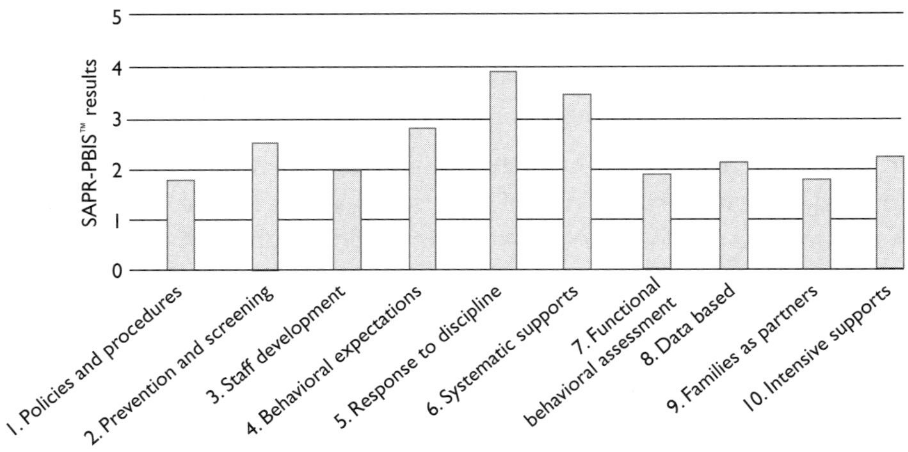


**Figure 6.1.** Example of a district's results in each practice area of the Self-Assessment and Program Review for Positive Behavior Interventions and Supports (SAPR-PBIS™) in 2007.

practices were rated as only partially in place (scores of 2 or 3). The data served as a guide for the district coordinator in discussing the information with the school board and district administrators. In speaking with them, the coordinator emphasized that district schools were stronger in their response to discipline and systematic supports for behavior and that she would work with them immediately to enhance systemwide approaches to student behavior. In addition, the district might look at some strategic goals in school improvement plans to enhance its policies and procedures regarding student behavior and provide some resources for staff development. Once these goals were established, the district could put in a plan to enhance these areas in the first cohort of schools before enlisting other schools into the PBIS network. After these areas were targeted, the coordinator was able to show improvements on these practices, as shown in Figure 6.2.

These data played an important role in identifying and conducting professional development activities for the schools. That is, when one or two goals were established for improvement, others appeared to improve in relation to them. In this case, when policies and procedures (Practice 1) and staff development (Practice 3) were targeted, schools showed improvement in Practices 2, 4, 5, 6, and 8. This makes sense in that the staff development likely assisted the schools in their development of procedures to enhance such practices as the referral process, early identification of students with behavior problems, setting expectations, and teaching desired behavior. Staff development also assisted schools in responding more effectively to challenging behavior and improving data collection for these goals. Similarly, as systematic supports were already somewhat in place, additional effort on this goal helped boost its final rating. The professional development, in this case, enhanced the overall district results on these practices.

## Organizing and Collecting Data for Presentation

In our work with schools, the most typical use for the district data has been for presentations at administrative boards or councils for the district. These groups usually include the super-

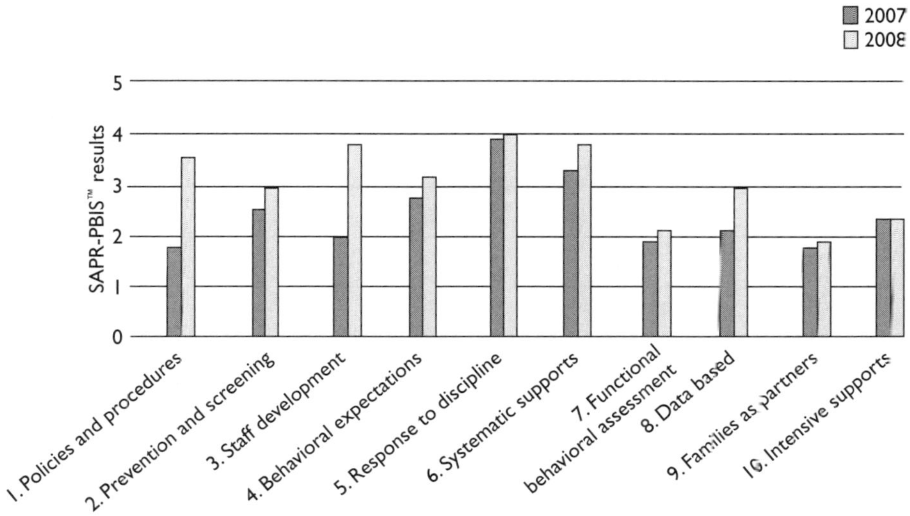


**Figure 6.2.** Example of district's results in each practice area of the Self-Assessment and Program Review for Positive Behavior Interventions and Supports (SAPR-PBIS™), showing improvement across 2 years.

intendent, assistant superintendents, and directors of units within the district. The group usually is interested in the overall impact of their districtwide initiatives in relation to the district's yearly goals. In the district in this case study, one goal was to improve the productive, social, and interpersonal skills of students and decrease problem behaviors by building positive school environments. The administrative team was, therefore, quite interested in the data that substantiated improvements in their schools that were related to their investment in professional development and personnel costs. The district coordinator decided to share the data in Figures 6.3, 6.4, and 6.5 in 2010, after 18 schools had joined the PBIS and RTI initiative. Figure 6.5 only shows data from the elementary schools.

In this district, the presentation had other data samples from schools, but the districtwide data were well received by the administrators, and they were able to conclude that the investment in a district coordinator and districtwide PBIS effort in 2008 had resulted in positive gains for the staff and students in the following 3 years. The superintendent was so pleased that she decided to put this as an agenda item for the school board meeting. The district coordinator organized all activities and results into a visual presentation to the school board that also included both a student's and a parent's perspective on the positive impact of the initiative in their schools, which was again very well received. At the district board meeting, the PBIS results from the SAPR-PBIS and behavioral data were related to districtwide gains on academic measures and state testing. These data were braided into the RTI and PBIS processes and the school board members were able to see how a multi-tiered model of academic and behavioral supports could result in positive outcomes for the students and staff that more than offset the cost of maintaining a full-time PBIS coordinator for the district. Most recently, the district administrative team was so impressed with the positive impacts of this initiative that they have added a second full-time PBIS coordinator to support implementation at the high-school level.

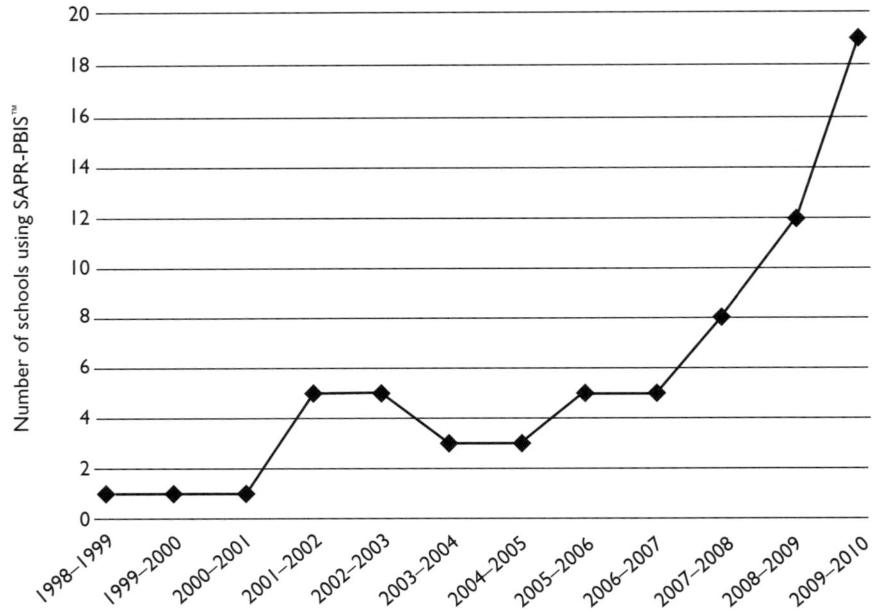


**Figure 6.3.** Data from a case study district: The number of schools over time implementing positive behavior interventions and supports. (*Key:* SAPR-PBIS™, Self-Assessment and Program Review for Positive Behavior Interventions and Supports.)

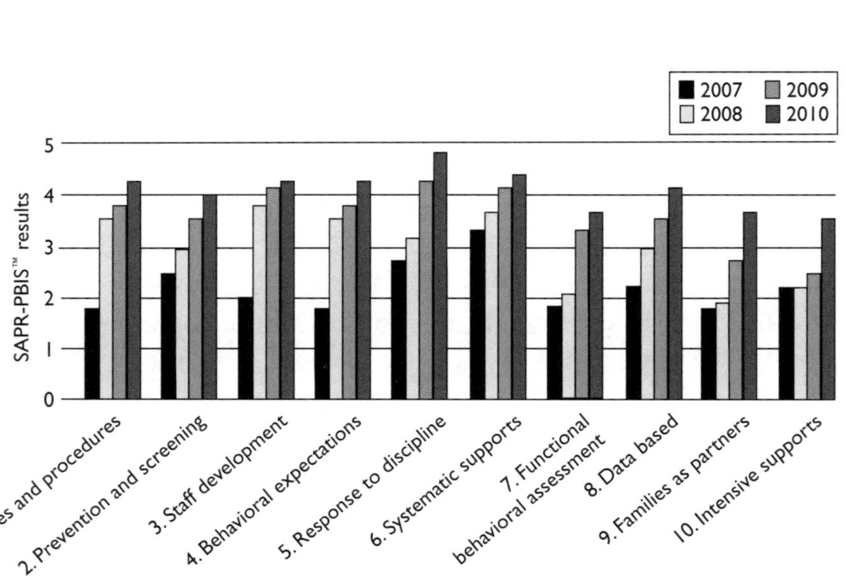


**Figure 6.4.** Data from a case study district: Improvements across 4 years in each practice area of Self-Assessment and Program Review for Positive Behavior Interventions and Supports (SAPR-PBIS™).

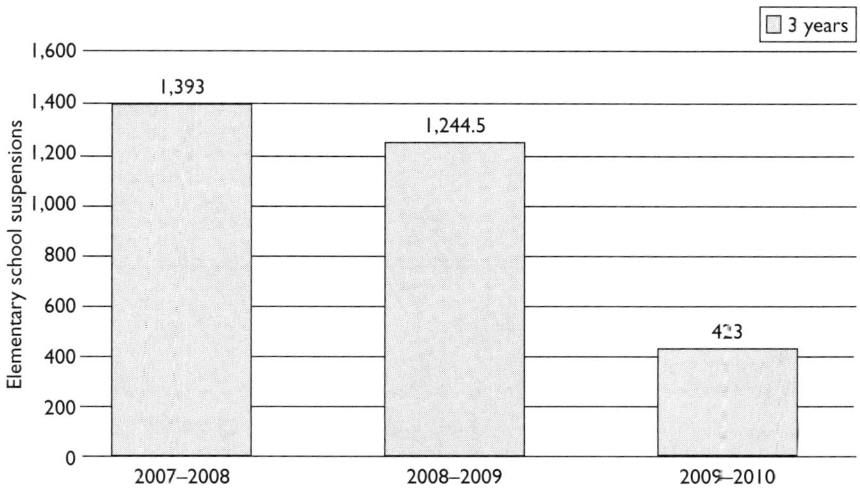


**Figure 6.5.** Data from a case study district: Decreases in elementary school suspensions for 15 schools.

The scaling up from a demonstration school to multiple schools and ultimately to entire districts was visible in many states in 2010. At that time, states such as Illinois were close to enrolling 1,000 schools in their PBIS initiative, and others such as New Hampshire, Maryland, and Florida had hundreds of schools participating. These states are finding that the investments involved in implementing the PBIS initiatives are cost-effective and efficient ways to support improvements in the academic and behavioral functioning of students. For example, in a study examining the fidelity of implementation of PBIS and related outcomes from a sample of 428 Illinois schools, Simeonson et al. (2012) found that the percentage of schools implementing PBIS with high levels of fidelity as measured by the SET increased from 36% in 2000–2001 to 78% in 2007–2008. All of the schools were supported by coaches and professional development offered by the Illinois state PBIS Network. In those schools that were found to be implementing PBIS with fidelity, the study found statistically significant improvements in academic performance on the state reading and math assessments, as well as statistically significant reductions in ODRs and out of school suspensions. Florida had similar results when reviewing outcomes of its statewide PBIS initiative as well (Elfner-Childs, Kincaid, & Peshak George, 2010).

The PBIS national network grows larger, stronger, and more effective yearly, and wise selection of measures and data collection tools help disseminate the positive results of this school reform approach to social behavior. The SAPR-PBIS is one of several empirically based assessment tools for teams that wish to monitor school and district progress on PBIS practices. The authors wish users of the tool the best in developing and enhancing PBIS practices in their schools and hope to hear that the efforts have helped to create a more positive learning environment for all students.

# References


Achenbach, T.A. (2001). *Achenbach's Empirical Behavioral Assessment manual for Teacher Report Form.* Burlington, VT: Achenbach System on Empirically Based Assessment.

Adelman, H., & Taylor, L. (2001). *Organization facilitators: A change agent for systemic school and community changes.* Los Angeles, CA: Center for Mental Health in Schools.

Adelman, H., & Taylor, L. (2007). Systemic change for school improvement. *Journal of Educational and Psychological Consultation, 17*, 55–77.

Anderson, A.R., Christenson, S.L., Sinclair, M.F., & Lehr, C.A. (2004). Check and connect: The importance of relationships for promoting engagement with school. *Journal of School Psychology, 42*(2), 95–113.

Behar, K., Peterson, R., Mannix, E., & Trochim, W. (2008). The critical role of conflict resolution in teams: A close look at the links between conflict type, conflict management strategies, and team outcomes. *Journal of Applied Psychology, 93*, 170–188.

Bender, W.N., & Shores, C. (2007). *Response to intervention: A practical guide for every teacher.* Thousand Oaks, CA: Corwin Press.

Bergan, J.R. (1977). *Behavioral consultation.* Columbus, OH: Charles E. Merrill.

Bradley, R., Danielson, L., & Doolittle, J. (2007). Responsiveness to intervention: 1997–2007. *Teaching Exceptional Children, 39*, 8–12.

Bradshaw, C., Barrett, S., & McKenna, M. (2008). *Implementation phases inventory.* Retrieved from http://pbismaryland.org/forms.htm

Bruce, J. (1993). *The self-renewing school.* Alexandria, VA: Association for Supervision and Curriculum Development.

Bruns, E.J., Walrath, C., Glass-Siegel, M., & Weist, M.D. (2004). School-based mental health services in Baltimore: Association with school climate and special education referrals. *Behavior Modification, 28(4)*, 430–439.

Bruns, E.J., & Suter, J.C. (2010). Summary of the wraparound evidence base. In E.J. Bruns & J.S. Walker (Eds.), *The resource guide to wraparound.* Portland, OR: National Wraparound Initiative. Retrieved from http://www.nwi.pdx.edu/publications.shtml

Calabrese, R.L. (2000). *Leadership for safe schools.* Lanham, MD: Scarecrow Press.

Caldarella, P., Young, E.L., Richardson, M.J., Young, B.J., & Young, K.R. (2008). Validation of the Systematic Screening for Behavior Disorders in middle and junior high school. *Journal of Emotional and Behavioral Disorders, 16*, 105–117.

Carr, E.G., Dunlap, G., Horner, R.H., Koegel, R.L., Turnbull, A.P., Sailor, W., ...Fox, L. (2002). Positive behavior support: Evolution of an applied science. *Journal of Positive Behavior Interventions, 4*, 4–16.

Cartledge, G., & Lo, Y. (2006). *Teaching urban learners: Culturally responsive strategies for developing academic and behavioral competence.* Champaign, IL: Research Press.

Cartledge, G., & Loe, S. (2001). Cultural diversity in social skills instruction. *Exceptionality, 9*(1 & 2), 33–46.

Cartledge, G., Singh, A., & Gibson, L. (2008). Practical behavior-management techniques to close the accessibility gap for students who are culturally and linguistically diverse. *Preventing School Failure, 52*(3), 29–38.

Center for Mental Health in Schools. (2007). *A resource aid packet on screening/assessing students: Indicators and tools.* Los Angeles, CA: Author.

Center for Mental Health in Schools. (2010). *School improvement planning: What is missing*? Los Angeles, CA: Author.

Center for Prevention Research and Development. (2004). *The school improvement self study.* Champaign, IL: University of Illinois.

Center on Positive Behavioral Interventions and Supports. (2002). *PBS implementation and planning self-assessment.* Eugene, OR: Author.

Cheney, D. (1998). *Washington assessment and intervention system for students with emotional disabilities (BEACONS Project)* (Federal grant #32M98014, U.S. Department of Education). Washington, DC: Author.

Cheney D. (2003). *BEACONS outreach: Scaling up positive behavioral supports to a statewide initiative* (Federal grant #84.324R, U.S. Department of Education). Washington, DC: Author.

Cheney, D., & Barringer, C. (1999). A transdisciplinary model for students' social and emotional development: Creating a context for inclusion. In J. Scotti & L. Meyer (Eds.), *Behavior intervention: Principles, models, and practice* (pp. 3–26). Baltimore, MD: Paul H. Brookes Publishing Co.

Cheney, D., Blum, C., & Walker, B. (2004). An analysis of leadership team's perceptions of positive behavior supports and the outcomes of typically developing and at-risk students. *Assessment and Evaluation for Intervention, 30,* 7–24.

Cheney, D., Flower, A., & Templeton, T. (2008). Applying response to intervention metrics in the social domain for students at risk of developing emotional or behavioral disorders. *Journal of Special Education, 42,* 108–126.

Cheney, D., & Osher, T. (1997). Collaborate with families. *Journal of Emotional and Behavioral Disorders, 5,* 36–44.

Cheney, D., Stage, S., Hawken, L., Lynass, L., Mielenz, C., & Waugh, M. (2009). A two-year outcome study of the check, connect, and expect intervention for students at-risk of severe behavior problems. *Journal of Emotional and Behavioral Disorders, 17,* 226–243.

Cicchetti, D. (1994). Guidelines, criteria, and rules of thumb for evaluating normed or standardized assessment instruments in psychology. *Psychological Assessment, 6,* 284–290.

Clancy, M. (2010). *Participatory evaluation in programs for students with emotional and behavioral disabilities.* Unpublished doctoral dissertation, Seattle University.

Cohen, R., Kincaid, D., & Childs, K.E. (2007). Measuring school-wide positive behavior support implementation: Development and validation of benchmarks of quality. *Journal of Positive Behavior Interventions, 4,* 203–213.

Collaborative for Academic, Social, and Emotional Learning. (2010). *Student social and emotional learning standards.* Retrieved from http://www.casel.org/standards/learning.php

Colorado Department of Education. (2008). *Response to intervention (RtI): A practitioner's guide to implementation.* Retrieved from http://www.cde.state.co.us/RtI/LearnAboutRtI.htm

Colvin, G. (2009). *Managing noncompliance and defiance in the classroom: A road map for teachers, specialists, and behavior support teams.* Thousand Oaks, CA: Corwin Press.

Conduct Problems Prevention Research Group. (2000). Merging universal and indicated preventions programs: The Fast Track model. *Addictive Behaviors, 25,* 913–927.

Conduct Problems Prevention Research Group. (2002). Using the Fast Track randomized prevention trial to test the early-starter model of the development of serious conduct disorders. *Development and Psychopathology, 14,* 925–943.

Crone, D., Hawken, L., & Bergstrom, M. (2007). A demonstration of training, implementing, and using functional behavioral assessment in 10 elementary and middle school settings. *Journal of Positive Behavior Interventions, 9,* 15–29.

Crone, D., Hawken, L., & Horner, R. (2010). *Responding to problem behavior in schools: The behavior education program* (2nd ed.). New York, NY: Guilford.

Crone, D.A., & Horner, R.H. (2003). *Building positive behavior support systems in schools: Functional behavioral assessment.* New York, NY: Guilford Press.

Crone, D.A., Horner, R.H., & Hawken, L.S. (2004). *Responding to problem behavior in the schools: The behavior education program.* New York, NY: Guilford.

Deno, S., & Mirkin, P. (1977). *Data based program modification.* Minneapolis, MN: Leadership Institute for Special Education.

DiPerna, J.C., & Elliott, S.N. (1999). Development and validation of the academic competence evaluation scales. *Journal of Psychoeducational Assessment, 17,* 207–225.

Drummond, T. (1993). *The Student Risk Screening Scale.* Grants Pass, OR: Josephine County Mental Health Program.

Dunlap, G., Heineman, M., Knoster, T., Fox, L., Anderson, J., & Albin, R. (2000). Essential elements of inservice training in positive behavior supports. *Journal of Positive Behavior Interventions, 2,* 22–32.

Dusenbury, L., & Hansen, W. (2004). Pursuing the course from research to practice. *Prevention Science, 5,* 55–59.

Dwyer, K.P. (2002). Tools for building safe, effective schools. In M.R. Shinn, H.M. Walker, & G. Stoner (Eds.), *Interventions for academic and behavior problems II* (pp. 167–212). Bethesda, MD: National Association of School Psychologists.

Eber, L., & Keenan, S. (2004). Collaboration with other agencies: Wraparound and systems of care for children and youths with emotional and behavioral disorders. In R. Rutherford, M. Quinn, & S. Mathur (Eds.), *Handbook of research in emotional and behavioral disorders* (pp. 502–521). New York, NY: Guilford Press.

Eber, L., Sugai, G., Smith, C., & Scott, T. (2002). Wraparound and positive behavioral interventions and supports in the schools. *Journal of Emotional and Behavioral Disorders, 10,* 171–180.

Ehrhart, M., & Naumann, S. (2004). Organizational citizenship behavior in work groups: A group norms approach. *Journal of Applied Psychology, 89,* 960–974.

Elfner Childs, K., Kincaid, D., & Peshak George, H. (2009). A model for statewide evaluation of universal positive behavior support initiative. *Journal of Positive Behavior Interventions, 12*(4), 198–210.

Elizalde-Utnick, G. (2002). Best practices in building partnerships with families. In M.R. Shinn, H.M. Walker, & G. Stoner (Eds.), *Interventions for academic and behavior problems II* (pp. 413–429). Bethesda, MD: National Association of School Psychologists.

Elliott, S., & Gresham, F. (2007). *Social Skills Improvement System.* Upper Saddle River, NJ: Pearson.

Elliott, S., Huai, N., & Roach, A. (2007). Universal and early screening for educational difficulties: Current and future approaches. *Journal of School Psychology, 45,* 137–161.

Fairbanks, S., Sugai, G., Guardino, D., & Lathrop, M. (2007). Response to intervention: Examining classroom behavior support in second grade. *Exceptional Children, 73,* 288–310.

Fox, L., & Dunlap, G. (2002). Family centered practices in positive behavior support. *Beyond Behavior,* 24–26.

Friesen, B., & Stephens, B. (1998). Expanding family roles in the system of care: Research and practice. In M. Epstein, K. Kutash, & A. Duchnowski (Eds.), *Outcomes for children and youth with emotional and behavioral disorders and their families: Programs and best practices* (pp. 231–259). Austin, TX: PRO-ED.

Fullan, M. (2007). *The new meaning of educational change* (4th ed.). New York, NY: Teachers College Press.

George, H.P., & Martinez, S.A. (2007). How to get SWPBS in your school. *PBIS Newsletter, 4*(1). Retrieved from the OSEP Technical Assistance Center on Positive Behavioral Interventions and Supports web site, http://www.pbis.org/common/pbisresources/publications/Newsletter_HowToGetPBISinYourSchool.pdf

Good, R.H., & Kaminski, R.A. (2002). *Dynamic Indicators of Basic Early Literacy Skills, administration and scoring guide* (6th ed.). Eugene, OR: Institute for the Development of Educational Achievement.

Gottfredson, G.D. (1991). *The Effective School Battery.* Odessa, FL: Psychological Assessment Resources.

Greenberg, M., Domitrovich, C., & Bumbarger, B. (2001). The prevention of mental disorders in school-aged children: Current state of the field. *Prevention and Treatment, 4,* 1–62.

Griffith, G. (2000). School climate as group evaluation and group consensus: Student and parent perceptions of the elementary school environment. *Elementary School Journal, 101,* 35–61.

Hagan-Burke, S., Burke, M., Martin, E., Boon, R., Fore, C., & Kirkendoll, D. (2005). The internal consistency of the Effective Behavioral Support Survey. *Education and Treatment of Children, 28*, 400–413.

Handler, M., Rey, J., Connell, J., Their, K., Feinberg, A., & Putnam, R. (2007). Practical considerations in creating school-wide positive behavior supports in public schools. *Psychology in the Schools, 44*, 29–39.

Harris, A. (2004). Distributed leadership and school reform: Leading or misleading? *Educational Management Administration & Leadership, 32*(1), 11–24.

Hawken, L., & Horner, R. (2003). Evaluation of a targeted intervention within a school-wide system of behavior support. *Journal of Behavior Education, 12*, 225–240.

Hawken, L.S., MacLeod, S.K., & Rawlings, L. (2007). Effects of the behavior education program (BEP) on office discipline referrals of elementary school students. *Journal of Positive Behavior Interventions, 9*, 94–101.

Hawken, L.S., Vincent, C.G., & Schumann, J. (2008). Response to intervention for social behavior: Challenges and opportunities. *Journal of Emotional and Behavioral Disorders, 16*(4), 213–225.

Hawkins, J.D., Smith, B., Hill, K., Kosterman, R., Catalano, R., & Abbott, R. (2003). Understanding and preventing crime and violence: Findings from the Seattle Social Development Project. In T.P. Thornberry & M.D. Krohn (Eds.), *Taking stock of delinquency: An overview of findings from contemporary longitudinal studies*. New York, NY: Kluwer Academic.

Heller, K.A., Holtzman, W.H., & Messick, S. (1982). Placing children in special education: A strategy for equity. *Management in Education, 22*(1), 31–34.

Higgins, M., Young, L., Weiner, J., & Wlodarczyk, S. (2009). Leading teams of leaders: What helps team member learning? *Kappan, 91*(4), 41–45.

Horner, R., Sugai, G., Todd, A., & Lewis-Palmer, T. (2004). School-wide positive behavior support: An alternative approach to discipline in schools. In L. Bambara & L. Kern (Eds.), *Positive behavior support*. New York, NY: Guilford Press.

Horner, R.H., Todd, A., Lewis-Palmer, T., Irvin, L., Sugai, G., & Boland, J. (2004). The School-Wide Evaluation Tool (SET): A research instrument for assessing school-wide positive behavior support. *Journal of Positive Behavior Intervention, 6*(1), 3–12.

Hoy, W., & Feldman, J. (1999). Organizational health profiles for high schools. In H.J. Frieberg (Ed.), *School climate: Measuring, improving, and sustaining health in learning environments* (pp. 84–102). London, England: Falmer Press.

Individuals with Disabilities Education Act Amendments (IDEA) of 1997, PL 105-17, 20 U.S.C. §§ 1400 *et seq.*

Individuals with Disabilities Education Improvement Act (IDEA) of 2004, PL 108-446, 20 U.S.C. §§ 1400 *et seq.*

Irvin, L., Horner, R., Ingram, K., Todd, A., Sugai, G., Sampson, N.K., ...Boland, J. (2006). Using office discipline referral data for decision making about student behavior in elementary and middle schools: An empirical evaluation of validity. *Journal of Positive Behavior Interventions, 8*, 10–23.

Irvin, L.K., Tobin, T.J., Sprague, J.R., Sugai, G., & Vincent, C.G. (2004). Validity of office discipline referral measures as indices of school-wide behavioral status and effects of school-wide behavioral interventions. *Journal of Positive Behavior Interventions, 6*, 131–147.

James, L.R. (1982). Aggregation bias in estimates of perceptual agreement. *Journal of Applied Psychology, 67*(2), 219–229.

Kamphaus, R., & Reynolds, C. (2007). *The Behavior Assessment Scale for Children–2: Behavior and Emotional Screening Scale*. Upper Saddle River, NJ: Pearson.

Kincaid, D., Childs, K., & George, H. (2005). *School-wide Benchmarks of Quality*. Unpublished instrument, University of Southern Florida, Tampa.

Kincaid, D., Childs, K., & George, H. (2010). *School-wide Benchmarks of Quality* (Rev. ed.). Unpublished instrument, University of Southern Florida, Tampa.

Knapp, M.S., Elfers, A.M., & Plecki, M.L. (2004). *Preparing for reform, supporting teachers' work: Surveys of Washington state teachers, 2003–2004 school year*. Seattle, WA: University of Washington.

Knoff, H. (2000). Organizational development and strategic planning for the millennium: A blueprint toward effective school discipline, safety, and crisis prevention. *Psychology in the Schools, 37,* 17–32.

Knoff, H. (2002). Best practices in facilitating schools reform, organizational change, and strategic planning. In A. Thomas & J. Grimes (Eds.), *Best practices in school psychology* (Vol. 1, pp. 235–253). Bethesda, MD: National Association of School Psychologists.

Knoff, H.M. (2007). Best practices in strategic planning, organizational assessment, and school effectiveness. In A. Thomas & J. Grimes (Eds.), *Best practices in school psychology* (Vol. 5, pp. 903–916). Bethesda, MD: National Association of School Psychologists.

Knoff, H.M. (2009). *Implementing response-to-intervention at the school, district, and state levels: Functional assessment, data-based problem solving, and evidence-based academic and behavioral interventions.* Little Rock, AR: Project ACHIEVE Press.

Knoster, T., & McCurdy, B. (2002). Best practices in functional behavioral assessment for designing individualized student programs. In A. Thomas & J. Grimes (Eds.), *Best practices in school psychology* (Vol. 1, pp. 1007–1028). Bethesda, MD: National Association of School Psychologists.

Kohl, G.O., Lengua, L.J., & McMahon, R.J. (2000). Parent involvement in school conceptualizing multiple dimensions and their relations with family and demographic risk factors. *Journal of School Psychology, 39,* 501–523.

Kutash, K., & Duchnowski, A. (1997). Create comprehensive and collaborative systems. *Journal of Emotional and Behavior Disorders, 5,* 66–75.

Lane, K.L., Kalberg, J.R., Parks, R.J., & Carter, E.W. (2008). Student Risks Screening Scale: Initial evidence for score reliability and validity at the high school level. *Journal of Emotional and Behavioral Disorders, 16,* 178–190.

Learning First Alliance. (2001). *Every child learning: Safe and supportive schools.* Washington, DC: Association for Supervision and Curriculum Development.

Leithwood, K., Mascall, B., Strauss, T., Sacks, R., Memon, N., & Yashkina, A. (2007). *Distributing leadership to make schools smarter.* Toronto, Canada: Ontario Institute of Studies in Education.

Leithwood, K., Seashore-Louis, K., Anderson, S., & Wahlstrom, K. (2004). *How leadership influences student learning: A review of research for the learning from leadership project.* New York, NY: Wallace Foundation.

Lewis, T., & Sugai, G. (1999). Effective behavior support: A systems approach to proactive school-wide management. *Focus on Exceptional Children, 31,* 1–24.

Lieberman, A. (2000). Networks as learning communities: Shaping the future of teacher development. *Journal of Teacher Education, 51*(3), 221–227.

Lindell, M., & Brandt, C. (2000). Climate quality and climate consensus as mediators of the relationship between organizational antecedents and outcomes. *Journal of Applied Psychology, 85,* 331–348.

Lynass, L., Tsai, S., Richman, T., & Cheney, D. (2011). Social expectations and behavioral indicators in schoolwide positive behavior supports: A nationwide behavior matrices study. *Journal of Positive Behavior Interventions.* (Advance online publication.) doi: 10.1177/1098300711412076

Marino, J. (2007). A new paradigm for organizational change: Involving customers and stakeholders in the improvement process. *Journal for Quality and Participation, 30*(1), 10–12.

Maryland Department of Education. (2008). *A tiered instructional approach to support achievement for all students: Maryland's response to intervention framework.* Retrieved from http://maryland publicschools.org/MSDE/newsroom/publications

Marzano, R., Waters, T., & McNulty, B. (2005). *School leadership that works: From research to results.* Alexandria, VA: Association for Supervision and Curriculum Development.

May, S., Ard, W., Todd, A., Horner, R., Glasgow, A., Sugai, G., & Sprague, J. (2000). *School-wide Information System (SWIS).* Eugene, OR: University of Oregon, Educational and Community Supports.

McIntosh, K., Campbell, A. L., Carter, D. R., & Dickey, C. R. (2009). Differential effects of a tier two behavior intervention based on function of problem behavior. *Journal of Positive Behavior Interventions, 11,* 68–81.

McKinney, J., Montague, M., & Hocutt, A. (1998). A two year follow up study of children at-risk for developing SED: Initial results from a prevention project. In C. Liberton, K. Kutash, & R. Friedman (Eds.),

*A system of care for children's mental health: Expanding the research base, tenth annual proceedings* (pp. 271–277). Tampa, FL: University of South Florida, Research and Training Center for Children's Mental Health.

McNamara, K., & Hollinger, C. (2003). Intervention-based assessment: Evaluation rates and eligibility findings. *Exceptional Children, 69*, 181–193.

Mellor, D. (2004). Furthering the use of Strengths and Difficulties Questionnaire: Reliability with younger child respondents. *Psychological Assessment, 16*, 396–401.

Muscott, H.S., Szczesiul, S., Berk, B., Staub, K., Hoover, J., & Perry-Chisholm, P. (2008). Creating-home school partnerships by engaging families in schoolwide positive behavior supports. *Teaching Exceptional Children, 41(6)*, 6–14.

Nelson, R., & Carr, B. (1999). *The think time strategy for schools kit.* Frederick, CO: Sopris West.

No Child Left Behind Act of 2001, PL 107-110, 115 Stat. 1425, 20 U.S.C. §§ 6301 *et seq.*

Nunnally, J. (1978). *Psychometric Theory.* New York, NY: Macgraw Hill.

O'Neill, R., Horner, R., Albin, R., Sprague, J., Storey, K., & Newton, S.J. (1997). *Functional assessment and program development for problem behavior: A practical handbook.* Pacific Grove, CA: Brooks/Cole.

Owen, J. (2007). *Program evaluation: Forms and approaches* (3rd ed.). New York, NY: Guilford Press.

Parise, L., & Spillane, J. (2010). How formal and on-the-job learning opportunities predict change in elementary. *Elementary School Journal, 110*(3), 323–346.

Patton, M. (2008). *Utilization-focused evaluation* (4th ed.). Thousand Oaks CA: Sage Publications.

Quinn, M., Gable, R., Rutherford, R., Nelson, C.M., & Howell, K. (1998). *Addressing student problem behavior—Part I: An IEP team's introduction to functional behavioral assessment and behavior intervention plans.* Washington, DC: Center for Effective Collaboration and Practice.

Ray, C., & Elliott, S. (2006). Social adjustment and academic achievement: A predictive model for students with diverse academic and behavior competencies. *School Psychology Review*, 35, 493–501.

Reid J.B., Eddy, J.M., Fetrow, R.A., & Stoolmiller, M. (1999). Description and immediate impacts of preventive intervention for conduct problems. *American Journal of Community Psychology, 27*, 483–518.

Rogers, E. (1995). Diffusion of drug abuse prevention programs: Spontaneous diffusion, agenda setting, and reinvention. *NIDA Research Monograph, 155*, 90–105.

Sadler, C. (2000). Effective behavior support implementation at the district level: Tigard-Tualatin School District. *Journal of Positive Behavior Interventions, 2*(4), 241–243.

Sadler, C., & Sugai, G. (2008). Effective behavior and instructional support: A district model for early identification and prevention of reading and behavior problems. *Journal of Positive Behavior Interventions, 11*(1), 35–46.

Safran, S. (2006). Using the Effective Behavior Supports Survey to guide development of schoolwide positive behavior support. *Journal of Positive Behavior Interventions, 8*, 3–9.

Safran, S.P., & Oswald, K. (2003). Positive behavior supports: Can schools reshape disciplinary practices? *Exceptional Children, 69*, 361–373.

School-Wide Information System. (2006). *Summary of SWIS data 2004–2005.* Retrieved from http://www.swis.org

Scott, T.M., Anderson, C.M., & Spaulding, S.A. (2008). Strategies for developing and carrying out functional assessment and behavior intervention planning. *Preventing School Failure, 52*, 39–49.

Scott, T., & Barrett, S. (2004). Using staff and student time engaged in disciplinary procedures to evaluate the impact of school-wide PBS. *Journal of Positive Behavior Interventions, 6*, 21–28.

Scott, T., & Caron, D. (2005). Conceptualizing functional behavior assessment as prevention practice within positive behavior support systems. *Preventing School Failure, 50*(1), 13–20.

Scott, T., & Eber, L. (2003). Functional assessment and wraparound as systemic school processes: Primary, secondary, and tertiary systems examples. *Journal of Positive Behavior Intervention and Supports, 5*, 131–140.

Scott, T., & Martinek, G. (2006). Coaching positive behavior support in school settings: Tactics and data-based decision making. *Journal of Positive Behavior Interventions, 8*, 165–173.

Senge, P. (2000). *Schools that learn: A fifth discipline fieldbook for educators, parents, and everyone who cares about education.* New York, NY: Doubleday.

Severson, H., Walker, H., Hope-Doolittle, J., Kratchowill, T., & Gresham, F. (2007). Proactive, early screening to detect behaviorally at-risk students: Issues, approaches, emerging innovations, and professional practices. *Journal of School Psychology, 45*, 193–223.

Shannon, G.S., & Bylsma, P. (2007). *The nine characteristics of high-performing schools: A research-based resource for schools and districts to assist with improving student learning* (2nd ed.). Olympia, WA: Office of the Superintendent of Public Education.

Simeonson, B., Eber, L., Black, A., Sugai, G., Lewandowski, H., Sims, B., & Myers, D. (2012). Illinois statewide positive behavioral interventions and supports: Evolution and impact on student outcomes across years. *Journal of Positive Behavioral Interventions, 14*(1), 5–16.

Simonsen, B., Myers, D., & Briere, D. (2011). Comparing a behavioral check-in/check-out intervention to standard practice in an urban middle school setting using an experimental group design. *Journal of Positive Behavior Interventions, 13*, 31–48.

Sinclair, M.F., Christenson, S.L., & Thurlow, M.L. (2005). Promoting school completion of urban secondary youth with emotional or behavioral disabilities. *Exceptional Children, 71*(4), 465–482.

Singh, A., & Muncherji, N. (2007). Team effectiveness and its measurement: A framework. *Global Business Review, 8*, 119–133.

Spillane, J., Hunt, B., & Healey, K. (2009). Managing and leading elementary schools: Attending to the formal and informal organization. *International Studies of Educational Administration, 37*(1), 6–12.

Sprague, J., Sugai, G., Horner, R., & Walker, H. (1999). Using office discipline referral data to evaluate school-wide discipline and violence prevention interventions. *Oregon School Study Council, 42*, 4–18.

Sprague, J., & Walker, H. (2000). Early identification and intervention for youth with antisocial and violent behavior. *Exceptional Children, 66*, 367–379.

Stone, D., Patton, B., & Heen, S. (1999). *Difficult conversations: How to discuss what matters most.* New York, NY: Penguin Putnam.

Stroul, B.A., & Freidman, R. (1986). *A system of care for severely emotionally disturbed children and youth.* Washington, DC: Child and Adolescent Service System Program Technical Assistance Center.

Suarez-Herrera, J., Springett, J., & Kagan, C. (2009). Critical connections between participatory evaluation, organizational learning and intentional change in pluralistic organizations. *Evaluation, 15*, 321–342.

Sugai, G., & Horner, R. (1999). Discipline and behavioral support: Practices, pitfalls, and promises. *Effective School Practice, 17*, 10–22.

Sugai, G., & Horner, R. (2002). The evolution of discipline practices: School-wide positive behavior supports. *Child and Family Behavior Therapy, 24*, 23–50.

Sugai, G., Horner, R.H., Algozzine, R., Barrett, S., Lewis, T., Anderson, C., ...Simonsen, B. (2010). *School-wide positive behavior support: Implementers' blueprint and self-assessment.* Eugene, OR: University of Oregon. Retrieved from http://www.pbis.org

Sugai, G., Horner, R., & Gresham, F. (2002). Behaviorally effective school environments. In M.R. Shinn, H.M. Walker, & G. Stoner (Eds.), *Interventions for academic and behavior problems II* (pp. 315–350). Bethesda, MD: National Association of School Psychologists.

Sugai, G., Horner, R., & Lewis-Palmer, T. (2001). *Effective behavior support team implementation checklist.* Eugene, OR: Author.

Sugai, G., Horner, R., & Lewis-Palmer, T. (2002). *Team Implementation Checklist.* Eugene, Oregon: Author.

Sugai, G., Horner, R.H., Lewis-Palmer, T., & Rossetto Dickey, C. (2011, May). *Team Implementation Checklist, Version 3.1.* Eugene, OR: University of Oregon, Educational & Community Supports.

Sugai, G., Horner, R., & Todd, A. (2003). *Effective Behavior Supports Self-Assessment Survey.* Eugene, OR: Author.

Sugai, G., Lewis-Palmer, T., Todd, A., & Horner, R. (2001). *School-wide Evaluation Tool.* Eugene, OR: Author.

Sutherland, K.S., Lewis-Palmer, T., Stichter, J., & Morgan, P.L. (2008). Examining the influence of teacher behavior and classroom context on the behavioral and academic outcomes for students with emotional or behavioral disorders. *Journal of Special Education, 41*(4), 223–233.

Tobin, T.J. (2006). *Use of the Team Implementation Checklist in regular and alternative high schools.* Eugene, OR: University of Oregon, Educational and Community Supports. Retrieved from http://pages.uoregon.edu/ttobin/alt_tic.pdf

Tobin, T., & Sugai, G. (1999). Using sixth-grade records to predict violence, chronic discipline problems, and high school outcomes, *Journal of Emotional and Behavioral Disorders, 7,* 40–53.

Todd, A., Horner, R., Sugai, G., & Sprague, J. (1999). Effective behavior support: Strengthening schoolwide systems through a team based approach. *Effective School Practices, 17,* 23–37.

Tuesday-Heathfield, L., & Clark, E. (2004). Shifting from categories to services: Comprehensive school-based mental health for children with emotional disturbance and social maladjustment. *Psychology in the Schools, 41,* 911–920.

U.S. Department of Education. (2000). *Twenty-second annual report to Congress on the implementation of the Individuals with Disabilities Act.* Washington, DC: Author.

U.S. Department of Education. (2005). *Twenty-seventh annual report to Congress on the implementation of the Individuals with Disabilities Education Act.* Washington, DC: Author.

U.S. Department of Health and Human Services. (2001). *Youth violence: A report of the surgeon general.* Rockville, MD: Author.

Van Horn, M.L. (2003). Assessing the unit of measurement for school climate through the psychometric and outcome analyses of the School Climate Survey. *Educational and Psychological Measurement, 63,* 1002–1019.

Vincent, C., Spaulding, S., & Tobin, T. (2010). A re-examination of the psychometric properties of the Schoolwide Evaluation Tool (SET). *Journal of Positive Behavior Interventions, 12,* 161–179.

Walker, B. (2010). Effective schoolwide screening to identify students at-risk for social and behavioral problems. *Intervention in School and Clinic, 46*(2), 104–110.

Walker, B., Cheney, D., & Stage, S. (2009). The validity and reliability of the Self-Assessment and Program Review Survey: Assessing school progress in schoolwide positive behavior support. *Journal of Positive Behavior Interventions, 11,* 94–109.

Walker, B., Cheney, D., Stage, S., & Blum, C. (2005). Schoolwide screening and positive behavior supports: Identifying and supporting students at-risk for school failure. *Journal of Positive Behavior Interventions, 7,* 194–204.

Walker, H.M., Horner, R.H., Sugai, G., Bullis, M., Sprague, J.R., Bricker, D., & Kaufman, M.J. (1996). Integrated approaches to preventing antisocial behavior patterns among school-age children and youth. *Journal of Emotional and Behavioral Disorders, 4,* 194–209.

Walker, H.M., Kavanagh, K., Stiller, B., Golly, A., Severson, H.H., & Feil, E.G. (1998). First step to success: An early intervention approach for preventing school antisocial behavior. *Journal of Emotional and Behavioral Disorders, 6,* 66–80.

Walker, H., Ramsey, E., & Gresham, F. (2003). Heading off disruptive behavior: How early intervention can reduce defiant behavior and win back teaching time. *American Educator,* 6–45.

Walker, H., & Severson, H.H. (1992). *Systematic Screening for Behavior Disorders.* Longmont, CO: Sopris West.

Webster-Stratton, C., Reid, J.M., & Hammond, M. (2004). Treating children with early-onset conduct problems: Intervention outcomes for parent, child, and teacher training. *Journal of Clinical Child and Adolescent Psychology, 33,* 105–124.

Webster-Stratton, C., & Taylor, T. (2001). Nipping risk factors in the bud: Preventing substance abuse, delinquency, and violence in adolescence through interventions targeted at young children (0–8 years). *Prevention Science, 2,* 165–192.

Wholey, J., Hatry, H., & Newcomer, K. (2004). *Handbook of practical program evaluation* (2nd ed.). San Francisco, CA: Jossey-Bass.

Woodruff, D., Osher, D., Hoffman, C., Gruner, A., King, M., Snow, S., & McIntire, J.C. (1999). The role of education in a system of care: Effectively serving children with emotional or behavioral disorders. In

*Systems of care: Promising practices in children's mental health, 1998 Series* (Vol. 3). Washington, DC: Center for Effective Collaboration and Practice.

Zins, J.E., & Elias, M.E. (2006). Social and emotional learning. In G.G. Bear & K.M. Minke (Eds.), *Children's needs III* (pp. 1–13). Bethesda, MD: National Association of School Psychologists.

Zins, J.E., Payton, J.W., Weissberg, R.P., & O'Brien, M.U. (2007). Social and emotional leaning and successful school performance. In G. Matthews, M. Zeidner, & R.D. Roberts (Eds.), *The science of emotional intelligence: Knowns and unknowns.* New York, NY: Oxford University Press.

SAPRpbis A

# Sample Individual and Team Meeting Forms

From Walker, B., & Cheney, D. [2012]. *The Self-Assessment and Program Review for Positive Behavior Interventions and Supports [SAPR-PBIS™]*. 

# SAPRpbis™ | Individual Form

School: Mountain View Date: 10/12/11

Name: Anne Walker Position: Teacher

Team meeting date: 10/15/11

## OVERVIEW

The first step of implementing schoolwide positive behavior interventions and supports (PBIS) involves a school self-assessment. Your leadership team will use this self-assessment tool to identify your school's strengths and needs related to evidence-based practices essential to the effective implementation of PBIS. Following each practice is a list of indicators that characterize this practice. Team members will use their ratings to assess the functioning level of the school. Many of the practices in this tool are relevant to every student in the school, whereas others are specifically focused on helping students who may be struggling with emotional or behavioral problems. For those practices that are focused on supporting students who may be struggling, throughout this assessment the term *emotional or behavioral problems (E/BPs)* is used to include all students with challenging behavior, not just those receiving special education services.

## INDIVIDUAL SELF-ASSESSMENT DIRECTIONS

You have been asked to complete this form because you are a member of the schoolwide leadership team. Please complete this survey prior to the scheduled team meeting. Look over each item and rate it using the rating scale below; determine the rating based on your specific knowledge and experience in the school. Circle *1* if you are not sure whether your school implements a particular practice as stated; then, share your responses and any questions at the team meeting.

Once you have rated all of the indicators, add the ratings for each practice and place the total in the spaces provided. Please be sure to rate all items. Use the scale that follows to determine your final ratings. Please consider the questions listed in each box to help you finalize your decisions. Circle any indicators that you would particularly like to discuss, and write down any comments or questions that you would like to share with the team. If you have any questions about this process, please talk with the designated facilitator for this process or with your school administrator.

*Remember:* Please do not discuss or compare ratings with other members of your team until the team meeting.

## THE SELF-ASSESSMENT SCALE

**5** = This indicator of the evidence-based practice is *fully in place.* Data and documentation indicate that it is functioning well and implemented with a high degree of consistency. The practice requires only maintenance of effort at this time.

**4** = This indicator of the evidence-based practice is *mostly in place.* Data and documentation indicate that it is consistently implemented in school practice. However, there may be some issues with the consistency of implementation that suggest it requires additional work to be fully in place.

**3** = This indicator of the evidence-based practice is *moderately in place.* Data and documentation indicate that it may only be implemented with consistency about half the time. It is clearly in need of additional work to be fully in place.

**2** = This indicator of the evidence-based practice is only *partially in place.* Data and documentation indicate that it is inconsistently implemented and needs much more work to be fully in place.

**1** = This indicator of the evidence-based practice is *not yet in place.* Data and documentation indicate that it is rarely implemented with any consistency and will require extensive work before it can be fully in place.

| 1 | Administrative policies and procedures support the education of all students, including those with or at risk of developing E/BPs. | | |
|---|---|---|---|
| 1.1 | **The school or district has a written statement that values the education of all students, including those with E/BPs.**<br>Does your school have a mission statement or overall philosophy that is shared with staff, students, and families through written documents such as the school handbook? If so, does it clearly state a commitment to the success of all learners, including those with learning and/or behavioral problems? | *Notes* | 1 2 3 (4) 5 |
| 1.2 | **Policies and programs in the school handbook focus on the *prevention* of academic and behavior problems.**<br>Does the school handbook describe strategies, practices, or programs designed to support students before they demonstrate significant academic or behavior problems? Does it explain to students and parents how they can gain access to these practices or programs? Does it explain how these programs can be helpful to students? | *Notes* | 1 (2) 3 4 5 |
| 1.3 | **Sufficient resources are allocated to implement these policies and programs.**<br>Are enough staff, time, volunteers, and materials available to ensure that these programs and supports are delivered consistently and efficiently? | *Notes* | 1 (2) 3 4 5 |
| 1.4 | **The school has a leadership team that meets regularly to review schoolwide discipline issues.**<br>Has a team of faculty and staff been created that meets monthly to review data, concerns, and issues related to schoolwide discipline? | *Notes* | 1 2 (3) 4 5 |
| 1.5 | **The team includes a school administrator, representative staff, educators, and families/community members.**<br>Does the team include the school principal or vice principal and individuals that represent the range of faculty, staff, and community members (including paraprofessionals, general and special educators, counselors, psychologists, and family members)? | *Notes* | 1 2 3 (4) 5 |
| 1.6 | **The school's leadership team develops annual goals and objectives to improve schoolwide PBIS.**<br>Does this team establish a written plan that outlines priorities at least once a year? Are these plans shared with the full school staff? | *Notes* | 1 (2) 3 4 5 |
| 1.7 | **The school's leadership team annually evaluates progress on goals and objectives.**<br>Does this team collect data that help it determine whether the plan has been successful? Does the team then adjust the plan as needed? | *Notes* | 1 (2) 3 4 5 |

Comments or questions for the team:

*The principal attends when she can—how can we get more consistent administrative involvement?*
*I would like to see our policies move to something more proactive. Currently they are more reactive.*
*We are just getting underway on this process and learning as we go.*

Total your score for this practice: 19

| 2 | School policies and programs emphasize prevention and the early identification of students with or at risk of developing E/BPs. | | |
|---|---|---|---|
| 2.1 | **A systematic schoolwide screening program is used annually to identify students with or at risk of developing E/BPs.**<br>Does your school have a screening tool, such as the Systematic Screening for Behavior Disorders or the Behavior and Emotional Screening Scale? Is it used in the first 2 months of school to identify students in need of Tier 2 intervention? Are office discipline referrals (ODRs) used to identify students who need extra support? | *Notes*<br>Only screening for reading/math are done right now. | (1) 2 3 4 5 |
| 2.2 | **A teacher assistance or prereferral intervention team is in place and is available in a timely manner to address problem behavior of students.**<br>Does the team meet twice monthly to review student progress and nominate students for additional supports? Does the team have efficient and effective interventions for use with students? | *Notes* | 1 2 (3) 4 5 |
| 2.3 | **Teams develop a method for ensuring that interventions are implemented with fidelity for all students identified as having E/BPs.**<br>Do the reviews lead to implementation of interventions? Do staff monitor and evaluate the interventions? Do team members visit classrooms to note implementation? | *Notes* | 1 2 (3) 4 5 |
| 2.4 | **An interpersonal problem-solving approach is taught and used by the entire staff with all students in the building.**<br>Do all school staff know how to discuss interpersonal problems with students? Do they use a multistep approach that identifies the problem, reviews the social expectations of the school, discusses positive solutions, and has students commit to using positive social skills/expectations? Do the faculty and staff review the effectiveness of the approach monthly by reviewing data, concerns, and issues related to the problem-solving approach? | *Notes*<br>What would this look like with older kids? | 1 (2) 3 4 5 |
| 2.5 | **The school counseling program is integrated with PBIS and is available to all students.**<br>Does your school have a school counselor? Is the counselor a member of your PBIS leadership team? Does the counselor help students learn and use the school's social expectations? Can students visit the school counselor for social-interpersonal problem-solving sessions? | *Notes* | 1 2 (3) 4 5 |
| 2.6 | **Families of students with E/BPs are engaged in school programs.**<br>Does your school have a family involvement program or goal? Do families assist students or teachers in classrooms? Is there an active family leadership group? Do families that are involved with the school contact those that may be hesitant to come to school? Do parents identify professional development activities to help them with their children's education? | *Notes* | 1 2 3 (4) 5 |

Comments or questions for the team:

We have a great psychologist and school counselor, and our special education staff help a great deal, but we don't use that team as effectively as we could.
I am pretty pleased with the level of family involvement at my grade level. Is this the same for everyone?

Total your score for this practice: 16

| 3 | Staff development activities focus on methods to educate all students, including those with or at risk of developing E/BPs. | | |
|---|---|---|---|
| 3.1 | **Ongoing staff development is provided to address the school's programs for social-emotional development of *all* students.**<br>Do some of the faculty and staff meetings and scheduled in-service days address topics related to social-emotional development of all students? If so, how often? How useful is the content presented? Does the staff development relate directly to schoolwide PBIS? | *Notes* | 1 2 (3) 4 5 |
| 3.2 | **In-service training focuses on evidence-based practices regarding behavior management strategies for students with or at risk of developing E/BPs.**<br>Does the training content include research-based strategies that are directly useful in the school and classroom? Do the strategies seem consistent with schoolwide PBIS? Do the strategies improve students' social behavior and reduce behavior problems? | *Notes* | 1 2 (3) 4 5 |
| 3.3 | **In-service training focuses on effective accommodations and instructional modifications for students with or at risk of developing E/BPs.**<br>Does the training include information on strategies to adjust academic and social activities to support success for students with E/BPs? Do the strategies support differentiating within the setting or activity so that all students can be successful? | *Notes*<br>*Districtwide training on differentiated instruction has been well attended.* | 1 2 3 (4) 5 |
| 3.4 | **In-service training focuses on risk and protective factors for the social development of all students.**<br>Does the training include information about how schools can make a difference and support success for students who are at risk? | *Notes* | 1 (2) 3 4 5 |
| 3.5 | **In-service training focuses on understanding common behavioral disorders of students (e.g., autism, attention deficit disorder, bipolar disorder) and effective supports.**<br>Does the training include helpful information for understanding the definition, issues, and challenges experienced by students with specific disorders and provide effective supports and strategies? | *Notes* | 1 (2) 3 4 5 |
| 3.6 | **A method is used to evaluate in-service effectiveness.**<br>After the training, are faculty and staff asked to provide feedback on its effectiveness and applicability to your situation? | *Notes*<br>*This is done inconsistently.* | 1 (2) 3 4 5 |

Comments or questions for the team:

*How can we get more focused on solutions? It is important that we know what these labels mean and look like—but how can we then emphasize positive, proactive solutions?*
*Do classified staff have access to any of this training?*

Total your score for this practice: 16

| 4 | Clear and consistent behavioral expectations are established for students across all school settings. | | |
|---|---|---|---|
| 4.1 | **Staff have adopted or developed a program to teach prosocial skills in classroom and nonclassroom settings.**<br>Does your school have a set of social expectations that are useful throughout the school? Do teachers take time to instruct students in the expectations and behaviors for these settings across the school? Does everyone know how to demonstrate, role-play, and teach social skills? | *Notes* | 1 2 3 (4) 5 |
| 4.2 | **This program is described in the school handbook.**<br>Does the school handbook describe strategies, practices, or programs to teach social expectations? Does it explain to students and parents how these practices or programs are implemented in classrooms? | *Notes*<br>We are getting there! | 1 2 (3) 4 5 |
| 4.3 | **Behavioral expectations are written and posted in classroom and nonclassroom settings.**<br>Are there posters throughout your school with your schoolwide social or behavioral expectations? Are they positive and engaging to students? Are students involved in developing or maintaining the posters? | *Notes* | 1 2 3 (4) 5 |
| 4.4 | **Behavioral expectations are taught, monitored, and reinforced systematically in classroom and nonclassroom settings.**<br>Is there a plan to teach social and behavioral expectations during the first day, week, and month of school, across all school settings? Are additional booster sessions taught throughout the year? | *Notes* | 1 2 (3) 4 5 |
| 4.5 | **Teachers and staff use effective approaches to discourage problem behavior.**<br>Do teachers give warnings, prompts, and redirections when they see misbehavior? Do the staff practice and use verbal problem-solving approaches for minor problems? Do teachers reinforce peers demonstrating responsible behavior when they see misbehavior in the classroom? | *Notes* | 1 2 (3) 4 5 |
| 4.6 | **The school leadership team monitors and evaluates the impact of the schoolwide program.**<br>Does the team review its data frequently and give feedback to the staff? Are there celebrations when the staff meet goals? | *Notes* | 1 2 (3) 4 5 |
| 4.7 | **The behavioral expectations and schoolwide program are regularly communicated to families.**<br>Do families receive newsletters, e-mails, or postings on web sites to learn about progress in schoolwide social programs? Is progress discussed at schoolwide family meetings such as parent nights at school? | *Notes*<br>This is just getting into place—we could do a faster job with translating key material in our three primary languages. | 1 2 (3) 4 5 |

Comments or questions for the team:

We have made a good start of this practice as part of our initial efforts. How are we going to focus our efforts to get this practice well established?
With our high student mobility turnover, how can we make sure new students and families get oriented to our schoolwide system?

Total your score for this practice: 23

| 5 | School procedures for responding to discipline referrals and emergency situations are implemented consistently and effectively. | | |
|---|---|---|---|
| 5.1 | **The discipline process includes criteria for office referrals, addressing the behavior of concern, and returning the student to the classroom.**<br><br>Does a clear, consistently implemented process exist? Is it written down? Are all students, faculty, staff, and families aware of the process? Is it followed consistently? | *Notes* | 1 (2) 3 4 5 |
| 5.2 | **Discipline and suspension policies are clearly stated in the handbook and effectively communicated to parents, students, and staff.**<br><br>Does a written statement of the policies exist? Are the consequences for certain behaviors clearly defined? Is the statement available in all the languages of the student community? Does everyone understand and follow the written process? | *Notes* | 1 2 (3) 4 5 |
| 5.3 | **Discipline procedures meet state and federal regulatory requirements (e.g., use functional behavioral assessments [FBAs] and behavior intervention plans [BIPs] when appropriate, employ documentation and parent contact as required).**<br><br>Are all of the policies and procedures related to discipline aligned with regulations? Do students who qualify for special education due to behavioral problems have an effective FBA and BIP in place? Does everyone involved in discipline understand federal and state laws related to reporting and implementing discipline? | *Notes*<br><br>Not sure—what are they? | (1) 2 3 4 5 |
| 5.4 | **Staff with specialized training are available to help resolve students' social-emotional conflicts.**<br><br>Have some or all of your staff members been formally trained to respond to and help students who are having difficulties, and are they available to help such students calm down and/or talk about their problems? Does the method used align with PBIS? | *Notes* | 1 2 (3) 4 5 |
| 5.5 | **A designated area is available in the office, hallway, or a classroom to resolve students' social-emotional problems (e.g., a problem-solving area, think time area, cool-off spot, buddy room).** *Note:* This is *not* a reference to a time-out room.<br><br>Are there supervised places where students can be sent when a problem is starting, where they can refocus, calm down, and make a plan to get back on track? Is this system used consistently and effectively? | *Notes* | 1 2 (3) 4 5 |
| 5.6 | **A team of teachers and staff is trained to use a crisis prevention and intervention program for emergency situations.**<br><br>Have some staff members been specifically trained in responding to crisis situations and helping students de-escalate in a way that protects student and staff safety if needed? Is the approach used in alignment with PBIS? | *Notes*<br><br>Not that I am aware of, and we have had need of this from time to time. | (1) 2 3 4 5 |

Comments or questions for the team:

There seem to be a lot of different perceptions and expectations about this practice throughout the building.
Teachers and classified staff often are not sure how the system should and does work. I think we have to talk more about how to address this.
Teachers use the "buddy room" options well, but it is mostly informal. What similar options exist for the cafeteria and recess?

Total your score for this practice: 13

| 6 | Systematic supports are developed to address the academic and social needs of students with E/BPs. | |
|---|---|---|
| 6.1 | **General educators receive support in their classrooms from certified specialists experienced with students having E/BPs (e.g., school psychologist, school counselor, behavior specialist, special educator).**<br>Does your school attempt to improve the social and academic environment by having specialists work collaboratively and purposefully in general education classrooms? Are time and resources allocated so that prescribed programs can be effectively implemented in classrooms? | *Notes* 1 2 (3) 4 5<br>Teachers help each other a lot, and our paraprofessionals are good at supporting lots of students. |
| 6.2 | **Tier 2 behavior interventions or support plans are developed for students with E/BPs.**<br>Does the student support team (SST) have time to meet and collaboratively develop behavior plans for students? Does the team help with professional development so that the plan can be coordinated across staff and implemented with fidelity? | *Notes* 1 (2) 3 4 5<br>Mostly kids who go to the office a lot or have an IEP get help. |
| 6.3 | **Academic supports help students with E/BPs receive passing grades in their classes.**<br>Are either teacher-mediated or peer-mediated academic supports available, such as small-group instruction, classwide peer tutoring, or cross-age tutoring? Do teachers adapt materials in terms of length and time allowable for completion? Are the academic supports monitored for effectiveness? Do struggling students seem to benefit from the supports provided? | *Notes* 1 2 (3) 4 5<br>Teachers work hard in this area. |
| 6.4 | **Specialized services such as a focused prosocial skills training help students with E/BPs succeed socially and behaviorally.**<br>Is there a Tier 2 intervention system that uses a check-in and check-out process, a daily progress report card, social skills instruction, problem solving, or another approach? Are these implemented and coordinated across the school's specialists and teachers? | *Notes* 1 (2) 3 4 5<br>We have some kids with behavior cards, but I'm not sure how you "qualify." |
| 6.5 | **Instructional approaches (e.g., Behavior Education Program; Check, Connect, and Expect; check-in and check-out process) are used to address individual students' cognitive, behavioral, and emotional needs.**<br>Do you have a special educator or a coach for students who understands and assists in social or academic modifications and accommodations? Does he or she help you understand how to break concepts into understandable units and how to make activities more meaningful to students who are unengaged in instruction? Does the social coach see students daily for checking in, monitoring daily progress, and checking out at day's end? | *Notes* 1 2 (3) 4 5<br>Teachers help each other a lot, and our paraprofessionals are good at supporting lots of students. |

| 6 | Systematic supports are developed to address the academic and social needs of students with E/BPs. *(continued)* | | |
|---|---|---|---|
| 6.6 | **Social supports facilitate positive interpersonal relationships for students with E/BPs (e.g., circle of friends, buddy system, peer mentors).**<br>Are peer-to-peer networks organized such that students help one another? Does instruction help enhance friendships and social interactions? Do staff teach the value of friendship and identify peers who will be helpful and empathic with students who have social difficulties? Are mentor systems in place to help struggling students? | *Notes* | 1 2 (3) 4 5 |

Comments or questions for the team:

*Again, I think the district's emphasis on differentiated instructional strategies helps in this area. But at a building level, we don't have good, consistent support for students who are starting to struggle with behavior. By the time a pattern is established, the SST appointments are FULL!*

Total your score for this practice: 16

| 7 | FBAs are completed for students with significant behavior problems to develop intensive interventions. | | |
|---|---|---|---|
| 7.1 | **The team uses FBA procedures for developing students' BIPs.**<br>Does an FBA team include staff with behavioral expertise for the FBA process? Does the team meet regularly to develop plans for students with behavior problems? Does the team identify the function of the student's behavior and then develop a proactive behavior plan that uses function-based interventions to teach students new skills to be successful? | *Notes*<br>It is only for students with IEPs. | 1 (2) 3 4 5 |
| 7.2 | **Each behavior plan addresses setting events, antecedents, prosocial skills, positive reinforcement, and the function of the behavior.**<br>Does the team understand the components of a student's behavior pattern and understand ways to help the student learn more appropriate behaviors for meeting the behavioral function? Do the BIPs include strategies for teaching the student prosocial skills and detail how adults will reinforce these new skills? | *Notes*<br>I have no idea! | (1) 2 3 4 5 |
| 7.3 | **BIPs are developed collaboratively with family members and are sensitive to cultural and linguistic differences.**<br>Are family members and caregivers included in the development of the plans? Are team members aware of the cultural, gender, and linguistic issues related to discipline and student behavior? Are positive behavior plans developed that feel supportive to the student and family members as well as school staff? | *Notes*<br>We involve families early on when problems come up. | 1 2 (3) 4 5 |
| 7.4 | **BIPs include systematic data collection to assess student progress.**<br>Do all behavior plans include clear strategies for tracking and monitoring the student's problem behaviors and prosocial skills to determine whether the plan is effective? Are changes made to the plan when necessary based on collected data? | *Notes*<br>It depends! Who is the teacher, and how busy is he or she? | 1 (2) 3 4 5 |
| 7.5 | **A case manager coordinates and monitors the BIP for each student.**<br>Are the plans followed by a trained staff member who helps to ensure that the plan is followed consistently and helps to answer questions and solve problems as they occur? | *Notes* | 1 2 (3) 4 5 |

Comments or questions for the team:

I think this idea of doing more detailed behavior problem solving before a student has an IEP has merit, but I think we will need a lot of training, and we have to be able to figure out who gets what support more consistently, not just a squeaky wheel!

Total your score for this practice: 11

| 8 | Data are routinely collected and systematically analyzed by the leadership team for program-evaluation and decision-making purposes. | | |
|---|---|---|---|
| 8.1 | **Staff collect and analyze patterns in ODRs using an electronic database.**<br>Does your school have an established referral process for disciplinary actions? Does it distinguish between minor problems that are classroom managed and major problems that are handled by an administrator? Are data collected on ODRs and analyzed by the leadership team or SST? | Notes | 1 2 (3) 4 5 |
| 8.2 | **Reports from the database are reviewed monthly to analyze patterns.**<br>Does the leadership or SST give reports to staff regarding ODRs and other behavioral issues or successes at least monthly? Are the reports used to improve the school's PBIS approach? | Notes<br>*The administration team does. I would like to see it shared with everyone.* | 1 2 (3) 4 5 |
| 8.3 | **Staff collect and analyze information on students' social and academic behavior in classrooms and nonclassroom settings.**<br>Are grades and other academic indicators, ODRs, or daily progress report (DPR) data used by classroom teachers and staff to improve the overall functioning of students in classroom and nonclassroom settings? Do the teachers and staff think these are meaningful data for improving academic and social functioning of students? | Notes<br>*They do this more academically than with behavior.* | 1 2 (3) 4 5 |
| 8.4 | **Data are analyzed to evaluate the relationship between ethnicity and disciplinary actions (e.g., referrals, suspensions, expulsions).**<br>Does the SST disaggregate data to look at issues of disproportionality based on race or ethnicity? Are any of the findings used to change practice regarding multicultural competence? Does the SST or administrator conduct professional development to address multicultural competence? | Notes | 1 2 (3) 4 5 |
| 8.5 | **ODR data are analyzed in the screening process to identify students with or at risk of developing E/BPs.**<br>Does the SST use ODRs or other screening tools to identify those students in need of Tier 2 intervention? Are the data looked at monthly to make this determination? | Notes<br>*There is no behavioral screening process except for students who get in trouble the most.* | 1 (2) 3 4 5 |
| 8.6 | **ODR data are considered when developing intervention plans for students.**<br>Are the types of ODR (e.g., disruptive, defiant, aggressive) reviewed to determine behavioral function? Are interventions matched with the type of behavioral difficulty to enhance efficiency and effectiveness? | Notes | 1 2 (3) 4 5 |

Comments or questions for the team:

*It is important for the administrators and student support people to share the discipline data with all of us. It would help us make better decisions.*
*What is our pattern over the past few years? Some commercial ODR tracking systems might give us more detailed information.*

Total your score for this practice: *17*

| 9 | Families are seen as partners in the development of their child's program. | | |
|---|---|---|---|
| 9.1 | **Family members are part of each child's team and are encouraged to participate in meetings and school activities.**<br>When students begin to have trouble at school, are parents and/or caregivers immediately notified and included in the problem-solving process? Are family members invited to be team members? Are family members encouraged to join other relevant school teams? Are family members welcome in classrooms during the instructional day? | *Notes* | 1 2 (3) 4 5 |
| 9.2 | **Parents of children with significant behavioral concerns have access to a family support group when needed.**<br>Are there supports available for families whose students are struggling significantly in school (e.g., parent network, community group)? Do school staff help connect families to these supports? | *Notes* | (1) 2 3 4 5 |
| 9.3 | **Families are supported in gaining access to additional community resources.**<br>When families need information on additional supports (e.g., health services, food or clothing bank, child care, recreational options), do school staff provide information and help families connect with these supports? | *Notes*<br>*Our office staff is great with this, but they are often so busy!* | 1 2 (3) 4 5 |
| 9.4 | **Family education programs and resources are available at the school.**<br>Does the school include references, resources, and supports to help families and students experience success (e.g., parent library, parent network, effective parenting strategies)? Do these programs occur at your school or in the community? Do school staff assist families in connecting with and participating in the programs? | *Notes*<br>*The PTA tries, but we often have parents with lots of questions.* | 1 2 (3) 4 5 |
| 9.5 | **A family's cultural and community perspective is valued and integrated into communication and student supports.**<br>Does the school provide information, materials, resources, and events that are meaningful and accessible to the various cultural groups within the school community? Are these events and resources translated so that they are accessible to families who speak other languages? Do school events, meetings, and activities reflect and respect the cultural traditions that make up the school community? | *Notes*<br>*I would like us to look at involvement patterns—are there groups we are not reaching?* | 1 2 (3) 4 5 |

Comments or questions for the team:

*Teachers work hard to engage and connect with families. But for the students who are struggling the most—how can we help those families see that they are part of the solution and that we can work best together?*
*What about a survey of families: What do they need, like, want to change, and so forth?*

Total your score for this practice: *13*

| 10 | Comprehensive plans are developed for students and families in need of intensive support. | | |
|---|---|---|---|
| 10.1 | **Students with severe behavior problems have timely access to medical, mental health, and other community social services.**<br><br>Does your school have connections with local service providers? Are these connections formal or informal agreements? Do the representatives of these agencies come to meetings at your school? Is your school nurse or school psychologist able to connect and coordinate services with these other private or public providers? | *Notes* | 1 (2) 3 4 5 |
| 10.2 | **A student's use of prescription medication is known by staff and is monitored frequently by school and family members.**<br><br>Does your school nurse, psychologist, or administrator have an understanding and documentation of medications used by students? Does someone know about the effects and side effects of the medications? Is there some form of monitoring of prescribed medications in the school? | *Notes* | 1 (2) 3 4 5 |
| 10.3 | **Students with individualized education programs (IEPs) have goals and objectives for their social and emotional needs.**<br><br>Are social-emotional assessments linked to the IEP? Are the goals for social-emotional development on the IEP measurable, and do they contain benchmarks for progress monitoring? Do behavior plans use methods to accomplish these goals? | *Notes*<br><br>Yes, on the IEPs I have seen, but I hear "no" from other teachers. | 1 (2) 3 4 5 |
| 10.4 | **Professionals from other agencies serve on students' IEP teams as needed.**<br><br>Is there a wraparound process for students who have complex or intensive needs? Do representatives from other agencies attend IEP or other planning meetings? Are these other professionals providing appropriate services to meet students' needs? | *Notes*<br><br>Not in my experience. | (1) 2 3 4 5 |
| 10.5 | **The school or district has a formal agreement with community agencies to provide services to meet the needs of students and their families.**<br><br>Have district or school administrators formalized any service agreements with medical, mental health, and other community social services for students with severe behavior problems? Are services determined by a multidisciplinary team including family members, a district or school administrator, educators, and community agency members? | *Notes* | 1 (2) 3 4 5 |
| 10.6 | **Interagency teams develop, implement, and evaluate treatment plans that are family centered, based on strengths and needs, and sensitive to cultural and linguistic differences.**<br><br>When there is an interagency team, does it use the wraparound process to develop a comprehensive treatment plan for the student? Is it person and family centered and culturally competent for the student and family? | *Notes*<br><br>What is this? | (1) 2 3 4 5 |

| 10 | Comprehensive plans are developed for students and families in need of intensive support. *(continued)* | | |
|---|---|---|---|
| 10.7 | **A family support liaison regularly contacts parents of students in need of intensive support.**<br>Does anyone in the school or district serve as a liaison to families and/or community agencies? Can members of the faculty assume responsibility for working with individual families? | *Notes*<br>*Usually it is a counselor or nurse.* | 1 2 (3) 4 5 |
| 10.8 | **A case manager coordinates all communication between the interagency team members.**<br>Is there a case manager for students who have multiple agency representation? Does the case manager coordinate, communicate, and evaluate multiagency care? | *Notes*<br>*I'm not sure.* | (1) 2 3 4 5 |

Comments or questions for the team:

*This is something I don't really understand at all. What options are there for students and families? Usually it is about qualifying for special education. Our nurse and counselor do try to help families with significant challenges.*

Total your score for this practice: *14*

# SAPRpbis™ | Team Meeting Form

School: Mountain View District: Kingston

Team meeting date: 10/15/11 Meeting facilitator: Patricia Carmen

Leadership team members: Ilene Juarez, Pat Kai, Anne Walker, Scott Marquette, Mindy Carlisle, Craig Michaels, Arvin Santos

## OVERVIEW

The first step of schoolwide program improvement involves a school self-assessment. This self-assessment tool was developed to assess evidence-based practices regarding schoolwide discipline, data collection, family and community involvement, and individualized student supports related to the effective implementation of positive behavior support. Your team will use this self-assessment tool to identify your school's strengths and needs related to these practices. This self-assessment contains a list of evidence-based practices for students with challenging behavior. Following each practice is a list of elements that characterize this practice. Team members will use their rating to assess the functioning level of the school. Many of the practices in this tool are relevant to every student in the school, whereas others are specifically focused on helping students who may be struggling with emotional or behavioral problems. For those practices that are focused on supporting students who may be struggling, throughout this assessment the term *emotional or behavioral problems* (E/BPs) is used to include all students with challenging behavior, not just those receiving special education services. It is suggested that a PBIS leadership team complete this process at least annually. Once the team has completed the self-assessment process, it uses the data to develop an action plan. *The SAPR-PBIS™ Manual* includes detailed instructions, samples, and other supports for this process.

## TEAM ASSESSMENT DIRECTIONS

### Step One: Plan for the Self-Assessment Team Meeting

Set a date for the schoolwide PBIS leadership team to meet and complete the Individual Form. The team will need approximately 60–90 minutes to complete the process.

### Step Two: Prepare for the Self-Assessment Team Meeting

Prior to the team meeting, each team member should be given the Individual Form to complete and bring with him or her to the team meeting. Specific directions for completing the Individual Form are included on that form, and details are provided in *The SAPR-PBIS™ Manual.* It is recommended that one member of the team be identified to facilitate the team meeting. The facilitator should serve as the team's recorder and will record the final ratings on this form, along with relevant comments and questions for each indicator. The facilitator should also collect current data on such things as office discipline referrals (ODRs), referrals to student support teams, and other practices referenced in the self-assessment discussion for the team's reference throughout the meeting. Documentation such as program descriptions and school policy manuals should also be referenced as part of the final rating process.

### Step Three: Conduct the Self-Assessment Team Meeting

As a school leadership team, you will discuss the results of each member's completed Individual Form to develop a consensus about how your school is functioning on the 10 evidence-based practices listed. For each practice, the facilitator asks each team member to share his or her total score from the Individual Form and records that along the scoring bar located under each item. As a team, discuss to what degree each practice is being utilized in your school, based on the scores being reported and the current data related to each practice.

## TEAM-ASSESSMENT DIRECTIONS

If there is a significant discrepancy between various team members' individual scores, we suggest that the team then discuss the ratings given to each of the indicators listed under the practice to clarify the different perspectives and come to a consensus. See Chapter 4 in the manual for detailed instructions and suggestions for how your team can come to consensus on the rating for a practice.

### Step Four: Identify Priorities for Improvement

As a team, review the results of the team assessment to identify up to three evidence-based practices to focus on improving during the school year as part of your schoolwide PBIS program. Use the indicators listed with each evidence-based practice to help you develop specific, measurable objectives for improvement. In the Action Plan on the final page of this form, record these objectives, briefly summarize the activities related to addressing each objective, and outline a plan for measuring progress. Throughout the year, the leadership team should revisit these objectives to determine the progress being made toward achieving them. See the manual for suggestions for developing effective goals and objectives as well as resources for strengthening each practice.

### Step Five: Share the Action Plan with School Faculty

Copies of the Action Plan should be given to each PBIS leadership team member for reference. We also suggest that you share these objectives and activities with the entire faculty.

## TEAM ASSESSMENT SCALE

(A detailed description for rating each practice is provided in *The SAPR-PBIS™ Manual* in Chapter 5.)

**5** = This indicator of the evidence-based practice is *fully in place.* Data and documentation indicate that it is functioning well and implemented with a high degree of consistency. The practice requires only maintenance of effort at this time.

**4** = This indicator of the evidence-based practice is *mostly in place.* Data and documentation indicate that most of it is consistently implemented in school practice. However, there may be some issues with the consistency of implementation that suggest it requires additional work to be fully in place.

**3** = This indicator of the evidence-based practice is *moderately in place.* Data and documentation indicate that it may only be implemented with consistency about half the time. It is clearly in need of additional work to be fully in place.

**2** = This indicator of the evidence-based practice is only *partially in place.* Data and documentation indicate that it is inconsistently implemented and needs much more work to be fully in place.

**1** = This indicator of the evidence-based practice is *not yet in place.* Data and documentation indicate that it is rarely implemented with any consistency and will require extensive work before it can be fully in place.

## EXAMPLE OF TEAM SCORING PROCESS

| 5 | **School procedures for responding to discipline referrals and emergency situations are implemented consistently and effectively.** |
|---|---|
| 5.1 | The discipline process includes criteria for office referrals, addressing the behavior of concern, and returning the student to the classroom.* See action plan for details. |
| 5.2 | Discipline and suspension policies are clearly stated in the handbook and effectively communicated to parents, students, and staff. |
| 5.3 | Discipline procedures meet state and federal regulatory requirements (e.g., use functional behavioral assessments [FBAs] and behavior intervention plans [BIPs] when appropriate, employ documentation and parent contact as required). |
| 5.4 | Staff with specialized training are available to help resolve students' social-emotional conflicts. |
| 5.5 | A designated area is available in the office, hallway, or a classroom to resolve students' social-emotional problems (e.g., a problem-solving area, think time area, cool-off spot, buddy room). *Note:* This is *not* a reference to a time-out room. |
| 5.6 | A team of teachers and staff is trained to use a crisis prevention and intervention program for emergency situations.* See action plan for details. |

Outliers

Tally marks represent scores from team members. Circle the range with the most scores. You may circle the overlap between two boxes if applicable.

| ✓ ✓ | ✓ | ✓✓✓✓ | ✓ | |
|---|---|---|---|---|
| **6–10**<br>1 = Not yet in place | **11–15**<br>2 = Partially in place | **16–20**<br>3 = Moderately in place | **21–26**<br>4 = Mostly in place | **27–30**<br>5 = Fully in place |

*Note:* The top numbers in bold represent the range of total scores from the Individual Form (e.g., 6 questions with 1–5 possible points equals a range of 6–30). The bottom numbers correspond with the rating scale, allowing the team to see where its total scores fall along that scale.

Place a tally mark above the box that includes the total score reported for the practice. If there is a significant discrepancy between ratings, or a low overall score, discuss the individual scores for each of the indicators in order to come to a consensus on the team rating and to identify priorities for improvement. In addition, record any specific questions, ideas, or comments that emerge from the discussion that the team would like to be able to reference in the future. See *The SAPR-PBIS™ Manual* for more suggestions about facilitating this discussion.

| 1 | **Administrative policies and procedures support the education of all students, including those with or at risk of developing E/BPs.** |
|---|---|
| 1.1 | The school or district has a written statement that values the education of all students, including those with E/BPs. |
| 1.2 | Policies and programs in the school handbook focus on the *prevention* of academic and behavior problems.* |
| 1.3 | Sufficient resources are allocated to implement these policies and programs. |
| 1.4 | The school has a leadership team that meets regularly to review schoolwide discipline issues.* |
| 1.5 | The team includes a school administrator, representative staff, educators, and families/community members. |
| 1.6 | The school's leadership team develops annual goals and objectives to improve schoolwide PBIS. |
| 1.7 | The school's leadership team annually evaluates progress on goals and objectives. |

Place a tally mark to reflect each of the scores of individual team members, and circle the box that reflects the scores from most team members. If there is a significant discrepancy or a very low score, discuss the individual scores of the indicators to help to develop consensus.

| | | ✓ ✓ ✓ ✓ | ✓ ✓ ✓ ✓ | ✓ |
|---|---|---|---|---|
| **7–12**<br>1 = Not yet in place | **13–18**<br>2 = Partially in place | **19–24**<br>3 = Moderately in place | **25–30**<br>4 = Mostly in place | **31–35**<br>5 = Fully in place |

**Notes and comments from the team:**

*We're doing fairly well for the first year. We need to focus on getting policies and procedures better articulated in handbooks, notes to substitute teachers, and parent communication. We added stars next to the indicators that we feel need the clearest focus.*

| 2 | **School policies and programs emphasize prevention and the early identification of students with or at risk of developing E/BPs.** |
|---|---|
| 2.1 | A systematic schoolwide screening program is used annually to identify students with or at risk of developing E/BPs.* |
| 2.2 | A teacher assistance or prereferral intervention team is in place and is available in a timely manner to address problem behavior of students.* |
| 2.3 | Teams develop a method for ensuring that interventions are implemented with fidelity for all students identified as having E/BPs. |
| 2.4 | An interpersonal problem-solving approach is taught and used by the entire staff with all students in the building. |
| 2.5 | The school counseling program is integrated with PBIS and is available to all students. |
| 2.6 | Families of students with E/BPs are engaged in school programs. |

Place a tally mark to reflect each of the scores of individual team members, and circle the box that reflects the scores from most team members. If there is a significant discrepancy or a very low score, discuss the individual scores of the indicators to help to develop consensus.

| | ✓ ✓ ✓ ✓ | ✓ ✓ ✓ | | |
|---|---|---|---|---|
| **6–9**<br>1 = Not yet in place | **10–15**<br>2 = Partially in place (circled) | **16–20**<br>3 = Moderately in place | **21–26**<br>4 = Mostly in place | **27–30**<br>5 = Fully in place |

**Notes and comments from the team:**

*This is a practice we feel strongly about moving forward on, and we have identified the actions of choosing a screening and exploring ways to better use our Student Study Teams as priorities for next year.*

*Craig and Anne will lead the team in review of some potential screening tools.*

| 3 | **Staff development activities focus on methods to educate all students, including those with or at risk of developing E/BPs.** |
|---|---|
| 3.1 | Ongoing staff development is provided to address the school's programs for social-emotional development of *all* students. |
| 3.2 | In-service training focuses on evidence-based practices regarding behavior management strategies for students with or at risk of developing E/BPs. |
| 3.3 | In-service training focuses on effective accommodations and instructional modifications for students with or at risk of developing E/BPs. |
| 3.4 | In-service training focuses on risk and protective factors for the social development of all students. |
| 3.5 | In-service training focuses on understanding common behavioral disorders of students (e.g., autism, attention deficit disorder, bipolar disorder) and effective supports. |
| 3.6 | A method is used to evaluate in-service effectiveness. |

Place a tally mark to reflect each of the scores of individual team members, and circle the box that reflects the scores from most team members. If there is a significant discrepancy or a very low score, discuss the individual scores of the indicators to help to develop consensus.

| | ✓ ✓ ✓ ✓ | ✓ ✓ ✓ ✓ | | |
|---|---|---|---|---|
| **6–9**<br>1 = Not yet in place | **10–15**<br>2 = Partially in place | **16–20**<br>3 = Moderately in place | **21–26**<br>4 = Mostly in place | **27–30**<br>5 = Fully in place |

**Notes and comments from the team:**

*In the first year, we have focused on universal-level training topics. We are ready to move toward helping staff understand issues related to at-risk students, screening, and other Tier 2 topics. Three of the early release dates will focus on PBIS topics, and PBIS will continue to be a standing topic during staff meetings once a month, with more scheduled time as needed when possible.*

| 4 | **Clear and consistent behavioral expectations are established for students across all school settings.** |
|---|---|
| 4.1 | Staff have adopted or developed a program to teach prosocial skills in classroom and nonclassroom settings. |
| 4.2 | This program is described in the school handbook. |
| 4.3 | Behavioral expectations are written and posted in classroom and nonclassroom settings. |
| 4.4 | Behavioral expectations are taught, monitored, and reinforced systematically in classroom and nonclassroom settings. |
| 4.5 | Teachers and staff use effective approaches to discourage problem behavior.* |
| 4.6 | The school leadership team monitors and evaluates the impact of the schoolwide program. |
| 4.7 | The behavioral expectations and schoolwide program are regularly communicated to families. |

Place a tally mark to reflect each of the scores of individual team members, and circle the box that reflects the scores from most team members. If there is a significant discrepancy or a very low score, discuss the individual scores of the indicators to help to develop consensus.

| | ✓ ✓ | ✓ ✓ ✓ | ✓ ✓ ✓ | |
|---|---|---|---|---|
| **7–12**<br>1 = Not yet in place | **13–18**<br>2 = Partially in place | **19–24**<br>3 = Moderately in place | **25–30**<br>4 = Mostly in place | **31–35**<br>5 = Fully in place |

**Notes and comments from the team:**

*Schoolwide expectations are pretty well established. We need to continue emphasis there. As part of emphasis on Tier 2, we need to provide better student supports more quickly once they are identified. Training on effective classroom and setting management for teachers and staff will be one topic to help in this practice also.*

| 5 | **School procedures for responding to discipline referrals and emergency situations are implemented consistently and effectively.** |
|---|---|
| 5.1 | The discipline process includes criteria for office referrals, addressing the behavior of concern, and returning the student to the classroom. |
| 5.2 | Discipline and suspension policies are clearly stated in the handbook and effectively communicated to parents, students, and staff.* |
| 5.3 | Discipline procedures meet state and federal regulatory requirements (e.g., use functional behavioral assessments [FBAs] and behavior intervention plans [BIPs] when appropriate, employ documentation and parent contact as required). |
| 5.4 | Staff with specialized training are available to help resolve students' social-emotional conflicts. |
| 5.5 | A designated area is available in the office, hallway, or a classroom to resolve students' social-emotional problems (e.g., a problem-solving area, think time area, cool-off spot, buddy room). *Note:* This is *not* a reference to a time-out room.* |
| 5.6 | A team of teachers and staff is trained to use a crisis prevention and intervention program for emergency situations. |

Place a tally mark to reflect each of the scores of individual team members, and circle the box that reflects the scores from most team members. If there is a significant discrepancy or a very low score, discuss the individual scores of the indicators to help to develop consensus.

| | ✓ ✓ ✓ ✓ | ✓ ✓ ✓ ✓ | | |
|---|---|---|---|---|
| **6–9**<br>1 = Not yet in place | **10–15**<br>2 = Partially in place | **16–20**<br>3 = Moderately in place | **21–26**<br>4 = Mostly in place | **27–30**<br>5 = Fully in place |

**Notes and comments from the team:**

*A clear process for ODRs is coming together. We need to reinforce staff for being consistent and clear. As part of getting policies better articulated in forms and communication with families, and so forth, we need to get this process more clearly laid out. Also, staff have expressed interest in a "buddy room" or think time–type process as an option before ODR in certain instances. Patricia and Arvin will bring some data and readings on this option to the leadership team in the next few weeks for consideration prior to bringing it to staff for discussion.*

| 6 | **Systematic supports are developed to address the academic and social needs of students with E/BPs.** |
|---|---|
| 6.1 | General educators receive support in their classrooms from certified specialists experienced with students having E/BPs (e.g., school psychologist, school counselor, behavior specialist, special educator). |
| 6.2 | Tier 2 behavior interventions or support plans are developed for students with E/BPs.* |
| 6.3 | Academic supports help students with E/BPs receive passing grades in their classes. |
| 6.4 | Specialized services such as a focused prosocial skills training help students with E/BPs succeed socially and behaviorally. |
| 6.5 | Instructional approaches (e.g., Behavior Education Program; Check, Connect, and Expect; check-in and check-out process) are used to address individual students' cognitive, behavioral, and emotional needs. |
| 6.6 | Social supports facilitate positive interpersonal relationships for students with E/BPs (e.g., circle of friends, buddy system, peer mentors).* |

Place a tally mark to reflect each of the scores of individual team members, and circle the box that reflects the scores from most team members. If there is a significant discrepancy or a very low score, discuss the individual scores of the indicators to help to develop consensus.

| | ✓ ✓ | ✓ ✓ ✓ ✓ ✓ ✓ (circled) | ✓ | |
|---|---|---|---|---|
| **6–9**<br>1 = Not yet in place | **10–15**<br>2 = Partially in place | **16–20**<br>3 = Moderately in place | **21–26**<br>4 = Mostly in place | **27–30**<br>5 = Fully in place |

**Notes and comments from the team:**

*A lot of these supports have been in place for a while on an informal basis. As part of exploring ways to use screening and the SST team more effectively, we would like to see if we can begin to emphasize the proactive and early intervention aspect of this practice.*

*The district's emphasis on differentiating instruction is helping in the classroom. Paraprofessionals would like some help with applying some similar thinking and problem solving to recess/common area options for students who often struggle in less structured settings.*

| 7 | **FBAs are completed for students with significant behavior problems to develop intensive interventions.** |
|---|---|
| 7.1 | The team uses FBA procedures for developing students' BIPs. |
| 7.2 | Each behavior plan addresses setting events, antecedents, prosocial skills, positive reinforcement, and the function of the behavior. |
| 7.3 | BIPs are developed collaboratively with family members and are sensitive to cultural and linguistic differences. |
| 7.4 | BIPs include systematic data collection to assess student progress. |
| 7.5 | A case manager coordinates and monitors the BIP for each student. |

Place a tally mark to reflect each of the scores of individual team members, and circle the box that reflects the scores from most team members. If there is a significant discrepancy or a very low score, discuss the individual scores of the indicators to help to develop consensus.

| ✓✓✓✓ | ✓✓✓✓ | | | |
|---|---|---|---|---|
| **5–8**<br>1 = Not yet in place | **9–12**<br>2 = Partially in place | **13–17**<br>3 = Moderately in place | **18–21**<br>4 = Mostly in place | **22–25**<br>5 = Fully in place |

**Notes and comments from the team:**

*In this area, the team is in consensus that we are just moving past awareness and beginning to think about this practice. We will continue to learn about this option, but the team agrees we should focus more on screening and other Tier 2 levels first. Pat, as school psychologist, will gather materials for the leadership team to read as we continue to try to understand this practice in action. Craig suggests sitting in on some meetings at Seaview, where they are using this approach pretty effectively.*

| 8 | **Data are routinely collected and systematically analyzed by the leadership team for program-evaluation and decision-making purposes.** |
|---|---|
| 8.1 | Staff collect and analyze patterns in ODRs using an electronic database. |
| 8.2 | Reports from the database are reviewed monthly to analyze patterns. |
| 8.3 | Staff collect and analyze information on students' social and academic behavior in classrooms and nonclassroom settings. |
| 8.4 | Data are analyzed to evaluate the relationship between ethnicity and disciplinary actions (e.g., referrals, suspensions, expulsions). |
| 8.5 | ODR data are analyzed in the screening process to identify students with or at risk of developing E/BPs.* |
| 8.6 | ODR data are considered when developing intervention plans for students.* |

Place a tally mark to reflect each of the scores of individual team members, and circle the box that reflects the scores from most team members. If there is a significant discrepancy or a very low score, discuss the individual scores of the indicators to help to develop consensus.

| | | ✓✓✓✓✓ | ✓✓✓ | |
|---|---|---|---|---|
| **6–9**<br>1 = Not yet in place | **10–15**<br>2 = Partially in place | **16–20**<br>3 = Moderately in place | **21–26**<br>4 = Mostly in place | **27–30**<br>5 = Fully in place |

**Notes and comments from the team:**

*Again, the team is pleased about where we are after year 1. We are getting better at using and analyzing the schoolwide discipline data using the School-Wide Information System. Priority will be on integrating that data with other sources as part of screening and early intervention planning in SST.*

| 9 | **Families are seen as partners in the development of their child's program.** |
|---|---|
| 9.1 | Family members are part of each child's team and are encouraged to participate in meetings and school activities. |
| 9.2 | Parents of children with significant behavioral concerns have access to a family support group when needed.* |
| 9.3 | Families are supported in gaining access to additional community resources.* |
| 9.4 | Family education programs and resources are available at the school. |
| 9.5 | A family's cultural and community perspective is valued and integrated into communication and student supports. |

Place a tally mark to reflect each of the scores of individual team members, and circle the box that reflects the scores from most team members. If there is a significant discrepancy or a very low score, discuss the individual scores of the indicators to help to develop consensus.

| | | ✓✓✓ | ✓✓✓ | ✓✓ |
|---|---|---|---|---|
| **5–8**<br>1 = Not yet in place | **9–12**<br>2 = Partially in place | **13–17**<br>3 = Moderately in place | **18–21**<br>4 = Mostly in place | **22–25**<br>5 = Fully in place |

**Notes and comments from the team:**

*The team is pleased with this practice overall, but there are some discrepancies in experience. Classroom teachers are feeling more directly connected with families than some of our classified staff, who are less involved in these kinds of interactions with families. Pat is going to talk with the PTA about assistance in some of these areas for families new to the area or who are facing challenges.*

| 10 | **Comprehensive plans are developed for students and families in need of intensive support.** |
|---|---|
| 10.1 | Students with severe behavior problems have timely access to medical, mental health, and other community social services. |
| 10.2 | A student's use of prescription medication is known by staff and is monitored frequently by school and family members. |
| 10.3 | Students with individualized education programs (IEPs) have goals and objectives for their social and emotional needs. |
| 10.4 | Professionals from other agencies serve on students' IEP teams as needed. |
| 10.5 | The school or district has a formal agreement with community agencies to provide services to meet the needs of students and their families. |
| 10.6 | Interagency teams develop, implement, and evaluate treatment plans that are family centered, based on strengths and needs, and sensitive to cultural and linguistic differences. |
| 10.7 | A family support liaison regularly contacts parents of students in need of intensive support. |
| 10.8 | A case manager coordinates all communication between the interagency team members. |

Place a tally mark to reflect each of the scores of individual team members, and circle the box that reflects the scores from most team members. If there is a significant discrepancy or a very low score, discuss the individual scores of the indicators to help to develop consensus.

| ✓ ✓ | ✓ ✓ ✓ ✓ ✓ | ✓ | | |
|---|---|---|---|---|
| **8–14**<br>1 = Not yet in place | **15–21**<br>2 = Partially in place (circled) | **22–28**<br>3 = Moderately in place | **29–35**<br>4 = Mostly in place | **36–40**<br>5 = Fully in place |

**Notes and comments from the team:**

*The team overall sees this as another practice that is going to take time to develop. Pat, the school psychologist, does interact with some of these services for students and families with significant needs, but usually when exploring more intensive special education supports. The team needs to learn more about this practice and how better to implement it.*

SAPRpbis™ | **Action Plan**

1. Review the results of the team evaluation and identify up to three evidence-based practices to focus on improving throughout the next year as part of your schoolwide PBIS system. Review the indicators of these practices to help you develop specific, measurable objectives for improvement. See *The SAPR-PBIS™ Manual* for examples and suggestions for developing an effective action plan as well as for strategies and resources to strengthen each of the practices.

2. In the space below, record these objectives, briefly summarize the activities related to addressing each objective, and outline a plan for measuring progress. Throughout the year, review progress made toward fully implementing these objectives. In order to visually display changes in the scores across time, the leadership team can enter the total scores for each evidence-based practice into a spreadsheet program after each meeting. This will allow the team to generate line or bar graphs that display changes in scores over time. This provides an "at-a-glance" summary of the team's ratings across time.

| Objective 1 | Activities | Evaluation |
|---|---|---|
| Ensure that all schoolwide practices and discipline policies are clearly and consistently written up and shared with key stakeholders. | Review existing documents and compare with minutes from staff meetings, as well as schoolwide expectation training events, etc. Make sure most current policies and procedures are included. Share with students, staff, and families. Use as opportunity to review and reinforce expectations, and so forth. | a. Hold fun "pop" quizzes with students and staff throughout the fall and midwinter to be sure that knowledge is there.<br>b. Complete the Schoolwide Evaluation Tool (SET) this spring to determine how well the schoolwide/universal practices are in place. |
| **Objective 2** | **Activities** | **Evaluation** |
| Implement a social/behavioral screening process this winter and begin implementing a more proactive focus to half of our student study team (SST) meetings. Begin implementing in conjunction with academic screening next fall. | 1. Identify screening tool by December 1. Train teachers in early January to implement it as well as in how the new Tier 2 aspect of the SST will work. Integrate ODR data into screening also.<br>2. SST will review identified students and begin matching to existing services based on need. Begin tracking student performance.<br>3. Bring information on potential Tier 2 targeted interventions to staff to determine one approach to pilot in the early spring. | a. Ask staff and families for survey feedback on the Tier 2 support process.<br>b. Review student functioning per reports on Tier 2 supports.<br>c. See how many students are again identified when screening occurs in the fall.<br>d. Review pilot data on students involved in the targeted behavioral support intervention to determine whether ready for full implementation the following fall. |
| **Objective 3** | **Activities** | **Evaluation** |
| Provide staff development and coaching on effective classroom management and supervision strategies. Include an approach for "buddy rooms." Once finalized, write down the procedure and guidelines in the staff handbook and give summary to parents. | 1. Use the three early release days to cover the following topics:<br>• Introduction to universal screening and Tier 2 interventions and supports<br>• Effective classroom management and supervision strategies<br>• Risk and protective factors and the role of relationships at school to support students who are at risk<br>Paraprofessionals will participate in these trainings.<br>2. Provide overview of these topics and approaches to PTA and share at parent/family nights.<br>3. Hold monthly staff meetings to focus on schoolwide systems updates and boosters, as well as SWIS ODR summaries. | a. Provide opportunities for confidential staff feedback after all staff development activities and as we roll out the Tier 2 program elements.<br>b. Have fun "pop" quizzes with faculty and staff on key aspects of the topics and procedures to help with review and motivation as new strategies are being implemented. |

# Summary of Technical Development

## ESTABLISHING THE RELIABILITY AND VALIDITY OF THE SAPR-PBIS

During the 2004–2005 school year, a study was implemented to establish the psychometric properties of SAPR-PBIS™. We completed the literature review to establish the content of the tool, described in Chapter 2, and the leadership teams at the 23 elementary schools that were participating in the BEACONS Outreach Project completed the SAPR-PBIS. Data from these schools, along with a survey of an expert panel for PBIS, were used to assess the validity and reliability of the SAPR-PBIS. Findings from this study are presented in this appendix. Although this study was conducted only with elementary schools, the content of SAPR-PBIS was developed in a way that is also relevant to secondary school settings. *Note*: These findings have been previously reported in Walker, Cheney, and Stage (2009).

## PARTICIPANTS AND DEMOGRAPHICS

The SAPR-PBIS was developed with the support of schools from throughout Washington State. This allowed us to obtain input from schools representing the diverse communities found throughout the state. The following section provides an overview of the demographics of the schools involved in the development of the tool.

### Setting

The elementary schools participating in this study were all engaged in the BEACONS PBIS Outreach Project and, therefore, were receiving training and technical assistance on implementing PBIS practices in their schools. A total of 13 of the schools were in their second year of PBIS implementation (Cohort 1) and 10 schools were in their first year of PBIS implementation (Cohort 2) at the time of this study. The schools were located in seven school districts from around Washington State, including urban, suburban, and rural regions of the state, and as a result they represent a range of demographics. Table B.1 summarizes the demographics for each of the school districts involved in the study.

From Walker, B., Cheney, D., & Stage, S. (2009). The validity and reliability of the Self-Assessment and Program Review Survey: Assessing school progress in schoolwide positive behavior support. *The Journal of Positive Behavior Interventions, 11*, 94–109; adapted by permission.

**Table B.1.** Demographics of participating school districts

| District | Enrollment | Ethnicity % | Primary ethnic group(s) | Free and reduced-price lunch % | Special education % |
|---|---|---|---|---|---|
| Mountain | 1,416 | 30 | Latino | 42.7 | 10.8 |
| East Mountain | 5,539 | 26 | Latino, with 15% migrant | 36.5 | 10.8 |
| Southern | 22,556 | 17 | Asian American | 33.8 | 10.2 |
| West City | 17,752 | 51 | Asian American and Latino | 46.4 | 10.4 |
| Northern | 7,093 | 16 | American Indian and Asian American | 20.0 | 10.0 |
| East City | 12,761 | 47 | Black and Asian American | 32.2 | 10.9 |
| Eastside | 3,576 | 11 | Latino | 39.0 | 9.9 |

## Participants

The SAPR-PBIS was developed with support and involvement of education professionals from schools throughout Washington State, while the content validity of the tool was established with the input of PBIS experts from throughout the country. Demographic details on these participants are summarized in the following sections.

### *School Leadership Teams*

The participants of the study were all members of their school's PBIS leadership team, established as part of the PBIS implementation process. Each team had six to eight members who were representative of the school faculty, typically including the school administrator, special educator, school counselor or psychologist, general educators from both the primary and intermediate grade levels, and paraprofessionals. A total of 23 school leadership teams participated in the study, with 150 individual staff members. The average leadership team in this study included seven members.

A descriptive analysis of demographic data found that approximately half of the leadership team members were general education teachers. The remainder of the group was composed of other professional roles. Sixty percent of the participants reported their ethnicity as Caucasian. All other ethnicities combined equaled only 5% of the participants, whereas the remaining 35% of the participants chose not to report their ethnicity. The leadership team participants had a wide range of experience in education, with an average of 14 years of experience and a range from 1 to 40 years.

### *PBIS Expert Panel*

A list of potential members for the PBIS Expert Panel was generated in two ways. The first group was identified by the list of state and district PBIS coordinators found on the OSEP Technical Assistance Center on Positive Behavioral Interventions and Supports' web site (http://www.pbis.org). In addition, the literature review we completed to develop items for the SAPR-PBIS generated a second list of 10–15 researchers who had made substantial contributions to PBIS development and research in the previous several years. These individuals were also included on the contact list. A total of 40 requests for participation were sent out; 21 individuals agreed to participate and 18 completed surveys were returned by the deadline. The mean years of experience with PBIS was 10, with a range from 2 to 25 years. Half of the respondents held Ph.D.s, slightly less than half had master's degrees, and one had a bachelor's degree.

## TECHNICAL ADEQUACY

The technical adequacy of the SAPR-PBIS was established using a variety of approaches, including an expert panel review, statistical analysis of the internal reliability of the items, as well as hierarchical linear modeling to explore the impact of role and school involvement in the overall process. The results of these analyses suggest that SAPR-PBIS has good to strong reliability and validity, making it a meaningful tool and process for schools implementing PBIS. Details on these analyses are included in the following sections.

### Content Validity Through Expert Panel Review

The survey completed by the expert panel used a four-point Likert-type rating scale, with 1 = *not relevant* and 4 = *fully relevant*. A descriptive analysis was used to compute the mean and standard deviation (*SD*) of each item based on participant responses. None of the items was rated below the midpoint of the scale (2), which was designated as the cut-off score for item inclusion. The *SD* in all but one item was less than 1. In fact, only two items were rated below a 3 (*moderately relevant*). Item 2.5, "in-school counseling is available," received the lowest rating of 2.88 (*SD* = 0.75). Item 3.5, "training includes information on common behavioral disorders in schools," was rated 2.9 (*SD* = 0.99). Item 8.4, "discipline data are analyzed for relationship between ethnicity and disciplinary actions," was rated 3.38 but had an *SD* of 1.03, the largest in the scale. The total mean score for all of the items was 3.46 (*SD* = 0.75). The scores of each of the items were above the criteria for elimination, indicating that each should remain in the self-assessment. These results suggest that the expert panel found all the items in the SAPR-PBIS to be very relevant to the implementation of SWPBIS.

### Internal Reliability

An internal reliability analysis was completed on the entire SAPR-PBIS as well as on each of the 10 subscales based on the item scores from the PBIS Project Individual PBIS Self-Assessments completed by school leadership team members in the winter of 2005 (*N* = 150). Table B.2 displays the results of these analyses. The alpha level of the entire self-assessment was $\alpha = .96$. Analyses of the 10 subscales found that all were above the recommended level of $\alpha = .70$, indicating that the self-assessment as a whole has a high level of internal reliability

**Table B.2.** Internal reliability of Behavior, Emotional, and Academic Curriculum on the Needs of Students (BEACONS) positive behavioral interventions and supports (PBIS) self-assessment subscales

| Participants (*N* = 150) | | | | |
|---|---|---|---|---|
| Subscale | Mean | Standard deviation | Alpha (α) | Number of items |
| 1. Policies and procedures | 28.27 | 4.85 | .80 | 7 |
| 2. Prevention and screening | 21.27 | 4.65 | .78 | 6 |
| 3. Staff development | 16.41 | 6.13 | .92 | 6 |
| 4. Behavioral expectations | 28.53 | 4.67 | .84 | 7 |
| 5. Response to discipline referrals | 24.07 | 4.21 | .76 | 6 |
| 6. Academic and social supports provided | 21.12 | 5.58 | .76 | 6 |
| 7. Functional behavioral assessment as needed | 15.14 | 6.18 | .95 | 5 |
| 8. Data collected and analyzed | 21.54 | 5.70 | .88 | 6 |
| 9. Families as partners | 13.35 | 3.89 | .81 | 4 |
| 10. Comprehensive plans for intensive needs | 27.67 | 7.64 | .90 | 8 |
| Scale total | | | .96 | 61 |

and the subscales have moderate to high levels of internal reliability (Cicchetti, 1994; Mellor, 2004; Nunally, 1978). Furthermore, review of the item–total correlation results on individual items within all of the subscales found item–item total correlation means ranging from 0.50 to 0.88, falling within an acceptable range for inclusion. At a practical level, these results, along with those from the expert panel, indicate that school teams can confidently reference the items included in the SAPR-PBIS because they provide a reliable and meaningful set of effective practices from across the three levels of the PBIS model.

## Hierarchical Linear Modeling Analysis

Table B.3 summarizes the results of the two-level hierarchical linear modeling (HLM) fixed effects analysis, mentioned in Chapter 2, that modeled individual total self-assessment scores by professional role nested within school leadership teams' total self-assessment scores. Under the fixed effect model at Level 1, individual assessment scores were not related to professional roles. However, at Level 2 the effect of leadership team's total score was found to be significantly related to individuals' scores (coefficient = 209.73; $p < .001$). The reliability estimate indicated that 43% of the variance in individuals' self-assessment scores was explained by the nested effect of team leadership scores. In addition, Table B.3 shows the random effect results of Level 2, which found a significant level of individual variation in school leadership team self-assessment scores ($p < .05$). Overall, these results indicate that an individual's professional role does not significantly affect his or her contribution to the team self-assessment.

The results of the HLM analysis indicate that membership in school team better predicted team self-assessment results than an individual's professional role. This suggests that the group self-assessment ratings accurately represent a "shared psychological meaning" for the leadership teams in each of the schools. Therefore, the team scores can be considered accurate measures of organizational function. If individual perception were the critical element of analysis, then differences based on individual role should have influenced the outcome of the HLM analysis more significantly (Van Horn, 2003). Had the reverse proven true, the implication would be that the shared or unifying perspective is more dependent upon what

**Table B.3.** Fixed and random effects of individual self-assessment ratings by role and school/team total

| Fixed effect | Coefficient | Standard error | *t*-ratio | Approximate *df* | *p*-value |
|---|---|---|---|---|---|
| **Level 1: Slope in scores by professional role[a]** | | | | | |
| Administrator | 11.79 | 37.29 | .316 | 143 | .752 |
| General education teacher | 8.07 | 36.39 | .222 | 143 | .825 |
| Special education teacher | 15.27 | 38.24 | .399 | 143 | .690 |
| Counselor/psychologist | 3.49 | 37.72 | .093 | 143 | .927 |
| Paraprofessional | 13.89 | 35.73 | .389 | 143 | .698 |
| **Level 2: Total team scores[b]** | | | | | |
| SAPR-PBIS™ school/ team total score | 209.73 | 36.70 | 5.71 | 21 | .001** |
| Intercept | 1.810 | .343 | 5.270 | 21 | .001** |
| Random effects | Standard deviation | Variance component | *Df* | Chi- square | *p*-value |
| **Level 2: Individual total by role and school team totals** | | | | | |
| Intercept1, U0 | 11.91 | 141.97 | 21 | 37.16 | .016* |
| Level 1, R | 34.36 | 1180.86 | | | |

[a]*n* = 150
[b]n = 23
*Key:* SAPR-PBIS™, Self-Assessment and Program Review for Positive Behavior Interventions and Supports
*$p < .05$
**$p < .001$

professional role the individual is involved in, regardless of where that position is located. This would call into question both the validity of the team self-assessment process overall as well as the reliability of the team scores. However, as they stand, these results provide strong convergent validity to both the team self-assessment process and the team scores themselves.

## Schoolwide Evaluation Tool and SAPR-PBIS Criteria Ratings

A descriptive analysis was completed to determine which schools met the 80% criteria for effective implementation across the SAPR-PBIS and the SET. These data were used to compare how often the scores across both measures concurred on whether a school was above or below criteria in a given area. A total of six schools in both cohorts were above the 80% criteria on both measures across all of the related subscales. An analysis of the error patterns across each cohort found that in Cohort 1, five schools had only one SET subscale score below criteria and those scores were within 5% of bringing both measures above criteria. By accepting that level of 5% as a reasonable range of error for one subscale, this brings a total of eight schools in Cohort 1 above criteria across all the paired subscales on both measures. Error analysis of the scoring across measures of Cohort 2 schools found that even accepting the same 5% range of error for one subscale, only three schools scored above criteria on both the SAPR-PBIS and the SET. However, whereas three schools scored under criteria on some of the related subscales, the scores matched consistently across the measures.

An analysis of the percentage of time both the SET and SAPR-PBIS subscales are in agreement across the related subscales, concurring that a school is either above or below criteria in a specific area, found that it was 71% when including all errors. When accepting 5% as an acceptable range of error when only one subscale is below criteria, this increased to 82%. Using the same criteria, a total of 13 schools matched scores on both measures as being either above or below criteria in all areas, and another six schools failed to match in only one area. The remaining four schools failed to match in two or more areas, with three of these schools in Cohort 2.

These results indicate that the related subscales on the SET and SAPR-PBIS were fairly consistent in assessing positive schoolwide discipline practices, suggesting that there is concurrent validity between the measures. The fact that results for Cohort 1 schools were higher and more consistent than Cohort 2 schools, which were only in their first year of PBIS implementation, suggests that the SAPR process differentiates between schools based on time in training and implementation of a PBIS initiative. The more time a team participates in PBIS training and practice, the more experienced and proficient it becomes with evaluating and implementing the practices.

## Descriptive Analysis of Self-Assessment and Discipline Referrals

The mean score for ODRs per year, per 100 students, in 2004–2005 for the BEACONS schools is 68, which was slightly below the national average of 70 per year for elementary schools during the 2004–2005 school year (School-Wide Information System, 2006). Four schools with total SAPR-PBIS score of 80% or above (*strongly in place*) had mean ODRs per 100 students of 40. Nine schools with total SAPR-PBIS score of 69%–79% (*moderately in place*) had mean ODRs per 100 students of 75, moderately above the national average. Ten schools with total SAPR-PBIS score of 44%–68% (*partially in place*) had mean ODRs per 100 students of 95. This places them well above the national average in discipline referrals. These results suggest that schools with higher SAPR-PBIS scores may have a broader range of effective PBIS practices well established, which affects the level of discipline issues in the school. These findings correspond to those summarized by Irvin, Tobin, Sprague, Sugai, and Vincent (2004) in their analysis of ODRs and schoolwide behavioral programs. In their review of several studies, they found that higher numbers of ODRs were associated with problematic behavior climates in schools. As schools consistently implemented schoolwide social and behavioral initiatives, ODRs decreased. Overall, the descriptive analysis of ODRs and SAPR-PBIS scores contribute to the overall validity to the assessment and effectiveness of the SAPR-PBIS, as schools with higher total SAPR-PBIS ratings tend to have lower ODRs.

The results of these studies suggest that the SAPR-PBIS offers a number of benefits to schools, including improved understanding of effective practices, a higher level of buy-in to improvement activities, and assistance to leadership teams in planning and implementing PBIS initiatives. Overall, the results clearly point to both the practical utility of the SAPR-PBIS and its relevance to reform initiatives in today's schools.

# Index

Page numbers followed by *f* indicate figures; those followed by *t* indicate tables.